PILOT MATH
TREASURE BATH

Jason Depew

www.pilotmathtreasurebath.com

Published by:
Hydroplane Aerospace LLC
www.hydroplaneaerospace.com

Treasure Bath and Pilot Duck Illustrations by:
Robert Lang Sr.

First Edition: November 2019

ISBN: 1-7341404-1-0
ISBN-13: 978-1-7341404-1-5

To my wife
for her encouragement and ridicule,
each in perfect measure

See what fictitious critics aren't actually saying about the Pilot Math Treasure Bath!

"I bought this book expecting him to tell me how I could actually acquire a bathtub full of gold coins. It did not have that information. What a rip-off!"

- Dmitry Alekseevich Kuznetsov, Russian hacker using a bogus Newsweek account to post fake news

"Depew shamelessly appropriated the combined knowledge of the Financial Independence, Retire Early (FIRE) movement and repackaged it for professional pilots. Any fool should know about this stuff already. Couldn't this no-talent hack figure out something new to write about? I'm going for a bike ride!"

- Definitely not Mr. Money Mustache

"Sure, this guy may have figured out a way for all of us to be richer and happier, but have you seen a picture of him? His poor wife! If I had a dog that ugly, I'd shave his behind and teach him to walk backwards!"

- One of Depew's old college roommates

"There is no place in this world for such unbridled optimism and love of life. This dude needs to learn to be a little less satisfied with what he has…like the rest of us. Oh, and in case you haven't heard, the damn company stole my pension and it's your job to make me whole!"

- Joe Pilot, Airline Captain

"Pilot Math Treasure Bath? Yah, I know that guy…great guy, great guy. He's a big fan of mine. None of those ideas are his…I taught him everything he knows. I practically wrote that book for him. In fact, people are always asking about my treasure bath and I tell them it's the greatest treasure bath there is. Everyone wants a treasure bath like mine because it's the best. What we need

is a country where every man can have his own treasure bath. The rest of the world is going to see our treasure baths and be insanely jealous. They'll be like, 'America truly is the best country in the world because of their treasure baths.' It's going to be great. It's going to be wonderful. You're going to be amazed when you see how great I'm going to make America's treasure baths."

- Certainly not Donald Trump, President of the United States of America

TABLE OF CONTENTS

Foreword

This book exists because you, as a pilot, are probably bad at math.

Bear with me on this.

I know that you probably have a bag full of mathematical approximations, cheats, and Rules of Thumb that you successfully employ every time you fly. Lovingly known as "pilot math," this collection of tricks is an important and generally unavoidable part of professional aviation.

I also know that, like me, some of you actually like math. We find it invigorating and engaging to apply things like thermodynamics and calculus to our aviation pursuits. It makes us safer, more efficient, and overall better pilots. (Not that any pilot needs something as lame as math to confirm his or her sense of overwhelming superiority.) These advanced mathematical disciplines are also good and important, but we're not going to talk about any of this math here.

Our profession provides us with outstanding opportunities in life. We get paid more money than most Americans (or any other humans) could ever hope to earn. Despite that, I'm shocked at how many pilots I meet who are terrible with money. Many of these pilots have incomes in the top 10% of all Americans, yet manage to be dirt poor.

We're here to fix that.

This book aims to teach you Pilot Math with the kind of lasting impact that will set you up for an amazing life. I'm talking about a life where you only ever do things that you want to do, yet you never have to worry about your family's needs being met. It's a life free from fear, and rich with actualization of your loftiest goals.

If you ask around, you'll be told that you can't have a life like this… that no normal person can. This kind of life, they'll tell you, is reserved for families with generational wealth and the chosen few who win the lottery.

Well my friends, you just won the lottery.

My job is to help you understand the magnitude of your winnings, and help you figure out how to hang on to them and fill your Bathtub with Treasure.

This is not some "get rich quick" thing. There is no scheme here, and it's not an "easy" path for the average victim of lifelong American consumerist brainwashing. This is a relatively long process that requires discipline, patience, and hard work. And yet, the Math is straightforward and elegantly simple. Stick around and we'll have you soaking luxuriously in your Treasure Bath before you know it.

—

If you're reading this, you're probably a pilot. I'm guessing that you either fly for the airlines, or that you aspire to do so someday. Pilot Math works the way it does because airline pilot pay is absurdly high, especially compared to the income of the average US citizen.

I wrote this book for pilots, and a lot of the examples and terminology will be unintelligible if you don't fly. However, the general principles behind Pilot Math work very well for people in other professions. Doctors, dentists, and lawyers can certainly make use of it. The average engineer or person who "works in finance" can probably find useful principles here as well…and that's a short list off the top of my head. Don't let the pilot jargon or attitudes in here turn you off. You have the potential to achieve a life just as amazing as any pilot (as long as you eventually get your act together and take some flying lessons.)

—

I also hope that some of the pilots who read this book will be able to convince their spouses to give it a try. If you're a spouse, I apologize again for the pilot-centric attitude in here. I hope you'll understand that I've employed this attitude intentionally, expecting it to be more effective in communicating my message to your hard-headed aviator.

Pilot Math is important for your family, and it's something you should actively discuss with your pilot. Please look past my bombastic tone and find the underlying message.

—

Welcome everyone. I hope you have some time on your hands because you aren't going to be able to put this book down. Now, let's get to work.

CHAPTER ONE

What is a Treasure Bath?

We have an awesome deal as professional pilots. We get paid a huge amount of money to perform a job that offers pretty great working conditions. (You certainly can't beat the view!) My compensation as a new-hire first officer at a major US airline put me in the 89th percentile for income among all Americans in 2016. (Yes, I'd "paid my dues" for more than a decade to get there, but even my previous job as a pilot in the US Air Force paid pretty well. We'll look at how the dues-paying period plays into our overall Pilot Math later in this book.)

Counting everything, your total compensation could easily reach the $8-10 million range, or more, over the course of a career. (And I remember being a kid who thought $100 was a fortune!) This should set each of us up for everlasting financial success. The goal of this book is to help you make that happen.

Why do you need a book to show you how to do this? Because many pilots suck at it. I don't know whether it's that our financial system is just complicated, or simply a lack of education in our society in general, but many people are so overwhelmed by the idea of saving and investing for the future that they try to ignore it altogether.

Sorry, but it's not going to take care of itself.

This book outlines the specific steps you need to take and dollar amounts that you need to be spending, saving, and investing each year to meet your future goals. This book explains exactly what you need to do to fill up a Treasure Bath.

Before we talk about what a Treasure Bath is, we need to take a quick look at what it isn't. The best person I know to help illustrate this is Poor Old Joe. I'm shocked at how frequently I fly with him.

You probably know Joe. He's been with the company since you were in high school. He's a captain at one of the biggest airlines in the world, and yet he hates life. He's earned millions of dollars over his career, and yet he's dirt poor. He's tired and cynical and lives in constant fear that he's going to retire and then run out of money before he dies. He's stressed, unhealthy, and generally burned-out.

Once you get him talking, you start to understand how Joe got to his position:

He "owns" (has a mortgage on) a giant house. He may also "own" a vacation home or timeshare. He "owns" (makes loan payments on) several really cool automobiles for himself, his spouse, and his kids. He has a boat, or ATVs, or a camper, or an airplane, or some other expensive toys. (He rarely gets to use them because he's always working, as we'll see.) The absolute latest iPhone hangs from a clip on his belt, the latest iWatch is wrapped around his wrist, and he has an iPad Pro and/or new MacBook tucked away in his flight bag. His wife and kids each own similar arrays of gadgets, fueled by an expensive unlimited data plan that allows each device to be used to its fullest potential.

Joe loves hosting parties at his house where he presents football games with a 90-inch UltraHD 4K TV and 7.1 surround sound speakers. He provides only the best refreshments for his parties because "life's too short to drink cheap booze." He's always proud as his guests marvel at the expensive furnishings and gadgets they see when they're at his house.

Speaking of parties, Joe managed to only go $10,000 (a *mere* 20%) over budget on each of his daughters' weddings. He had to because he loves his kids, right? That's also why he paid 100% of any tuition, fees, room, and board not covered by scholarships for his kids to attend some top-name schools...because the school's name is as important as the degree on your resume. Right?

Sometimes these costs are all compounded by the fact that Joe has been divorced once or twice. In addition to providing all this for his current family, he's still paying some form of spouse or child support to his old family.

Joe is very proud of all his "treasure." He probably thinks he's rich because he "owns" all of that stuff. That's probably what most of his friends think too. We know better though, don't we?

The only way that Joe could afford to spend (and can continue to spend) like this is to cut back on (or completely eliminate) his savings while simultaneously accruing a crushing load of debt. Though nearing the mandatory pilot retirement age of 65, he only has a few hundred thousand dollars in his IRA and 401K accounts. He acknowledges that these figures are lower than they should be, but they're far better than the national average of less than $25,000 in retirement savings.

Part of the problem is that the damn company took away his pension. When he started at his airline they promised him 60% of his Final Average Earnings (FAE) from the day he retired until the day he died. He thought he could afford to spend like he does because of this promise. Times were tough in the 2000s, but he'll tell you that the company intentionally let things get bad enough to declare bankruptcy because they knew this would allow them to escape the burden of funding this ungainly pension plan. He may be correct, at least in part, but that doesn't help his situation today. His pension is not coming back.

Old Joe tells you that he's not too worried because he still has four years to work. He's a captain so his annual income is over $350,000. That means he'll bring in at least $1.2 million before he retires. You don't need to read this book to know that at least 30% of that income will go to Uncle Sam as taxes. Then, given Joe's average annual spending, he's not going to end up with more than a couple hundred thousand extra dollars in additional savings when it's all said and done.

Now you understand why Joe flies as much as he can. He scrapes to get 100+ hours a month when the average pilot only flies 75-80. He's gone from home more than anyone else in the airline...he has to be to take care of his family. It's straining his marriage, it's causing him to miss out on some of the most important years of his kids' lives, it's having a big impact on his health and fitness.

He's had to run like this for years to maintain this "standard of living" for his family, but he *only* has to do it for another four and then he'll finally get to retire and relax.

I feel terrible for Poor Old Joe every time I see him. He's absolutely swimming in...stuff...but the truth of his situation is that he's poor. His income puts him in the 99th percentile of all Americans...that contemptible 1% against which the Occupy movement protested years ago. And yet, despite that sky-high income, he has very little actual wealth. If Joe lost his pilot medical certificate today, his family would almost immediately find themselves in desperate financial trouble.

Do you want to be like Joe?

I sure don't!

I'll admit: I like toys too. Are the toys really necessary to have a good life though? Are the toys worth the costs?

I don't want to be flying 100+ hours a month when I'm in my 60s. (I don't think I'd want to work that much now either.) I certainly don't want to give up my health in exchange for money. How many years do you think Old Joe will last after he retires? How much will he actually be able to enjoy those years? He's out of breath and drenched in sweat just from pulling his suitcase from the jet to the curb to catch the crew van at the end of a flying day. He's not going to be able to enjoy hiking, or golfing, or traveling the world, or playing with grandkids. He's going to be stuck at home in a recliner watching TV news stations all day. (Barf!) He's going to be riddled with health issues caused by his decades of trading fitness and health for money. That's not my idea of a great retirement.

Thankfully, we don't have to end up like this!

Many airline pilots are sad that pensions are gone. I understand their pain. It must have been frustrating to start a career with certain expectations, and then suddenly have to pivot late in the game. For my part though, I'm extremely happy that we don't have pensions anymore! Without any delusions of being taken care of by someone with conflicting interests, I knew from the beginning that I was the only person in control of my future.

One of the biggest problems with pensions is that they lock you in to a job for a long period of time. At Joe's company, you only got the full 60% FAE if you worked there for 25+ years. Every year you left before you hit 25 cost you 4% of your pension benefits. That's a powerful psychological incentive to continue working full-time into old age. I'm not sure I would want to do that.

Since the annual pension payment was based on FAE, there was a strong incentive to work harder than ever during your last three years with the company to boost that "Average Earnings" number. In my mind, that's not the time to be sprinting. That's the time to coast gracefully across the finish line. Thankfully, since pensions are gone, I'm not subject to any of those pressures…and neither are you.

Throughout this book I'll joke about the idea of a Treasure Bath. We'll conjure images of Scrooge McDuck swimming through piles of gold coins and precious gemstones. Spoiler alert: that stuff isn't actually treasure. Neither are houses, cars, electronic gadgets, expensive clothes, or designer handbags. There will never be a human being who, on his or her deathbed, says any of the following:

- "Damn, I'm glad I upgraded to the iPhone 6 the day it came out instead of sticking with my iPhone 5. That made such a difference in my life!"
- "I'm sure glad I paid extra to have a house with a formal living room, and that I spent $12,000 furnishing it nicely. I got so much enjoyment out of that room!"
- "I'm so glad I missed my daughter performing the lead role in her high school play to earn a few thousand extra dollars flying a last-minute trip for premium pay. That let me buy her fancier centerpieces on the tables at her wedding, and those made both her and me far happier than watching her on stage ever could have!"

Ouch. Sorry. Let's stop swinging so low and get to the good stuff.

Now that we've considered what a treasure bath *isn't*, ask yourself: What do I actually treasure in life?

In case that's a tough question for you, here's part of my answer to get you started:

I treasure time with my wife and kids, with my friends, and with the rest of my family. I love seeing my kids get excited when they learn something new, and watching them gain mastery of new skills. I enjoy taking them to places that bring me joy, and seeing that these places have the same effect on them. I love joking around with them and hearing them laugh. I love watching my daughter at dance class. It's just "foundations of ballet" and she hates it because it's all learning basic movements instead of actual dancing. Still, watching her learn and practice those basic movements is one of the most beautiful things

I've ever seen. For me, a true Treasure Bath is a life of time spent in these ways—meaningfully, with people I care about.

I also treasure some activities. I love hiking in mountains and forests. I enjoy hiking on cross country skis in the winter and "hiking" at high speed down those mountains on downhill skis. I love swimming and playing on the beach. I enjoy sitting back and reading a good book, and I even enjoy watching a good movie or TV show. I like that even more when I'm cuddling with my wife or kids. These books and shows are best when I can then find someone to discuss them with —to laugh together at the jokes, express our shock when we're surprised or disgusted, to cheer when our favorite characters are victorious, or pretend we're uniquely astute in our ability to meaningfully apply the storys' lessons to the world around us. I love building and creating things...projects with my kids, computer programs, and even writing books. I aspire to build an airplane and then take my family and friends flying in it. For me a Treasure Bath is a life full of time spent in these pursuits.

Speaking of flying, I do love it! (I understand that for many pilots an airplane is nothing more than a cubicle with a view and that you could happily give it up tomorrow. I feel bad that you don't enjoy it more, but that definitely means that you need to read the rest of this book!) For me a Treasure Bath must include a lot of flying. Some of that will include teaching others to fly...something I enjoy almost as much as I enjoy flying myself.

Ideally, somewhere in my mind, I also envision myself trying to make a difference in the world. We'll look more at this idea in the next chapter.

The one thing I know is that I can't accomplish much changing the world (or any of this other stuff) while I'm on the road flying trips for my airline. Time is a precious resource, and every hour we spend working is an hour we can't spend on these other pursuits. We've already noted that money is not treasure in and of itself. However, if we want the freedom to use our time the way we want to, we need enough money to free us from having to spend all our time working.

That's what I mean when I say "Treasure Bath": having enough money that the passive income from your investments will cover your family's basic needs for the rest of their lives, whether you earn more money actively working or not. Once you reach this state, your time is truly yours to do as you wish. You can then use your newfound freedom from mandatory work to spend your life doing what you love.

Many people in America try to make everything regarding money into a fight. The idea that you or I could be free from the demands of mandatory full-time work and live on passive income offends them. Either we're greedy for frugally saving so much money rather than giving it to others, or we're lazy for not wanting to spend every waking moment at work. To these people, anyone who manages to fill up a treasure bath really is Scrooge McDuck laughing at others as he swims around among his millions.

If you encounter these people tell them where to shove their hurt feelings and then walk away.

We're not going to delve deep into the ideas of the Non-Aggression Principle here, but the bottom line is this: nobody has any right to force you to work to support them. They have no rightful claim on the fruits of your labor. (And yet, you're probably going to give them upwards of 35% of everything you earn for the rest of your life anyway.)

You don't ever need to feel bad for profiting when you produce something of value, or for living in such a way that you don't immediately consume everything you earn.

If you feel a desire to help others, it should grow out of the goodness of your heart and because you value their human potential for greatness—not out of some arbitrary obligation.

The great news is that you're free to find ways to help those around you. You can even give some of your time and resources right now, while you're also working in a full-time job. I believe that it's morally good for each of us to do this.

However, how effective can you really be at helping others if you spend most of your time working to support a high level of personal spending? Imagine how much more meaningfully you could help others if you had the ability to give them the time you're currently spending at your job? Imagine how much better your focus could be if a steady stream of passive income covered all your needs, freeing you from constantly having to figure out how to make enough to support your family.

The point of drawing a Treasure Bath isn't to then spend the rest of your life lazily soaking in it. It's to spend your life doing things that have true meaning for you (and probably many other people as well.)

Many of those things weren't options before because they don't pay a salary high enough to support your family. Others weren't possible because you can't do them part-time when you have to rely on a full-time job to support your family. We'll get into more detail on this in the next chapter.

While we're here, we need to take one more look at the idea that there's nothing wrong with deciding you're done with mandatory full-time work.

There is a growing community in our world focused on the idea of FIRE (Financial Independence, Retire Early.) The idea is to work hard for 5-15 years, saving the vast majority of your income. By learning to enjoy life with low spending levels, it's possible to accumulate enough wealth in 10 years (or less) that the passive income from your investments will cover your family's spending needs.

Forever.

And the principal dollars and cents sitting in your investment account will never decrease.

Once a person reaches that point, reaches FIRE, he or she could technically stop "working" forever, and be just fine.

There's a lot of opposition to the ideas of the FIRE movement. Our culture is completely brainwashed to equate income and/or hours spent at work with individual human worth. (You may reject that assertion on a gut level, but look around yourself and tell me I'm wrong.) The idea that a person might only work for 10 years and then "play" for the rest of his or her life offends people. We've already decided that these people are morons, right?

The truth is that most people who achieve FIRE end up continuing to earn money, even though they don't need it. The difference is that they earn this money by doing things that they're passionate about, rather than grinding away endless days in a cubicle at Innitech. Their idea of "retirement" is very different from the definition common in modern society.

I'm not writing this book to specifically encourage you to pursue a life of FIRE. I enjoy watching that community and take a lot of useful ideas from it. I spend more money than the average FIRE acolyte, and I intend on working longer than many of them do. Their ideas did help inspire this book though.

Whether you want to "retire" early or not, I don't want you to end up like Poor Old Joe. There are many ways to avoid becoming him, but if you apply a few straightforward principles in your life, what we're calling Pilot Math here, I can almost guarantee your success.

A Treasure Bath is all about freedom. If you fill one up, it will give you the freedom to decide exactly how you want to live your life and spend your time. You don't have to abandon your day job out of principle, but if at any point in time that job starts interfering with your ability to freely live your life, your Treasure Bath will give you the confidence to make a change. You might walk away entirely, or you might just reshape the way you work at that job.

My wife and I have a pretty decent Treasure Bath filled up, and we're using it to make our jobs work for us. I've mentioned that my ideal life includes lots of flying. I aspire to have full-time access to a variety of aircraft. I want to pursue mastery flying each of them, and enjoy teaching others to fly in them as well. However, I'm perfectly happy to scratch part of my flying itch by continuing to work for my airline. Why pay hundreds of dollars an hour to operate my own aircraft when my airline will pay me hundreds of dollars an hour to operate theirs? You won't see me flying 100 hours a month like Poor Old Joe, but as long as I'm still enjoying it, why not let my company pay me to do some of that flying for now?

One of the reasons the FIRE movement is so fixated on the idea of "early" retirement is that most jobs are five-days-a-week-fifty-weeks-a-year-or-nothing sort of arrangements. The economics of running the average business require employees be in the office or factory producing value every day. The average worker only has two options: work full-time every day, or have zero income.

Thankfully, the airlines don't work that way! We fly our trips and then we go home. When we're home there's nothing for us to do. If we want to work less, we bid for fewer trips or drop/swap away the ones we don't want. Some other part-time or contract jobs allow this kind of flexibility, but the catch is that none of us gets paid for work we don't do. If a daycare provider or barber just up and decided to only work 10 days a month (and didn't get fired) he or she might not make enough money to survive. Our pay rates are a lot better. I flew about 75% of a full schedule during my second year at my major airline and my total compensation still put in the top 6% on income earners in America. I flew 22% less than that in my third year and made the same amount of money. A captain could probably hit that level of income on less than half of a normal schedule.

If your Treasure Bath is full, an airline job offers ultimate flexibility. You can fly a trip or two a month and still enjoy as many days off to spend pursuing your interests as most people spend working. If you suddenly decide you'd like some more money for a special purchase, it's no problem. Our jobs also give us the unique ability to adjust the amount of work we do every month based on our needs. You can bid for a heavier schedule and/or pick up extra flying, hopefully for premium pay. It's not unreasonable for even a full-time airline pilot to double his or her monthly pay during the right time of year, on the right type of aircraft. You can work hard until you have enough money to cover your big purchase, then throttle back again and return to the luxury of your Treasure Bath to cover your everyday needs.

Although I'm not specifically trying to convince you to retire early, I do want you to at least think through the possibility. Some people want to pursue bigger things in life. Do you aspire to be a doctor, coach college sports, do missionary work in Africa, start a company, or become an astronaut? You might be shocked when you discover how quickly Pilot Math can get you to the point where you have more than enough passive income to support you and your family for the rest of your life. Once your Treasure Bath is full, you will absolutely be free to pursue any other goal you could come up with.

(The crazy thing is, our profession offers so much free-time and flexibility that you can pursue almost any of these goals without quitting your day-job. I know pilots who already do many of these things, and more, while still working occasionally for their major airline.)

I don't feel bad saying that I think our industry as a whole would be better off if more people chose to leave it altogether at younger ages. I feel bad for Poor Old Joe when I see him, but I also get frustrated. He's no fun to fly with because he does nothing but complain. He upholds the minimum standards of safety, but does nothing to improve our brand or our customers' experience. He's so disgruntled and self-centered that he couldn't possibly be bothered to consider anyone else's needs. If Joe had been able to fill up a Treasure Bath sooner, or if I could have gotten him to realize how full it already was, he could have left this job he no longer loves a long time ago. He could have been spending more time with his family, or golfing, or fishing, or doing whatever else it is he'd rather be doing. He'd truly be better off.

This would work wonders for the younger pilots in the company. First off, they wouldn't have to endure Old Joe's bad attitude reducing the quality of their working environment. In the longer-term, his departure would free up a seat for younger pilots to move up more quickly. This means pilots could spend less time stuck in regional airline purgatory, and we could all have the option of upgrading to captain or flying a nice cushy widebody a lot sooner.

The airlines would have to scramble to fill the extra vacancies at first, but once things reached steady-state, they would actually prefer it. They'd have a larger number of pilots on the low (less expensive) end of the pay scale. The pilots who did stay would be happier and take better care of their customers.

Our industry could also see improvements if Old Joe had just realized he could use his Treasure Bath to work less, rather than walking away completely. It's demoralizing to grind away as a pilot when you think you have no other choice. If Joe had been able to work less in the past, spending a larger portion of his time pursuing other meaningful things, maybe he wouldn't have stopped enjoying his job at all. He could have been more rested and less stressed when he did come to work...making the entire operation safer and more effective.

This "work less" paradigm would also require airlines to change their staffing picture. They'd need more pilots on staff to cover their flights; however, this could also reach a mutually-beneficial steady-state. Younger pilots trying to fill up their Treasure Baths would do some of the extra flying that Old Joe is currently using his seniority to scoop up. Companies could negotiate benefits into contracts that encourage all-or-nothing choices to get pilots to retire early, and unions could counter by preserving our right to work part-time if desired. Nay-sayers will argue that this is impossible. I say that it's completely possible...as long we we're willing to figure out a solution that is different than the one in our current contracts.

Whether you're looking at our industry as a whole, or just worried about yourself, there's no debating the fact that pilots are better off when they know and apply Pilot Math. By reading this book, you're putting yourself in a little danger. Once you see the simplicity and power of Pilot Math, you can't unsee it. You'll want to put it to use in your life, and that may require you to rethink some of your lifelong assumptions.

Although Pilot Math is simple, I won't say that applying it is quick or easy. It will require you to exercise at least a modicum of self control for several years. Perhaps at this point you're thinking, "Well Emet, this all sounds intriguing. However, it also sounds like a lot of effort. Why would I want to change my entire mindset on work and life?"

Well my friend, you're right. This is a bit of extra effort...in the short-term. However, it's a hell of a lot less work than trudging away as a full-time employee until you're 65!

It's also very astute of you to ask "why." As it turns out, Why is what makes all the difference.

CHAPTER TWO

Start With Why

I just mentioned that choosing to apply Pilot Math requires you to rethink some of your assumptions about the purpose and meaning of work. Our society has some very strong views on work, and, quite frankly, they suck![1]

Our society has decided that human beings should spend almost their entire lives working. This means going to a 9-to-5 job, 5 days a week, essentially until we're too old to physically or mentally keep up. Knowing that each individual reaches this age at a different point, and realizing that it's bad for corporate morale when workers to die in their cubicles, we set an average limit around age 65.

We estimate this as an age where a worker's performance has decreased enough that it isn't a big loss for the company to let him or her go. At this age a given worker's savings, family, and/or the social welfare system are probably sufficient to support his or her basic living requirements until he or she dies—without running out of money. At current life expectancies, this worker can hope for at least a decade or two of life without work—enough of a carrot to convince us, the toiling masses, to keep our heads down and continue working.

And oh what a time that retirement is! After 4-5 *decades* spent working we're more likely to have health problems. That immediately diverts much of our time and money to doctor's visits and limits the ways we can spend the rest of our free time. It's okay though. We can gather in communities of other old people to tell stories, play cards,

---

[1] The title of this chapter quotes the 1st Book of The Pilot Math Bible, *Start With Why: How Great Leaders Inspire Everyone to Take Action*, by Simon Sinek.

16

and golf. We get to spend time visiting our families and finally enjoying our grandkids. For those who manage to save more than the absolute minimum, we now have the time available to travel the world. We probably won't be doing any involved hiking, scuba diving, or mountain climbing on those travels because we're not as strong or fit as we once were, but we'll still enjoy walking around looking at things...and of course lots of shopping! We might be able to afford some things we couldn't when we had children constantly in tow, though we have to be careful lest we run out of money.

There's nothing wrong with this picture, per se. I'll be 65 (or 95) someday and I suppose I'll enjoy this type of life at that point. However, it's not a big enough carrot to convince me to work and live like Poor Old Joe for the next 26 years. There has to be more to life.

So, let me ask you a question: what would you do if you won the lottery?

I know, I know...this question has almost become a sort of trite excuse for a thought experiment in our society. It's a question posed by high school teachers before assigning some piece of tangentially related homework. Bear with me for now though as we take this question more seriously.

Let's assume you hit one of those big jackpots...the kind where even after giving half of your winnings to Uncle Sam you'd never have to worry about money again.

Would you go back to work the next day?

Would you ever go back?

Most people will answer this with a resounding "NO!" I have a theory that most people don't actually like their jobs that much. Frankly, I can see where they're coming from. If the job was really that enjoyable, why would the company have to pay so much money for someone to do it?

There are a chosen few in the world who actually love their jobs and wouldn't quit. I think I'm probably one of them. As I've mentioned, I love flying so much that my definition of a Treasure Bath includes a lot of flying. I can see myself continuing to enjoy this job even if I didn't need the money. Even if I decided to give up airline flying, I'd still look for other excuses to get in the air on a somewhat scheduled basis.

"Sorry babe. I'd love to lounge around in the pool with you all day, but they're counting on me to fly that P-51 to the airshow...."

Maybe part of the reason you don't love your job this much is because you *have* to do it to keep your family afloat. Removing that pressure can completely change the way you experience something.

As I was finishing up college at the US Air Force Academy, the required sophomore-level "Intro to Psychology" class appeared on my schedule. The Academy requires a *lot* of core classes. I graduated with over 175 credits in four years. (I understand that an average college requires 120 credits for a 4-year degree, meaning I packed nearly 6 years of college into 4.) I enjoyed some of the core classes, but hated others. I majored in Computer Engineering and was too busy building circuits and writing code to care deeply about things like Management or Economics or English.

However, by my senior year I'd basically won the college lottery. I'd accrued more than enough credits to graduate and my grades were pretty good. Yes, this class might require some work, but that total amount of effort was not going to be a big pain compared to everything else I had going on. All I really needed in this class was a mercy C and I'd be on my way. Cake walk.

So, instead of approaching this class as a burden that I had to do well in, or else, I approached it as an opportunity to learn something interesting. One of my best friends happened to be in the class with me and we had an outstanding professor, Dr. Steven Samuels. My friend, Ted, and I spoke up in every conversation in class. We volunteered for every demonstration. We even encouraged our other classmates to be more active in class. The results were awesome. Ted and I had a great time, and enjoyed being able to participate actively rather than just sit through a bunch of boring lectures. Dr. Samuels enjoyed our participation in the class, and that only made him a better professor for all of us.

In the end, I did better than a mercy C. I learned a great deal that I've been able able to use in my personal relationships and my career as a pilot. (I even went on to enjoy earning a Master's Degree in Human Factors Psychology.) My "Intro to Psychology" experience would have been nothing like that if I'd been under the pressure of having to perform for the sake of my future.

Although I hope you enjoy flying as much as I do, or that you *could* enjoy it that much after filling up your Treasure Bath, I'll understand if you don't. In that case, what would you do instead after your lotto win?

Would you sit on a couch in your boxers all day with a 6-pack of Miller Light and a bowl of Cheetos watching Sports Center? Would you hike the Appalachian and Rocky Mountain Trails as a warm-up for some serious mountaineering elsewhere in the world? Would you change your name to Johnny Utah and go on a surfing safari to all the best beaches on the planet? Would you read through the greatest literary works that humankind has produced?

These all seem like decent ways to spend some time, but I don't know that I'd want to spend the entirety of my life on any of them. I feel like I can do better than this.

If you read biographies, one of the great regrets you'll notice in many lives is people not spending enough time with their families. That could be parents wishing they had more time with their kids, or kids wishing for more time/attention/involvement from their parents. If this isn't an incentive to abandon mandatory full-time work, then I don't know what is.

My wife and I were both on active duty in the Air Force when our kids were born. My wife's parents took care of the kids for us during the day, so they at least got love and quality time with family. I missed out on those hours though. Worse, deployments and assignments kept me away from them for several extended periods of time.

If I had known better (maybe having read a book about Pilot Math when I was your age,) I could have already been working toward some type of financial freedom that would have given me more time with my kids. I owed the USAF a full decade of my life, but had we realized all our options, my wife and I may have chosen different career paths or chosen to delay having kids a few years to give us the opportunity to be there more for them.

These aren't light decisions. We both loved our jobs. We wanted our kids to know their grandparents. We liked the idea of the GI Bill paying for their college. We didn't want to be geezers before they even finished high school. We didn't want to risk older-age pregnancy complications for my wife or our children.

Although I didn't let it affect me, my church preaches that it's actually sinful to delay having kids to spend some time setting up your career and finances. While I can agree that delaying kids for purely selfish reasons is probably bad, I can't imagine the intent is to raise kids who don't know their parent(s)...because said parent(s) had to work all the time to provide for kids who were born before a family became financially stable.

The beauty of Pilot Math is that when you employ it properly, you'll find yourself presented with a variety of options that gets increasingly wide as time goes on. Your living expenses will be low enough that you can afford to have kids sooner without having to work all the time. Or, if you wait just a few years, you really will have the option to choose part-time work or quit work altogether and enjoy your relationship with them every day.

Several of the prominent exemplars in the FIRE community, like a blogger who writes under the pen name of Mr. Money Mustache, chose to give up full-time work early in life precisely because they wanted more time with their kids, and I applaud that mindset. The thing about that is: it doesn't last forever. Eventually your baby will start school. An early retiree is much better set up for homeschooling, but that's not the right path for everyone. Sooner or later, that kid will grow up and even people like MMM will be again faced with the question at hand: Why?

There are plenty of activities out there—flying, other jobs, or just other hobbies—that I enjoy a lot more when I'm doing them for the pure pleasure of the experience, rather than to meet some external (usually monetary) demand. What hobbies or jobs would you pursue if money and/or time weren't issues?

I recently signed on as a part-time flight instructor for Icon Aircraft. They build the A5, an amphibious Light Sport Aircraft that is more fun to fly than I could possibly explain in a book. The A5's unique capabilities require targeted training, so Icon has opened up two primary training centers...one of which is just down the road from my house at Peter O. Knight airport in Tampa, FL. They pay better than most flight instructing jobs, but not nearly enough to attract the average pilot with my level of experience. Most of my contemporaries would never consider teaching for Icon because it just doesn't pay enough. However, my Treasure Bath is filling up nicely and I have enough free time to pursue activities that reward me with fulfillment other than money. I absolutely love working for Icon because the flying and teaching are rewards in and of themselves. Yes, Icon pays me for my time, but that's just icing on the cake. I'm able to enjoy this part-time "job" because I've already won the Pilot Math lottery.

I've also thought about pursuing flying opportunities like being an Alaskan bush pilot, racing gliders, doing competition aerobatics, or doing other flight instructing. I know enough about the industry to realize that the items on that list can't possibly provide the kind of salary that I make as an airline pilot. However, if I was free from worrying about money, I would also be free to pursue these kinds of flying.

I've met many people who aspire to do some type of missionary flying. In most cases, these volunteer jobs require a lot of time and require a pilot to pay his or her own way. Again, not a great option for someone who has to work full time just to keep the family afloat. Wouldn't it be fun to start working as a missionary pilot in just a few years instead of some ambiguous "someday" after you've turned 65?

I've thought many times about becoming a teacher...probably college because high school kids can be pretty annoying. I'd enjoy teaching aviation, math, programming, engineering, psychology, or economics. I could be the kind of professor for other people that Dr. Samuels was for me. I feel like a person could make a lasting, meaningful difference in some young lives in a job like that.

I also aspire to build an airplane. Experimental kit aircraft have come a long way and offer far more performance and capability for your money than you'll ever find in certified aircraft. I enjoy working on airplanes, and like the idea of knowing every rivet on my machine. Some kits only take a few hundred hours to build. When you try to squeeze that into a life of full-time work, family, and who knows what else, it frequently takes builders a decade or more to complete a kit. What a nightmare! I like to think that a pilot with a decent Treasure Bath could easily find the time to complete a kit in just a year or two. Once that's done, you have a whole new airplane to enjoy and master. It could be something to teach in, or something to display at airshows. If the building process is as enjoyable as I expect, I could see it becoming an addiction of its own.

There are even people out there who make great money building and selling airplane kits, one after another. It'd be a fun and lucrative way to get some high-quality, capable aircraft out into the world. Who knows, I might eventually learn enough to come up with my own design. More than one aircraft company has been born that way.

Barring all that, I'd consider being a forest or park ranger. If I wasn't flying for a living I think it'd be tough to beat a job where you get to spend your time hiking around the mountains, building/fixing stuff, and helping people. The pay and hours weren't attractive enough for 18 year-old Emet, but I think it'd make a fantastic part-time gig now.

That's just a short list of things I'm considering doing with my life. Any of these jobs/avocations/hobbies are enough to spend a couple enjoyable decades mastering. I expect that somewhere along that path I'd encounter something else that interests me and make another transition. Understanding the beauty of Pilot Math will give me the freedom to make moves like that if I want to.

Although I can find ways to use most of these avocations to benefit others around me, I'll admit that they're largely self-centered undertakings. Freed from having to use a full-time job to support my family, I'd be doing them primarily because I want to. While I believe there's nothing wrong with that, I think we can still go a step further: why not try to really change the world?

You're scoffing at me right now, aren't you?

Don't feel bad...I get it. What can an airline pilot do to change the world? It's a valid question. Then again, what can a couple engineers do in a college dorm room or a garage?

Bill Hewlett and Dave Packard built a tech empire from a garage. Steve Jobs and Steve Wozniak did the same thing and became the biggest company on the planet. Larry Page and Sergey Brin started Google as a side-project in their college dorm room.

Elon Musk started companies that provided a web tool for newspapers and then an online payment system. He's gone from that to building some of the highest performance cars on the planet, radically changing the entire auto industry, and founding a company that builds and operates rocket ships.

Jeff Bezos started a company to sell books online. He's one of the richest people on Earth and has his own rocket ship company, Blue Origin, that will eventually provide Musk's SpaceX with some healthy competition.

Sir Richard Branson started out importing records with a van. He now owns an entire empire of businesses, including a company that will likely start flying tourists to space on its own rocket ship in the next year or two.

While all of these individuals have their share of brilliance, I assert that none of them is any more capable than you or me.

One of the things you'll notice is that these people had to find a way to free themselves from mandatory 9-to-5 jobs in order to have the time and money to undertake these projects. The Steves behind Apple were college drop-outs—no problem with time for them. Musk, Bezos, and Branson had filled up nice Treasure Baths in the form of financially self-sustaining business empires before they were able to start building rockets. Page and Brin weren't undergrads desperately trying to make it through college before their scholarships or mom-and-dad lifelines ran out. They were PhD candidates, probably bringing in some money through research grants and/or work as teaching assistants...and their little side-project fit neatly into the research they were required to do for their degrees anyway.

I believe that the biggest thing holding most of us back from changing the world is that we're tied to a 9-to-5 job. Part of the problem is financial—without the job we'd be unable to support our families. The other part is temporal—between a job and the rest of having a family/life, there just isn't time to pursue a significant, long-term project. You need the opportunity to spend at least a couple hours a day, most days, for years, to accomplish something truly big.

Humanity has always feared technological development. The introduction of the automobile was going to destroy an economy based on producing and operating horse-drawn carriages...and then that invention changed the world in ways that horses never could have. Today many people are horrified at the thought of driverless cars. What about all the taxi, bus, and truck drivers of the world? They'll all be unemployed. The economy will be ruined forever, oh no!

Isaac Asimov is, in my mind, the Great Grandmaster of science fiction. He was also a professor of Chemistry at Columbia and spent a lot of time writing contemplations on the future of humanity. He foresaw a day when robots would take care of most day-to-day things for us (not *just* driving, telephone line switching, banking, etc., like they already do.) Yes, he acknowledged, this would mean fewer of those kinds of jobs for humans. It'd be okay because the market price for goods and services would drop when they didn't require paying a human producer/operator. He predicted that all this automation would leave individual human beings with much more time on their hands. After an initial period spent getting over an ingrained habitual laziness, we would start using all our newfound time to accomplish great things.

How many potential Musks, Brins, and Jobs are out there today toiling away just to make ends meet? Are you one of them? Can you picture a world where we could unlock the potential and creativity of all those people?

If you use the Pilot Math we'll look at in this book to free yourself from the constraints of time and money, you will find yourself free to pursue something world-changing.

Don't worry, I won't think less of you if you fall short of starting a colony on Mars or starting a social network larger than any country on Earth. There's plenty of important work to be done short of that.

I mentioned the possibility of being a teacher. I don't think anyone would deny that our world has a shortage of great teachers. Imagine the difference you could make in kids' lives if you weren't worried about your job security being based on your students' standardized test scores. Maybe you don't want the commitment and bureaucracy of teaching full-time in a public school. Why not start giving lessons on something meaningful after school? You'd have the best students because the only ones willing to put in the extra time after classes would be the ones who really care about what you're teaching.

I'm not an amazing computer programmer, but I enjoy it. Google developed a programming language for making Android apps that is incredibly easy to use.[2] I'd love to teach a class on app development to high school kids. It'd be an after-school thing. I'd set the price somewhere around $50-100 to make sure that the kids who showed up were serious about it. With the right setup, I believe that I could give kids usable skills in the fundamentals of computer programming in 20-40 hours of class without them even realizing the practicality and scope of the things they were learning. When we were done, they'd have everything they needed to start developing apps on their own— apps that they could sell in the app stores, starting the first trickle toward filling their own Treasure Baths and inspiring them to continue developing their programming abilities. All it takes to host a class like this is a schedule with free time more predictable than that of a full-time airline pilot.

I'd also like to teach the fundamentals behind Pilot Math to high

---

[2] Google gave up the care of this programming language to MIT. It's now called MIT App Inventor. It's 100% free to install and use: https://appinventor.mit.edu/.

school or even middle school students. Imagine how much better off humanity would be if we all understood these principles from a young age.

What are you good at that you could teach?

I don't even expect you to choose something as directly focused on "giving back" as teaching. I personally believe that music is a very important thing in our world. From Mozart to the Beetles to Bob Marley, musicians have influenced the world and made a difference in the lives of billions of people. If you love music, quitting regular work could give you the time to really put in the effort required to be great at it. You could absolutely make a difference in our world with music.

There are other worthwhile artforms out there too. Are you a good writer? Thanks to authors like JK Rowling, our society has rediscovered an insatiable appetite for good fiction. Kids who might have grown up never reading anything more complex than a txt msg have discovered a love for 700-page fiction novels. Why not contribute to humanity's ever-expanding compendium of great literature?

Maybe you're great at building things. You could make sculptures, weld fancy light fixtures, or design and build entire houses that are both beautiful and energy efficient.

I also regard some TV and movies as forms of art. Why not start writing and/or producing some of your own? Web resources like YouTube, Kickstarter, drones, and GoPro cameras have made this attainable even for amateurs like you and me. You could go on to make the next Schindlers' List, Fight Club, Matrix, or maybe, if you practice really hard and get good enough, the next Happy Gilmore.

If you're good at programming, you could come up with the next great app. Services like Amazon, Google, Air BnB, Uber, Skype, and many others have radically altered our world. (Hopefully for the better.) Humanity is only just now getting started with quantum computing. Once we figure it out our world will change drastically. The people who teach them selves quantum programming in the next 10 years will be the Jobs, Hewletts, and Packards of the 21st century. You could be one of those people.

If you're not good at programming now, you'd have plenty of time to learn it. I won't say that it's especially easy, but if you worked on it nearly-full-time you could attain the skills necessary to do some serious app development in under a year. There are several free or very cheap courses on the web that would teach you enough to get started. (If you're interested, start by checking out Treehouse.)[3] You absolutely have the potential to develop a world-changing app in a matter of years.

You could also use your time to work for or even start some sort of service organization. I have some friends from my time in Air Force Special Operations Command who do a lot with organizations like the Wounded Warrior Project[4] and the Special Operations Warrior Foundation.[5] A group of Pilot Network members have started PreFlight,[6] a summer camp that inspires young women to pursue careers in aviation and other STEM disciplines. If you're having trouble thinking of something, just go volunteer with Habitat for Humanity[7] until you figure something else out. You'll make a lasting difference in others' lives, and learn some useful skills in the process.

None of these are things you have to wait to start on. However, you'll find it much harder to succeed at any of them if you're burdened with a regular full-time job. Pilot Math is all about getting your finances to a point where you don't need to rely on a job to support your family's needs. Once you're there, you have the option of making every "job" you take for the rest of your life a passion project because the amount of the compensation you receive will have zero influence on your ability to provide for your family's needs. Without the burden of mandatory full-time work, you'll finally have the kind of time needed to really throw yourself into something that matters to you.

I've suggested a lot of ideas here. Most of them are based on my personal preferences and goals, but don't let that limit you. There are

---

[3] Treehouse has several courses that walk you through teaching yourself to code. They focus on practical capabilities, rather than theory and some fancy degree accompanied by zero skills. Part of their courses includes building a portfolio of real applications that you could absolutely use to land a job, if desired. Even if you aren't looking for a full-time programming job, doing these projects will give you the skills to do serious programming for your own purposes. https://teamtreehouse.com/

[4] https://www.woundedwarriorproject.org/

[5] https://specialops.org/

[6] https://www.preflightcamp.com/

[7] https://www.habitat.org/

so many things in this world more worth pursuing than sitting in a cubicle (or even flying ATL-BHM-ATL every day,) 20 days a month, for the next 26 years.

I expect that as you've been reading you've already identified at least one really big Why with the potential to get you out of bed in the morning. If you haven't yet, take a few minutes to ask yourself if there's a Why you may have forgotten about. It's sad how quickly the grind of full-time-work-or-my-family-starves can kill our dreams. You may need some serious introspection to remember a really great Why that you gave up on years ago.

This Why is important for many reasons. It's meaningful as a goal, but you'll also find that Pilot Math is impossible to apply without it.

Our society is so brainwashed that most people you talk to will actively try to discourage you from using Pilot Math. Many will tell you that it's just impossible to get a Treasure Bath full enough. They'll reject the math without having seen it. They'll say that it's lazy to pursue anything other than full-time work. They'll accuse you of being selfish, entitled, or something else undesirable. Without a serious Why, you might end up shamed into conformity.

Most people around you are also brainwashed into thinking that the purpose of life is acquiring things. They believe it's appropriate to spend every dime you earn, and then some, buying stuff. Even those pretentiously enlightened enough to "buy experiences, not things" will spend all their money on trips and outings to slather across their social media accounts, rather than working toward freedom. Sure, we're pilots so we think we're better than them and don't care what we think. Unfortunately though, it's tough to protect yourself from the pressure of being surrounded by friends and acquaintances who are always showing off some shiny new toy.

One of the most important parts of Pilot Math is the idea that you shouldn't spend all your money as soon as you earn it. I'm going to ask you to save a lot of your income. (Though, we'll see shortly that this doesn't deprive you at all. Pilot Math is not about extremism.) It will be very difficult to apply Pilot Math while living a world driven by consumerism.

If you want to successfully fill up a Treasure Bath for yourself and your family, you must find at least one compelling Why to keep you on course. (If you find more than one, you'll be even better off.) This process of applying Pilot Math will take years and it won't always be easy. Don't worry though. Ten years from now you'll be living a life of ultimate freedom that will make everyone around you jealous. They'll still be buried in debt and looking at another decade (or two or three) in a job that is at best tolerable, and at worst abject misery. I promise you'll thank me for showing you Pilot Math.

And with that, let's take a look at how it works.

CHAPTER THREE

The Fundamental Theorem of Pilot Math

Okay, enough with starry-eyed platitudes. Let's get to some specifics, shall we?

Picture a person living paycheck-to-paycheck. He or she has no spare money to save for the future. In the event of a catastrophe, this person will have to borrow money from somewhere to deal with the problem. The danger here is that this person had to borrow money in the first place because he doesn't have any excess. He doesn't have any savings. If this person already spends every dollar he makes every month, how can he ever hope to pay off his new expense?

Without any excess income to pay off this new debt, that individual could be setting himself up for a lifetime of what amounts to financial slavery. We don't want to be like that.

Let's say instead that one of our favorite pilot buddies, Indie, is able to save 10% of her income. (This is a good start, though certainly not enough. I'm appalled at how many self-proclaimed financial advisors will tell you this is all you need to save!) If Indie has a catastrophe, chances are she'll be able to deal with it using her savings. Good for her!

Better yet, she avoids catastrophe and invests that 10% somewhere so that her money will grow for her over time. Even without interest we can see that after 9 years of saving like this, Indie will have saved up enough cash to support one year's worth of spending...one year of retirement, if you will. (Actually, thanks to the beauty of compounding interest she does slightly better than this, as we'll see shortly.)

(Yes, your goal may not be a full early retirement in the FIRE community's vernacular. Don't worry, you'll see shortly that this concept is still meaningful for you.)

Let's say Indie's salary is $100,000 per year. She spends $90,000 and invests $10,000. We're going to assume a 5% return on investment (ROI) and that she starts saving at age 30.

If she continues to invest at this rate for all nine years, she'll end up with $111,004 at the start of year 10. Of that, $90,000 is cash that she put in and the remaining $21,004 is interest that her investment earned with zero effort on her part. That extra $21,004 is like getting two free years worth of savings thanks to interest. Her $111,004 isn't enough money to quit working forever, but it'd fund slightly more than one year's worth of life without full-time work. Or, if she decides to use the 4% Rule to only live off the interest from her invested money, this little pool of Treasure at the bottom of her Bathtub will give her an annual "passive" income of $4,440. That's also not enough to retire on, but can you see where we're headed?

Let's say Indie decides to double her efforts—a total of 18 years of saving. She'll end up with $282,470...enough for *three* full years of retirement though she only did *two* cycles of saving. That's pretty nice, but it's even more impressive to see that if she uses the 4% Rule to only live off interest at this point she'll get $11,298 per year. That's still not enough to live on, but we're getting closer.

We can continue this calculation out indefinitely to figure out how long it'd take for her to build up a passive income equal to her annual spending. Unfortunately, the answer isn't pretty. It'd take her 51 years to achieve that level and she'd be 81 years old. Poor Old Indie.

At this point the value or her investment portfolio would have grown to an impressive $2.2 million. She would actually have wanted to start spending her principal at some point in there because she's going to die long before she runs out of cash.

In case you can't tell, I'm not a huge fan of this strategy. Your investments will have some bad years somewhere along the line. If your principle depreciates enough, your passive income in those years won't be enough to cover your expenses and you'll be in trouble. Even assuming nothing but gumdrops and rainbows in the investing world, it'd still require her to work for a lot longer than she should have to. 51 years is too long to wait to gain full control of your life.

Let's try another strategy. Instead of only investing 10% of her income, Indie gets gnarly and invests half of everything she makes.

She spends $50,000 per year and invests $50,000. Since she's able to reduce her spending so much, every year of savings will fund a full year in retirement. (Even more than that with interest.) She's achieved a critical 1:1 ratio that we will call a 50% "savings rate."

After 17 years, and at the much less-ripe age of 47, Indie will have amassed a Treasure Bath filled with $1.3 million. This is enough to provide a passive income of $51,899 every year...enough to cover her annual spending forever, assuming that her spending doesn't increase.

It's critical to note an almost magical property of Pilot Math at this point. By reducing her annual spending, Indie has gained a double benefit. First, the more she saves, the faster her Treasure Bath fills up. (Our next example will take this one step further.) Second, by choosing to live a life of reduced spending while she's still working, Indie essentially trains herself to enjoy a frugal life. That mindset is critical!

Many retirement planners or pension funds arbitrarily choose a percentage of Final Average Earnings (FAE) as a target for retirement. Until a decade or so ago, airlines and pilot unions used FAE to determine their pension plan payouts. A common industry baseline was 60% FAE. This is stupid from every possible angle.

If you're spending 100% FAE the year you retire (you're spending every dollar you bring in,) but your pension is only going to provide 60% of that amount (60% FAE) each year in retirement, then you'll instantly find yourself 40% short of the funds you need to continue spending in retirement like you did before retiring.

If you always spend everything you make without putting enough into savings, you will never have enough money to cover your needs in retirement.

If you know that you'll receive 60% FAE in retirement, then it behooves you to learn to live a happy, fulfilling life while only spending 60% FAE while you still have a job. If you can manage this, your lifestyle won't have to change at all in retirement.

This 60% FAE number is a somewhat arbitrary figure from a long-gone era. I feel that many companies and unions did their pilots a disservice by training them to put too much focus on that value. The truth is that once you stop receiving an income from actively working, all you have left is the passive income from your savings. It doesn't matter what percentage of FAE that gives you because you just don't have any more money. If you spend more than your investments earn each year, the amount of principle in your investment accounts will start depleting...your Treasure Bath will start leaking.

However, if your passive investment income is enough to cover your spending, your Treasure Bath will last forever. If you've trained yourself to live happily on the amount of spending that your passive income can provide, you should never have to dip into the principal in your accounts. If your investments have a bad year, you can reduce your spending slightly or do a little part-time work to make up the difference. If your investments have a good year, use the excess to pad your balance and make your Treasure Bath that much deeper (or just enjoy some extra luxuries for a year.)

Indie won't need 60% FAE in retirement, because she's already learned to live happily on 50% of her current annual earnings. If she's smart, she'll continue enjoying life at that spending level, even while her income increases during her career. If she pours all that extra income into her Treasure Bath, her savings rate will continue to increase over time, allowing her to reach financial freedom that much sooner.

That said, Pilot Math isn't good for anything if it means living an unhappy life where we actually feel deprived. We're going to look at some real-world numbers in the next chapter and see that you and I should easily be able to turbocharge our savings without having to feel deprived at all.

Now, bear with me and let's look at one more case. Let's say that Indie decides to be a saving monster and limits her spending to $25,000 per year. She's now saving $75,000 per year, a whopping 75% of her income. Even without interest, we see that every year of work earns Indie *three* years of freedom! Ten years of working at this rate means she's set through age 70, even if she never earns a penny of interest. It gets even better though.

In this scenario it only takes Indie 7 years to amass the roughly $650,000 that will provide her an annual passive income of $25,000. Yes, it's possible to start from zero savings to reaching complete freedom from mandatory full-time work in just 7 years. All it takes is the discipline to control your spending and invest the rest.

Perhaps you're saying to yourself right now, "That's ridiculous. Nobody can live on $25,000 per year!"

Although there are people who would disagree with you, I'll concede your assertion for now.

The beauty is that this principle of Pilot Math scales. If you make $200,000 a year, you can spend $50,000 per year and still have this amazing 75% savings rate. It still only takes 7 years to hit the point where you can retire forever...with a passive investment income of $50,000 in this case. (If you're wondering, you can hit an annual total compensation of $200,000 somewhere around Year 3 at a major airline, depending on your airline, the type of aircraft you're flying, and whether you choose to live in base. That's for First Officer pay. You'll be well above $200,000 the moment you make Captain.)

"But Emet, airlines used to promise their pilots pensions of 60% FAE? That equates to $120,000 per year, or more, in retirement. If I choose to only spend $50,000 per year I'm missing out on a lot of toys I could have bought, right?"

That's a good point. Could I spend $120,000 a year in retirement? You bet! Do I need to though?

We'll look at some actual data shortly, but for now we need to understand that our economy has basically morphed into a raging monstrosity of unchecked consumerism. It's not good enough for a company to have strong sales every year, a company has to grow—to *increase* total sales—every quarter or else everyone panics. (Actually, things are so out of whack that this quarterly growth has to be within pennies of an arbitrary number that analysts choose by gazing into a crystal ball. Panic ensues if real-world growth numbers fail to match this guess each quarter.)[8]

Yes, the population is increasing overall, but the only way to sustain constant growth is to get people to buy more stuff. Your phone can last longer than a year or two. Your car should be drivable for decades. Good clothing can last nearly that long. (The best socks I ever owned lasted through 15 years of daily punishment.) You don't need all the stuff that companies spend billions every year convincing you to buy. It's the companies selling it who need *you* to buy it.

Don't worry, I'm not talking about spending hours of your life clipping coupons, having extra children to use as slave labor on a family farm, or having your spouse give you haircuts with a pair of rusty scissors that you fished out of a garbage can. Pilot Math is not about deprivation or extremism!

---

[8] There's a fascinating book about this. I highly recommend: The Number: How the Drive for Quarterly Earnings Corrupted Wall Street and Corporate America.

Pilot Math says that you can rapidly achieve financial freedom while living the life of an average, middle-class American family. I even have the numbers to prove it. Let's take a look!

CHAPTER FOUR

How Much Is Enough?

So, I just told you that you have to live on no more than 25-50% of your salary and invest the rest. You saw that number and panicked. Is everyone caught up? Good. Let's move on.

The big question here is: "How much money is enough to live on?"

I just asserted that a 3rd year major airline FO should spend a total of $50,000 per year, max. Yes, it seems like a very low amount of spending given that pilot's income, but plenty of families do just fine on less. Let's engage in some consumerism shaming by looking at some examples:

Exhibit A is one of my personal heroes, Mr. Money Mustache.[9] He worked for a grand total of 9 years between college and retirement. His average combined family income was only $125,000 for those 9 years. He reached financial independence by spending less than $25,000 every year and saving everything else.

His 2016 spending was just over $30,000 (his house is paid off.) He's one the most zealous examples I know of frugal living and uses some strategies that are tough for some of the whimper members of society, but he doesn't do anything truly crazy. He lives in a fancy house, eats fancy organic food, and seems to enjoy a fun and fulfilling life with friends and family. Although he's officially retired, he still has side projects that earn far more than he spends every year. He pursues side projects for pure enjoyment, and the money he earns from them is just

---

[9] Just go read his whole blog. It's as entertaining as it is full of great ideas: www.mrmoneymustache.com/

a nice fringe benefit. His 'stache has continued to grow so far beyond his needs that he gave $100,000 to charity in 2016.[10] Where did the first 9 years of your working career get you?

Next up is Exhibit B, Mr. Root of Good.[11] Married with three kids, Mr. RoG retired after 10 years of mandatory full-time work with $1.3 million in the bank. Neither he nor his wife ever made a six-figure income and they never had any significant windfalls. We've already run the math to know that the RoG family can afford to spend $50,000 per year forever, given the comforting, bubbly depth of their Treasure Bath. However, they have yet to come close to that level of spending. Their annual spending was in the 30s for a while and hit $38,000 in 2016. Despite not having any significant active income, the overall balance of their portfolio has now surpassed $2 million!

You can see the specifics of MMM's spending on his blog.[12] Here are the monthly expenses for another FIRE blogger, Nick, a husband and father who writes at pretired.org:[13]

- Groceries/Eating out: $350
- Utilities (water/sewer/garbage) $101
- Electricity: $78
- Gas (heating and stove): $66
- Internet and TV: $63
- Cell phones: $129
- Car insurance: $256
- Life insurance: $88
- Property tax house: $440
- Homeowners insurance house: $46
- TOTAL: $1,618

He admits that he left out a couple expenses here and estimates his

---

[10] https://www.mrmoneymustache.com/2016/10/26/notes-on-giving-away-100000/

[11] Root of Good isn't as entertaining as MMM, but it's an excellent example of a family that applied the principles behind Pilot Math, achieved financial independence, and quit full-time work forever, all while making far less money than a Year 2 major airline pilot. http://rootofgood.com/

[12] https://www.mrmoneymustache.com/2017/05/19/2016-spending/

[13] Another smaller-scale, but very interesting FIRE blog: http://www.pretired.org/.

actual spending at somewhere around $1800. That's well below the annual $25,000 goal we set for our pilot friend, Indie, in the last chapter.

You'll note that Pretired Nick doesn't have a house or car payment. My wife actually laughed the first time she saw these numbers. I don't present them as a goal, but as a lower boundary to show where spending can potentially be for a real family living happily in the US.

Any skepticism that applies to Nick could apply to any of the examples I just mentioned. These are just a bunch of bloggers, right? Nobody starts a blog to talk bout how they failed. I see where you're coming from. How about we look at some numbers from a source we can trust like the US Government? (Because it's so great with finances.) Well, we're in luck.

It turns out US Bureau of Labor Statistics (BLS) publishes the results of an annual Consumer Expenditure Survey in Excel format every year.[14] We're going to use their "Income Before Taxes" spreadsheet to try and find some real-world numbers.[15] I'm impressed at the treasure trove of data available here for "free." Let's see what it does for us.

First off, the numbers in this spreadsheet are all averages, even though there is probably no such thing as the "average" household. Your particular numbers will almost certainly be higher or lower than these figures in most categories. (The spreadsheet includes variance numbers if you're statistically savvy enough to make use of such things. Our discussion doesn't require us to dive that deep. Also, I hate statistics and don't feel like slogging through all that math on your behalf. Thanks to the security of my own Treasure Bath, my family won't starve because of my personal aversion to rigorous statistical analysis.)

Speaking of averages, it's important to note that this data set gives double credit in some areas. It shows both the average amount spent on rent and the average amount paid toward a mortgage each year and adds those two figures as part of its total annual spending amount for housing. Since we're trying to reach financial independence, we going to choose to not have both a house with a mortgage *and* an apartment

---

[14] You can download these tables yourself, for free, right here: https://www.bls.gov/cex/tables.htm.

[15] Here's the spreadsheet for the 2016 BLS numbers that I used: https://www.bls.gov/cex/2016/combined/income.xlsx.

as our primary residences at the same time. We'll just pick one or the other. We'll be adjusting the value the spreadsheet has for "total spending" for double-credit situations like this where appropriate. (It also reflects a surprisingly small value for mortgage payments. We'll actually have to adjust this value *up* to make it feel more realistic.)

Also, I'm shocked and appalled to see that the groups of lowest-income Americans *all* spend more on average than they earn each year! It isn't until we reach an income level of $50,000-$69,999 per year that people actually do better than breaking even (looking at their after-tax income.) No wonder so many people in our country are in financial trouble!

Let's focus on the good news though. In the last chapter I arbitrarily set $50,000 as an upper limit for annual spending for a major airline pilot. It turns out that 63% of the households in this spreadsheet spend at or below that level. (Yes, I'm cheating here to get a better number. I'm including the $50,000-$69,999 cohort because, at $52,088 in annual spending, they're "close enough" to hit our $50K mark with only minimal adjustments.) This means my arbitrary spending limit is probably attainable for most Americans without forcing your family to dress in rags and eat only cat food while living in a van down by the river. We're actually going to base all of our future calculations on an adjusted final value we come up with for "average" spending in America.

I'm going to challenge you live your life such that your spending doesn't exceed this amount of money each year. This isn't some arduous challenge...I'm basically asking you to spend the same amount of money as the majority of other middle-class Americans.

I realize that your family's numbers won't match perfectly with the ones we come up with here. You're welcome to download a copy of my spreadsheets and input your actual spending numbers.[16] If you're a pilot for the military or a regional airline, you family's spending is probably in this range already.

Now let's take a look at the Bureau of Labor Statistics (BLS) numbers and adjust them slightly for reality. We'll discuss a few of them both to convince you that the numbers are realistic, and to prompt you to think about how much of your own spending is

---

[16] https://pilotmathtreasurebath.com/calculators/

necessary.

We're going use the numbers from the $50,000-$69,999 per year cohort as the baseline from which we adjust. (Why? Their spending is actually quite similar to the next lower level and reasonably close to our $50,000 per year limit...making them convenient.)

That said, let's start with food:

Category	Line Item	Average
Food (Total)		$6,739
	Food at Home	$3,893
	Food Away from Home	$2,847
	Alcoholic Beverages	$420

This figure of $6,739 per year works out to just $561 per month. It seems low to me, but maybe that's because I'm not a very disciplined grocery shopper. (I have a long way to go there, in fact.) It seems like a family working hard to achieve financial freedom could cut back on eating out, do some deliberate meal planning, clip some coupons, and save a lot of money here. However, I'm going to assume that $6,739 is a reasonable amount to spend on food and not make any adjustments. (If you don't drink alcohol you'll be up $420 per year here, assuming you don't spend that cash on fancy coffee, smoothies, or protein shakes instead.)

Next up, let's take a look at the BLS's numbers for housing:

Category	Line Item	Average	Adjustment
Housing Total		$17,331	
Other Dwellings			
	Mortgage interest and charges	$2,451	$8,000
	Property tax	$1,657	
	Maintenance, repairs, insurance, other expenses	$1,228	
	Mortgage principal	$0	$4,500
Rented dwellings		$4,150	-$4,150
Other lodging		$494	
Utilities, fuels, and public services			
	Natural gas	$339	
	Electricity	$1,459	
	Fuel oil and other fuels	$83	-$83
	Water and other public services	$590	
Telephone			
	Cellular phone service	$1,255	
	Residential phone service, VOIP, and phone cards	$288	-$288
Household operations			
	Personal services	$269	-$269
	Other household expenses	$820	
Housekeeping supplies			
	Laundry and cleaning supplies	$155	
	Other household products	$342	-$171
	Postage and stationary	$124	-$90
Household furnishings and equipment			
	Household textiles	$92	
	Furniture	$333	
	Floor coverings	$19	
	Major appliances	$280	
	Small appliances, miscelaneous housewares	$128	-$100
	Miscelaneous household equipment	$778	
Adjusted total			$24,683

The BLS numbers here didn't look quite right, so I made some significant adjustments. I subtracted out the $4,150/yr for renting, because we're assuming you either rent or own...not both. When looking at home ownership costs though, the BLS numbers only come out to $5,336 for mortgage interest, taxes, and maintenance. Their spreadsheet also doesn't mention anything about any part of mortgage payments going toward principal. Those interest payments seemed way too low to me, so I added $8,000. I also assume that if a pilot is going to buy a house, he or she intends to pay it off someday. I put $4,500 per year toward principal, hoping that's a low-end estimate.

These adjustments are based on a home with a purchase price somewhere in the $200,000 - $250,000 range, with a loan at 4%. (You can do a little better than 4% right now, but I went with something conservative.)

Note that this mortgage is a crazy amount of money. My adjustments have us paying the bank more than twice as much in interest every year as we pay in principal. There are many arguments for and against paying off a mortgage early. I assert that if you want to reach a state of financial independence, you'll be a lot better off living in a home that is paid off. If you can make that happen, you'll reduce your annual spending needs by $15,000, if not more. Knowing this, we suddenly realize that the comparably microscopic spending of people like MMM and Mr. RoG usually reflects families who have paid off their houses.

You can save a lot of money in this category by choosing a more affordable type of housing. A community called Bigger Pockets[17] is dedicated to helping people like you and me figure out how to get more out of real estate. They have blogs, books, podcasts, and an active forum where you can find all kinds of strategies for saving or even making money with your housing. Most of that content is free on their website. It's worth your time to at least stop by and think about how you can exploit their knowledge to your advantage.

Moving on, there were some other housing-related items I chose to adjust:

I eliminated the $83 expense for fuel oil. I figured it was redundant with natural gas and electricity on there. I think most homes will pick one of those three options for heating, so I eliminated the smallest expense to be conservative.

Since this is the 21st century I eliminated the cost of home phone service and calling cards. If you're desperate for a home phone number then use a free service like Google Voice.[18] Long distance is free on your cell phone and you can get long-distance *video* calling for free using services like Skype, FaceTime, Google Hangouts, etc.

The average figure of $1,225 for cell phone service is actually only

---

[17] Be careful clicking this link. You will find so much great information that it could be hours before you make it up for air: https://www.biggerpockets.com/.
[18] https://www.google.com/voice

about 10% more than my wife and I pay for Google's Project Fi with 2 lines and a shared 5 GB of data. I consider that a pretty luxurious phone plan, and we opt for it because we have a lot more than $70K annual income. (If you have a side-hustle, you may be able to expense some or all of this phone bill.)

If you're in the trenches trying to fill up your Treasure Bath to meet a specific goal, you aren't yet set up to waste money on luxuries like a fancy phone plan. Google FI[19] only costs $20 per line for unlimited texting and calling in the US, unlimited international texting, and $0.20 per minute calling in dozens of countries. They also make your life easier by giving you free calling and texting over wifi. After that, your family shares all data at $10 per GB and you only ever pay for data you use. Data costs the same overseas as it does in the US. If you have unused data at the end of the month that amount is credited back to you in full as cash, rather than macaroni minutes.

You can get two lines and 1 GB of data to share for a grand total of $45 per month. (The base price for additional lines is only $15 each.) If you go out of your way to use wifi whenever possible, it's perfectly realistic to enjoy modern life on a plan like this. I challenge myself to avoid using cellular data whenever possible. I luxuriate here, but I could easily do a lot better. If you're trying hard to fill up a Treasure Bath, you can definitely make this work.

Many people consider extra data plans for iPads or other devices essential. I assert that you can live a fulfilling live without them. They are nice luxuries, but they're not for people who want to get rich. You lived just fine before tablet computers existed, so you can survive now limiting your tablet to wifi.

While $45 per month is easily attainable for a couple by themselves, I realize that most parents have good reasons for wanting to provide their kids with a cell phone. That doesn't mean your kid needs unlimited data! You want the ability for them to call or text if they're in trouble, and you want to be able to call and hound them at will. None of that requires covering a data plan for them.

Get your kids a phone, but ration their data. Or, better yet, tell them they have to pay for their own phone and data by getting a job! (Spoiler alert: this will not kill your children.) Since adding a couple

---

[19] Google FI now allows most types of phones, including iPhones. The customer service is great, and you'd be hard-pressed to convince me you need a more expensive service. https://fi.google.com/

kids can quickly elevate the cost of cell phone service, I let the $1,225 figure stand. If you don't have kids (yet or at all) you'll be banking money faster here.

(Google FI recently announced unlimited data plans that could protect you from kids who have a tough time controlling their data use habits. You could subscribe to these plans and make the kids pay for their share each month, or continue to charge them by the GB to try an teach them about budgeting.)

Our next adjustment is for "Personal Household Services." It took me a minute to figure out what the BLS meant by this before it occurred to me that some people do things like hire maids to clean for them. Your immediate response to that should be: "Hell no!" You can scrub your own toilets and mow your own lawn. If you enjoy it, you can make extra money providing these services for your eternally-low-net-worth neighbors. However, no self-respecting pilot should outsource this stuff, at least not until you have a Bath brimming with Treasure.

(Men: it wasn't that long ago that American culture said women are responsible for all the cooking and cleaning around the house. If nothing else, Mad Men showed us that this is no way to be happy.[20] You and your spouse are partners. Work together to take care of these things. Don't put it all on someone else.)

The one exception I'll make on outsourcing household services is for funding your kid's cell phone plan or other spending needs. Pay them to mow the lawn, scrub toilets, and wash windows, so that they can turn right around and pay you for their cell phone data and cover their other expenses. You don't have to do the work yourself, and your kid learns the value of earning his or her own money to support his or her wants and needs. Win/win!

It's worth noting here that the smaller your house, the fewer chores everyone has to do. You'll save money on your home's purchase price as well as costs and time or upkeep. Perhaps the answer to "how much home is enough?" is: "as much as I can stand to clean."

The next line in the spreadsheet is for "other household expenses." I wanted to significantly reduce the budget for this category, but my

---

[20] https://www.amc.com/shows/mad-men/exclusives/where-to-watch

wife reminded me that this covers things like: school field trips, family pictures, gymnastics lessons, and an array of other items. There are many ways to reduce the costs of things on that list, but we'll leave it alone for now.

I initially thought that $155 per year for laundry services was ridiculous. If you look into the cost of detergent though, you'll find that this may be a pretty good value. (If you look further though the internet you will find some ways to economize significantly here, but we'll accept this expense as is.)

I wanted to reduce the budget for furniture, major appliances, and household textiles ($92 per year on drapes? Really?) However, I think many of us will realistically need to replace a major appliance or want to replace a major piece of furniture every few years. We'll let these two figures stay as they are so they can build up over time. The "expense" here is you stashing those dollars away in an investment to cash-out when your refrigerator dies...not permission to go out and buy a major appliance every year because Samsung decided to turn the door into a giant tablet computer.

I can't imagine spending $128 per year for small appliances though. Appliances like microwaves, toasters, or coffee makers last a long time. Need a new one? Most are surprisingly cheap at Walmart or Target. If you can't stomach those prices, look on Craigslist, or wait for Black Friday / Cyber Monday on Amazon.

After all these adjustments our annual expenditures for housing actually went up. That's based entirely on an assumption that you're going to spend more than this cold, mathematical average for home ownership. If you go with a cheaper house, or choose to rent, you may be able to economize significantly here. However, I feel like these values offer most pilots a good shot at a safe and comfortable home.

If you can pay that home off, you'll free-up a lot of money! Yes, you can make more interest in the stock market right now than you can from making extra payments on a house with a 3.5% mortgage. However, if your family is deeply indoctrinated in our culture of consumerism will you actually invest that money instead of blowing it on junk? If not, you may be better off paying your mortgage down sooner, rather than later.

Next up is clothing:

Category	Line Item	Average	Adjustment
Apparel and services		$1,662	
Men and boys (Subtotal)			
	Men, 16+	$318	
	Boys, 2 to 15	$83	
Women and Girls			
	Women, 16+	$521	
	Girls, 2 to 15	$69	
Children under 2		$72	
Footwear		$324	
Other apparel products and services		$235	-$135
Adjusted Total			$1,487

When it comes to clothing I divide the world into two types of people: those who base their self-worth on their clothing and those who don't.

Chances are you didn't design and sew the clothes yourself. I'm not impressed by your ability to walk through a store and choose clothing. I'm equally unimpressed by your ability to stand in front of a closet and put together an outfit. If you don't have anything in your life worth being more proud of than what you wear, you need to go re-read Chapter 2 and spend some time coming up with a Why instead of going on your next shopping trip. Don't take my word for any of this though.

The 3rd Book of The Pilot Math Bible is *The Millionaire Next Door*, by Thomas Stanley and William Danko.[21] The authors have spent their careers studying millionaires (frequently funded by companies trying to figure out ways to sell things *to* millionaires.) What they discovered is critical to your future happiness. Hopefully it won't be surprising.

It turns out that when you look at most people who live in expensive neighborhoods, drive fancy cars, wear fancy clothes, and show what most people think of as outward signs of wealth, you'll find that they aren't actually wealthy. In fact, most of them are buried in debt and living one missed paycheck away from financial ruin. The

---

[21] link: https://amzn.to/2LkYmtW

majority of real millionaires (people with an actual net worth at or above $1,000,000) are people who life frugal lives and don't appear "rich" at all. Stanley and Danko list the average and maximum prices for things that true millionaires own, and it's downright humorous. Real millionaires wear Timex watches, drive Toyotas, and shop for clothing at TJ Maxx.

For a large part of human history, displaying expensive possessions was useful for attracting a mate because this actually was a sign of underlying wealth. The advent of things like mass-production, credit, and e-commerce have invalidated that assumption. In my mind, Stanley and Danko have demonstrated, conclusively, that if someone has a bunch of expensive stuff, he or she is a terrible potential mate because chances are he or she has no actual wealth...probably accompanied by a lot of bad spending habits.

In case I haven't been clear enough: I don't respect you more if you wear expensive clothing. In fact, I probably notice your clothing and immediately think a lot less of you. I know that you're trading some fancy clothes for long-term financial stability and that someday you'll be the one insisting, just like Poor Old Joe, that *I'm* responsible for funding *your* social security to support you in retirement because you couldn't be bothered to take care of your own needs in life.

My wife and I have some friends who are embarrassingly bad with money. The wife, we'll call her Nancy, has *hundreds of thousands of dollars* of student loan debt. The husband, we'll call him Fred, spent several years not working and just picked up an entry-level position. Despite that, they have closets full of fancy clothes. One day at their house, Fred proudly showed us his new pair of deck shoes. (No, he does not regularly spend time on or near boats.) The shoes looked kind of goofy, but whatever.... Later, my wife looked them up and saw that they cost $300. Fred has two pairs. (One in red, one in blue.) Another time, Nancy showed up for a double date with a plastic bag in addition to her designer handbag. Before we went into the restaurant for dinner, she pulled out a pair of fancy heeled boots. After dinner, she swapped back into her original shoes and carefully put the boots back in the bag. My wife looked the boots up online: $900!

I would have considered each of these shoes ridiculous on any pair of feet. The fact that they were being worn by people with that much debt was staggering. When I see you wearing expensive clothing, I assume that you're as clueless as these friends. In the words of Shawn

Spencer: "Gus, don't be the Mystery Mousekatool!"[22]

Where does this leave us? I almost reduced the limit for spending on men's clothing by a lot. It's been ages since I paid more than $30 for a pair of jeans. I prefer shirts from somewhere like TJ Maxx, and I'm still trying to wear out old Air Force squadron t-shirts as workout attire. My primary jackets were either issued to me by the USAF (your tax dollars at work) or purchased from a clearance rack.

Remember: I will judge you when I see you wearing anything more expensive. Someday I'll buy a really nice outdoor jacket from REI or Patagonia. It'll be expensive, but I'll plan on wearing it for at least a decade. For now, I'll settle for older jackets and a Bath brimming with Treasure.

However, I also acknowledge that some situations require spending more on clothing than others. With my kids' clothing, it's always a race between growing out of it, or putting so many holes in it that I feel like a bad parent taking them out in public. I left the full spending figure here, though if you can do better you'll be saving more.

It's also unlikely that you'll go your entire career spending $72 per year on clothing for children under two years old. Either you can continue to spend those $72 per year replacing worn-out clothing for your kids, or you can bank the rest and get further ahead on the savings game.

You may have noticed that I didn't touch the average spending for women's clothing. I did this for two reasons. First, it seems like decent women's clothing costs more than what I prefer to wear. It's a racket, but what can you do?

Second, my wife is only starting to come around to this whole concept of giving up full time work and living on the passive income provided by a Treasure Bath. Society has spent her entire life telling her that a human being's worth is based on how many hours he or she spends working at a mandatory full-time job. In her profession, and many others, society expects service providers to dress a certain way. That clothing costs a lot more than a couple sets of pilot uniforms and

---

[22] The television show *Psych* was comic genius. If you're going to waste a bunch of time watching TV, you could do worse than choosing this show. Warning: these clips will make you laugh: https://www.youtube.com/watch?v=sW3PuMGyv88

some casual clothing to wear off-duty.

Thankfully, my wife is still very frugal. She doesn't waste money because she would feel like she's taking food out of her babies' mouths. She is also an intelligent and talented person who makes more money than I do.

If "but what can you do?" isn't a good enough argument for you, TJ Maxx and Marshalls are good places to shop for nice clothing at a discount. My wife has also started occasionally looking at places like Goodwill for environmentalist, rather than economic reasons. She's found a surprising number of very nice, like-new items at prices around 1/10th of what they cost in a retail store. If you're focused on your driving Why in life, and you agree that a person's clothing does not reflect her worth, you may can significantly reduce your spending here.

If your spouse spends a lot on clothing, helping him or her find a really awesome Why in life will naturally push him or her toward identifying ways to save. He or she should easily be able to spend far less than these average figures for clothing. Filling up a Treasure Bath is not a solo sport if you have a family. Your desired end-state includes you and your significant other enjoying your Treasure Bath together. (Sharing a Treasure Bath with your spouse is always a good thing. You save on clothing because you can't wear it in the tub, and baths are always more fun when your spouse joins you!)

You may notice that I also didn't touch a shoe budget that appears pretty large at first glance. Although I don't advocate spending a lot on most shoes, and I'll think less of you for spending too much on them, I feel like there is a place for owning a decent pair of running or other athletic shoes. These are tools for cheap pleasure and long-term health. They last for a limited number of miles and ideally we're all doing enough running or other exercise to wear out at least one pair of shoes every year. I used to gag every time I spent $80 on a pair of running shoes, and prices have only climbed over the years. I'm leaving this expense as-is to account for one pair of athletic shoes for the BLS average of 2 adults and 0.6 children in a household per year. This potentially allows some leeway for rock climbers, hockey players, or athletes that use other specialized footwear.

We've been pretty generous with clothing allowances so far, which is why I cut out most of the "Other apparel products and services" category. I'm guessing they mean things like belts, purses, wallets, and jewelry here. I don't know about you, but my average wallet lasts about 10 years. Belts last several years and cost less than $15 at Marshalls anyway. Some women spend as much on handbags as they do on shoes. I hope by now you'll agree that this is just another sign of being a foolish spender who is accepting a lifetime of financial slavery and missed opportunity in exchange for a bag. Don't do it!

We've only saved a few hundred dollars in this category, but we can do better. I personally spend far less than $200 a year on clothing, and so can you. Don't be afraid to challenge yourself here. If you have a high-spending spouse, helping him or her identify a more meaningful Why could prompt him or her to spend less here too.

If my opinions on clothing haven't gotten through to you yet, maybe you'll respond more favorably to yet another pop culture reference. With that hope, I refer you to some enduring apparel wisdom from *Thrift Shopping* by Macklemore and Ryan Lewis (feat Wanz):

They be like, "Oh, that Gucci? That's hella tight"
I'm like, "Yo, that's 50 dollars for a t-shirt."
Limited edition, let's do some simple addition
50 dollars for a t-shirt, that's just some ignorant bitch shit
I call that getting swindled and pimped, shit
I call that getting tricked by business
That shirt's hella dough, and having the same one as six other people in this club is a hella don't
Peep game, come take a look through my telescope
Tryin' to get girls from a brand?
Man, you hella won't! Man, you hella won't!

And with that eloquent and classy argument, let's move on to the BLS's numbers for transportation:

Category	Line Item	Average	Adjustment
Transportation		$9,173	
Vehicle purchases (net outlay)			
	Cars and trucks, new	$1,332	-$1,332
	Cars and trucks, used	$2,342	
	Other vehicles	36	
Gasoline and motor oil		$2,069	
Other vehicle expenses			
	Vehicle finance options	$260	
	Maintenance and repairs	$910	-$410
	Vehicle insurance	$1,193	
	Vehicle rental, leases, licenses, and other charges	$577	-$277
Public and other transportation		$452	-$452
Adjusted Total			$6,702

When it comes to transportation, I'll again refer you to *The Millionaire Next Door*. Spoiler alert: Rich people don't drive BMWs, Mercedes, or Lamborghinis. I'm pretty sure I'd love to drive a BMW X5, Corvette, or Tesla Model S. They're all masterpieces of automotive engineering. However, nobody (yes not even you) *needs* one.

I can come up with a lot of reasons to own a Toyota Tundra, or at least a Tacoma. However, the truth is I'm not a farmer. I don't have a bunch of hay bales to move around. I'm also not a general contractor who can generate tens of thousands of dollars a year through a mobile carpentry operation.

In many parts of America, pickup trucks are as fundamental to our culture as baseball and apple pie. It'd be useless to try and argue that the average American suburbanite should not own a truck. I will say that if you are going to own one, make sure you're using it enough to justify the added expense. If your truck isn't regularly hauling more than people and groceries, you may be sacrificing a lot of your future for little immediate benefit.

Driving a specific car may provide short-term pleasure, but few vehicles are likely to provide any of us with long-term, lasting happiness. (For a deeper discussion on this, I refer you to the master.)[23]

If your self-worth should not be based on what you wear,

---

[23] One of MMM's best posts: https://www.mrmoneymustache.com/2016/06/08/happiness-is-the-only-logical-pursuit/

then it certainly shouldn't be based on the vehicle in which you spend even less of your life. If it is, you again need to go back to Chapter 2 and spend some time figuring out a Why that actually matters in your life.

If you evaluate potential mates on their choice of car, you're just setting yourself up for a lifetime of financial disaster. There may have been a point in time where owning a nice car reflected actual wealth, but I that's not the case today.

During my Air Force career, I could always tell when I was on a base populated by junior enlisted Airmen or young officers because the parking lots were packed with brand-new, tricked-out Mustangs, Corvettes, and giant trucks. It's no secret what those vehicles cost, and it's no secret what these people earned. Each person had doomed him- or herself to several years of financial slavery to obtain those vehicles. One of my friends did a tour as a commander in charge of enlisted troops and said that half of his time every day was spent on disciplinary actions for things like getting into financial trouble. It is dishearteningly easy in the United States for a person to buy far more car than he or she can afford.

So, looking at the BLS data we can see that Americans spend more on cars than they do on food. Wow! I'm not going to say that you absolutely can't have two cars, but you should consider the possibility of only having one. This is especially true if you're an airline pilot. Have your spouse or teenage kid drop you off and pick you up for trips. Remember, we're trying to spend more time with our families anyway. This could give you an extra 30-60 minutes of uninterrupted time with someone important at each end of your trip.

The "average" data has Americans making payments on both new and used cars every year. I decided that at most we only need to be making payments on one car in any given year. I eliminated the less-spendy category to be conservative. (Surprisingly, this happened to be new cars in the BLS data.)

This shouldn't seem like extremism or deprivation. The average (reasonable) car loan is 48-60 months. This means that my Pilot Math allows for you to own two cars, buying a brand new one every 4-5 years, and that each car you buy has to last you 8-10 years. If this seems outrageous to you, I'll again send you back to examine your Why.

I also made adjustments for vehicle maintenance, licensing, and rental cars. I've had some rough years for maintenance, but $910 is an awful lot. If you buy a reliable, proven car (a Honda or Toyota like all the Millionaire(s) Next Door you're trying to emulate) you're not going to be spending that much. Licensing your car in Florida costs a few hundred dollars the year you buy it, but is less than $100 per year thereafter. If you live in a state where you're paying hundreds a year to license yourself or your car, then the government probably charges you too much for a lot of other things and you might consider moving to a less expensive state.

I left some money there for rental cars or Uber/Lyft. As airline pilots it sometimes makes sense for us to take a ride somewhere on a layover. If nothing else, ride sharing is the absolute best invention I've ever seen for reducing drunk driving. I don't advocate frequent or excessive drunkenness. However, if you're going to drink, you absolutely have my permission to sacrifice a couple days of future financial freedom to catch a Lyft.

I also subtracted the $452 average expense for public transport. Don't get me wrong, I think public transit is a great thing in a big city. It reduces traffic, it's better for the environment, and it can eliminate a lot of headaches associated with car ownership (as long as the public transit is well-implmeneted.)

If you live in a city where public transit is good enough to use on a regular basis, you have no excuse for matching the average US spending figures for car ownership. Either only own one car, or get rid of all your cars and use ridesharing apps or rentals when you need to drive somewhere far away.

For the sake of simplicity, I estimated the savings of using this strategy by eliminating this $452 expense from the budget. Chances are that by owning zero or one reasonable cars and maximizing your use of public transit, you'll save a lot more in the overall transportation category than just $452. Adjust your personal version of our spreadsheets accordingly.

With these adjustments we're saving nearly $3,000 per year on transportation expenses. We're not even doing anything outlandish here. We're allowing ourselves to have a monthly payment on one new car at all times. We're not even limiting our annual mileage... something you could do to save even more. All we're doing is consciously choosing to not buy ourselves a fancy, expensive car that we don't really need.

It's possible to increase your savings here drastically. Most FIRE gurus will argue that you can easily find a reliable, used compact car on Craigslist for about $5,000. A car like this should last for hundreds of thousands of miles. This isn't something you go into debt for...you save your money and buy it outright. (Or, just sell your current Chevy Tahoe and use part of the cash to buy a used Toyota Corolla before investing the rest.)

The other theory that the experts will push is that you should not be driving an "average" amount. You should be driving far less and biking or walking as much as possible. It's also worth noting that the "average" of $2,069 on gas and oil accounts for an average amount of driving in a lot of trucks and SUVs with embarrassingly bad gas mileage. If you own a reasonably fuel efficient car you should have no problem doubling or even tripling the mileage that these trucks and SUVs get. All of this can drastically reduce your annual fuel bill and help you achieve freedom that much sooner.

With a smart used car purchase and an increase in bicycling you could easily cut this expense to less than half of the national average. The blogosphere is chocked full of people have done exactly that.

If you live in the right location, you can put a solar array on your roof that will pay for itself in just a decade or two. I have one on my house that meets this criteria and it provides more power than I use. With this setup, I could completely eliminate my fuel and oil expenses by purchasing an electric vehicle and charging it at home every night using credits I've earned by giving excess electricity to my power company. Most lower-end electric vehicles have at least enough range to cover a day of driving on a charge, and higher-end cars from companies like Tesla can potentially go days between charges. You can actually save a lot of money on both electricity and vehicle costs if you have the cash available to go solar. (Hmm...another good reason for having a Treasure Bath built up.)

Now that I've told you you're never allowed to own a "fun" car again, I want to backtrack and give you an option. One of the fundamental examples from the 2nd Book of The Pilot Math Bible, *Rich Dad, Poor Dad*, offers an interesting approach to fancy car ownership. The author, Robert Kiyosaki, talks about how he'd always wanted to own a Porsche. He watched some of his colleagues go into debt buying them and realized how stupid they were, yet he still aspired to own a Porsche of his own some day. He figured out a much more mature way of obtaining one.

He decided to work hard and invest his money intelligently. Each investment provided him with a stream of passive income. He decided to set aside some investments for his Porsche. Once the passive income from those investments covered the cost of owning the car, he went to the dealership and proudly bought it. Since it was funded entirely by passive income he knew that he could continue to make payments and drive it forever, even if he lost his job. It seems simple once you read it, but it's actually a brilliant approach in my opinion. Inflation has made these numbers a little crazy since Mr. Kiyosaki first published his book, but I think this is a better approach to take if you absolutely can't live without a fancy car.

Now, I don't recommend employing this technique before you're already financially independent. You're better off using the passive income from those investments to pay off debt, pay off your primary residence, and build your nest egg. However, we've already seen that if you are willing to maximize your savings, you can reach the point of safe retirement very quickly. Once you're there, you could potentially work for another few months after that point and earn enough to cover the cost of owning a fancy new car.

The trick here is to not get trapped in a cycle of working a couple extra months to be able to afford each item on a long list of toys. That's where most people are stuck today…always wanting more and never finding themselves satisfied with what they buy. They fail to recognize it because their average monthly spending eats up most of their paycheck and it takes forever to get each toy. By the time they've saved up enough money to get the next one they've forgotten the lesson they learned last time. Will a fancy car buy you happiness? No. Sorry, but it just won't. Neither will a boat, an airplane, an iPhone, or any other gadget. If you can learn to focus on what matters in life, not only will you spend less, you'll want fewer things.

Okay. We've covered food, shelter, clothing, and transportation. Let's look at health care next:

Category	Line Item	Average
Health Care		
	Health insurance	$3,171
	Medical services	$726
	Drugs	$464
	Medical supplies	$137

Health care is scary. My mother-in-law spent a month in the hospital before passing away. I'm glad my father-in-law had insurance because the bill was over $100,000. Without insurance, one catastrophe could would be enough to drain even the most frugal family's Treasure Bath.

I'm in the USAF Reserves, but sadly my service category doesn't get me access to the military health care system, Tricare. My family is on one of my company's health insurance plans and it's been good so far. My union publishes a maximum annual out-of-pocket cost for each of our plan options. This is a worst-case scenario assuming everyone in your family had the worst year ever and you maxed out each individual deductible, coinsurance, and copay amount. Their worst-case number for the top-of-the-line plan is $15,600 per year. That's a lot of money!

Thankfully, the national average numbers make it seem fairly unlikely to expect a year like that. Our premiums are less than $100 per month and we've spent an annual average of less than $3000 in copays and deductibles during our first few years on the plan. According to the BLS statistics, the average health care expenditure for a family of 2.6 who brings in nearly $70,000 per year is only 20% of my health care plan's maximum annual cost.

As such, I'm not adjusting these numbers at all. I don't want to paint an overly-rosy picture, but I feel like it's a powerful indication that the average annual health care cost across all income bands in our dataset is only $4,600. Part of the Treasure Bath we fill up will be banking against future health care expenses either with Tricare as part of a military retirement, or maximizing contributions to a Health Savings Account.

Some families will have unique challenges with healthcare. This is an extremely tough thing to deal with and I don't wish it on anyone.

However, for an airline pilot, working just one year past the point at which you're set for retirement could be enough to cover decades of medical costs. You shouldn't feel like you're sunk if your family has extra challenges here.

Our next major category is entertainment:

Category	Line Item	Average	Adjustment
Entertainment			
	Fees and admissions	$460	
	Audio and visual equipment and services	$1,096	-$256
Pets, toys, hobbies, and playground equipment (subtotal)			
	Pets	$600	
	Toys, hobbies, and playground equipment	$129	
Other entertainment supplies, equipment, and services		$470	-$370
Adjusted Total			$2,129

I'm actually surprised at how little falls into this category because I feel like we Americans spend a lot on entertainment. I should have cut out something under "fees and admissions" except I aspire to attend a lot more live music events than I do. I guess I'm already saving a lot here, though I'd prefer to save a little less.

I cut a lot on AV equipment and services because there is no excuse for cable or satellite TV in 2019. My father-in-law has a cheap HD antenna stuck to the wall behind his TV. It gets 37 local channels in crystal clear digital HD. On top of that, there are several great streaming TV services that end up getting most shows and movies.

Many of the best shows aren't available on cable anymore anyway. Netflix has been cleaning up at the Emmys lately. Amazon is giving them a run for their money. HBO does fantastic work, and relative upstarts like Disney, CBS, and even Apple are putting honest effort into original content for their own streaming services.

We'll allow up to $15 per month to cover one streaming service at a time. Want to watch a show on the streaming service you aren't subscribed to? Cancel the subscription with your current service, sign up for the other service, spend a month watching the latest season of their hit show, and then switch back as desired. Or, if someone in your family just can't give up your main streaming service, subscribe to a second service for a single month. Binge-watch the latest season of the show you can't miss, and then cancel.

Many will argue that they're so addicted to sports that they *need* cable to watch them. Bullshit. Although it's conversion is proving slower than other genres, televised sports will eventually be available on streaming services. Disney is offering their new streaming service, Disney+, with both Hulu and ESPN for about the same price as Netflix. If you're truly a sports addict, make this your primary streaming service and switch between the others each time a new season of your favorite show is released. Amazon is also dipping its toes into streaming sports. I hope they're able to give Disney/ESPN some competition because it'll make both services better for everyone.

In the meantime, if you really want to be poor all your life in order to spend hours sitting around and watching other people play sports, be my guest. You can get a lot of games for free, in HD, through regular old broadcast television. All you need is an antenna and some minimal effort to install it. Beyond that, use your restaurant budget to enjoy some brews at a sports bar to watch any big games. Better yet: just go watch at the house of a friend who wants to stay poor. Go to the grocery store, pay 20% (or less) of sports bar prices for beverages, and watch from the comfort of your friend's couch.

I'm also going to go out on a limb and suggest that if you're that much of a sports fanatic you should be out *playing* sports rather than sitting around watching other people do it. Your ability to watch or talk about other people playing sports won't impress me much. If you want to impress me, beat me at a pickup game in the park. Go play, be healthy. There are plenty of adult sports leagues if you're interested.

Sports also highlights an interesting fact about television in general. Answer honestly: how much time to you spend watching TV every year? If you're a sports fanatic, how many more hours do you spend reading, thinking, and talking about the sports you watch? When you are lying on your death bed, will you be glad you spent all those hours sitting around? I hope you're at least with your friends or family while you watch, but just imagine what else you could do with your life if, instead of sitting on the couch, you did anything else. There's no excuse for ever saying that you're "busy" or "don't have the time" to pursue a major life goal if you spend that many hours watching anything on TV.

For music, Spotify's family plan gives you unlimited access to most of the music on the planet for $15 a month. (You can also use free streaming services like Pandora to get nearly unlimited music with "limited commercial interruptions," saving even more.)

The expenditures I allow here grant you Spotify Family every month, in addition to your choice of one streaming TV service. I allow internet service only (not bundled with TV or phone.) A quick Google search showed me 10 different companies offering internet access for prices starting at $20 per month. I allowed $40 per month to be conservative, but you could certainly save a lot of money here.

If you look through the Entertainment category you'll note that pets are very expensive. I don't know if I could ever convince my wife to go without any pets. (I'm not sure I'd even risk suggesting it!) If you can forego this category, you'll save a lot of money.

This category also has a miscellaneous/catch-all line. I left $100 there for random expenses. We've already allowed ourselves a pretty health entertainment budget compared to the national average. I think we can survive on what we have.

Having saved at least $500 on entertainment, let's look at the last set of items in our dataset:

Category	Line Item	Average	Adjustment
Original BLS Total		$9,549	
Personal care products and services		$613	
Reading		$100	
Education		$739	
Tobacco products and smoking supplies		$368	-$368
Miscellaneous		$994	-$500
Cash contributions		$1,428	
Personal insurance and pensions (Subtotal)		$5,307	
	Life and other personal insurance	$260	
	Pensions and Social Security	$5,047	$2,829
Adjusted Total			$11,520

I didn't touch "personal care products and services" although I think it's possible to save a lot there. I'm not pretty enough that a really great haircut is going to benefit me any more than the $9.99 Monday Special at Super Cuts. This is another area that will cost more for women.

I'm disappointed that as a nation we're willing to spend more than $1,000 on average for television and music, but only $100 for reading. Still, if you buy books full-price you'll bust a $100 limit pretty quickly. Libraries, used book stores, and used books on Amazon are all great ways to save money here. However, I'd rather you exceed a $100 book budget every year than waste your life watching more cable TV.

An education expense of $739 per year is ridiculously low if you or any of your children are in college. However, the BLS dataset effectively averages this expense across an entire lifetime. As such, I'll assume that this "expense" represents you saving for future education costs, for yourself or your children, if you're not paying that much to cover college right now. (You'll be investing your education money in a 529 plan for some awesome tax advantages. We'll take a look at these types of accounts later.)

I was shocked to see how expensive smoking is. You are never smoking again. Whatever you think you might gain from it, you'll lose far more. It's unhealthy and disgusting. Given humanity's vast body of scientific knowledge about the negative impacts of smoking, there is no reason for anyone to ever smoke tobacco again. Vaping alleviates some of the risks of smoking, but it makes you look even less cool than smoking does. Vaping is out, for your long-term social welfare, not to mention the financial savings.

If you're still skeptical about the correlation between smoking and wealth, consider the following statement made by some RJ Reynolds executives when asked whether they smoke:

"We don't smoke that shit. We just sell it. We just reserve the right to smoke for the young, the poor, the black and the stupid."[24]

Even if you really, really do want suffocate to death or give yourself cancer, do you want your money going to a group of such racist, condescending assholes?

We're cutting out just over half the budgeted annual expense for the "miscellaneous" line. We have plenty of generous allowances for spending. We don't need to waste $1000 of our money every year on expenses too meaningless to even track.

You'll notice a massive adjustment in the wrong direction under "pensions and Social Security." This happens because the average

---

[24] Source: The World Health Organization's report entitled: *Tobacco Explained - The truth about the tobacco industry…in its own words*: http://www.who.int/tobacco/media/en/TobaccoExplained.pdf

airline pilot will max-out social security tax every year. (I did it on second year pay.) You "only" get taxed on the first $127,200 you earn, meaning each of us should expect to shell out a total of $7,886.40 each year. Costs here will eventually have to go up because the Social Security Administration freely admits that the trust fund will be completely depleted sometime in the 2030s. After that point, the only way to pay even drastically reduced benefits will be to increase this tax by a lot. Sucks for us. We'll forego estimating that tax increase for now.

I've made a lot of adjustments here and the numbers didn't work out entirely like I'd hoped when I started this research. Our estimated average yearly spending total comes out to $57,758. I'm happy to leave it there because the average airline pilot makes a lot more money than this. I was pretty pleased to see how close my arbitrary annual spending figure of $50,000 came to the published national average. I feel like any one of us can enjoy a rewarding life while limiting annual spending to this level.

That said, once you start trying to reduce your expenses and purposefully save money, you'll notice that it gets easier...even exciting. You'll want to save more because the path toward your ultimate Why becomes increasingly clear. A family willing to cut back on miscellaneous expenses, clothing, personal services, and a few more areas could easily get this spending well below $50,000. Plus, we've already identified the fact that paying off your house would immediately get you close to only having $40,000 in annual expenses without any other cuts.

If you're an older military pilot or a major airline pilot you probably earn more than the $69,999 at the top end of this spending cohort...and there's a good chance you currently spend more than we've allowed for our average numbers here. It doesn't have to be that way though. We haven't made any adjustments that equate to living in a van down by the river, watching grass grow for fun.

This spending level allows you to have reliable cars and a comfortable (though not opulent) house. You get more streaming TV and music than you could consume in a lifetime. Men get $200 per year to spend on clothing and women get three times that amount. Hell, you even get $92 per year to spend on drapes!

At some point in your life, you have already lived happily while spending $57,758 per year, or less. You are absolutely capable of living happily at that spending level right now. (You're actually capable of living happily spending a lot less, but I'll leave it to the rest of the internet to show you how to make further cuts.)

The beauty of this is that if you can live happily on $57,758 in spending while you're working full-time, you can also live happily on that amount in retirement. The 4% rule says that as soon as you've saved up 25x this number, or $1,443,950, you can retire and never work another day in your life. Some financial independence writers recommend getting your savings as high as 33x your annual expenditure requirements. This would require you to have just over $1.9 million in your Treasure Bath.

This seems like a lot of money, but the beauty of Pilot Math is that if you can learn to live happily at this level of spending, you can reach the point where mandatory full-time work is optional in a amazingly short amount of time. If you're making Year 3 major airline pay of roughly $200,000 and you only spend $57,758, you could be capable of permanently abandoning mandatory full-time work after just 10-11 years.

At that point you could continue to spend just as much money as you have been, while never working again. Or, you could just fly a single 4-day trip each month and still make more money every year than you spend. That $1.44 million you saved up will continue to grow both because you're earning interest on it while not withdrawing a penny, and because you're investing the difference between what you earn every year and your spending of $57,758.

I've chosen some arbitrary numbers for all this. The numbers we're throwing around in this chapter also assume that you start your major airline job without a penny to your name. However, you'll have to "pay your dues" by flying at a regional airline or in the military for at least a few years before you start at a major. If you can limit yourself to this same level of spending at those jobs, you'll have a big head start on filling up your Treasure Bath when you finally show up at your major airline job. We'll run numbers for each of those specific scenarios in upcoming chapters. (Spoiler alert: If you can limit your spending from the very beginning of your career to the the figure we've come up with here, you won't even have to work a full 11 years at the major airline before you reach financial independence!)

Since you're a pilot, I know that there is a part of you that, despite having just read this chapter, doesn't believe me. Sure, dozens of financial independence bloggers live happily on low levels of spending. Sure, US Government data says that 63% of all Americans spend less than $52K per year. You're just not sure you can (or want) to do it.

Part of me wants to play the cheerleader and say, "Ra! Ra! You can do it!" Since you're a pilot though, I'm going to try a different tactic and tell you that I don't really care what you want.

(Wow, this Emet guy is a jerk!)

You may be right, but just bear with me for a moment.

Another beauty of Pilot Math is that it works on an individual level (unlike the corporate, municipal, and other governmental pension programs all over the world that are rapidly revealing states of long-term insolvency for entire workforces.) My wife and I have applied Pilot Math in our lives and we're good. We could decide right now to quit working forever, and live happily at the spending levels I've described here. Whether you decide to apply Pilot Math in your own life, or not, won't affect me in any way.

In fact, the overall success of my investments requires a large swath of the population to continue spending as much money as possible. This spending makes money for companies that I own shares of. Those companies pay me dividends and their stock gains value over time. If the whole world stopped spending like fools and started trying to apply Pilot Math all at once, our whole system would collapse. (It'd be rough for a few years, but I believe that we could raise something much better and stronger from the ashes. I'd say more, but that's a topic better left to another book.) If you want to be one of our economy's foolish consumers, I'm happy to earn dividends from your spending!

However, I don't wish that upon *you*, as an individual. I want something better for you. I want you to be free to pursue a life with more meaning than producing some iWidget at Company X, or even driving glorified busses full of business people and tourists around the sky.

Part of this is because I believe a life lived for a good reason, a good Why, is a more pleasant life. I don't see any reason why you shouldn't enjoy that kind of life.

The other part is that I believe you are capable of more greatness than the world has ever seen. I have many brilliant pilot friends. They hold degrees in science (at least one friend has two degrees in *rocket science!*), engineering, literature and more. With the freedom to pursue projects like Elon Musk and Jeff Bezos do, my friends could be major players in shaping the future of our civilization.

However, they're stuck toiling away at far-more-than-full-time jobs as pilots/staff officers in the US military. Sure, they might make some difference in those jobs. As squadron or wing commanders they might even have positive effects on the lives of hundreds of people. However, chances are they'll work for 20+ years in those jobs and end up with little more than a $55,000 per year pension. No matter how great or sweeping their influence is while on active duty, they'll be mostly forgotten within a few years of retiring. After another 10 years, almost nobody left in the military will even remember their names.

I want you to process the idea that by understanding and limiting your spending, and saving aggressively, you can free yourself from the financial bondage that will keep you working 9-to-5 for most of your life, and instead go do something amazing in our world. As airline pilots, we can accelerate that timeline drastically and easily abandon mandatory full-time work within 11 years of starting at a major airline.

Before I give up trying to inspire you and move on, I want to look at this from another angle.

I don't know about you, but I love pizza. It may be my all-time favorite food. It's hot and filling and delicious. Since it can be topped with almost anything, there's no risk that it'll ever get boring.

Have you ever been really hungry when sitting down to eat some pizza? Isn't that first bite amazing? I almost always burn the roof of my mouth because I lack the self control to wait to take my first bite until the cheese cools to a temperature below "DANGER: LAVA!" When I'm really hungry, I can take out an entire slice of pizza in what seems like a matter of seconds.

The pleasure and satisfaction that comes from that first slice is amazing. In fact, it's usually so amazing that I immediately reach for a second slice. Unfortunately, the universe is a horrible, cruel place, and that second slice is never quite as good as the first. Don't get me wrong...it's still delicious and I still love it, but it's never as satisfying or enjoyable as the first one was.

There's actually a name for this characteristic. It's: "Marginal

Utility." It means that once you have a given amount of something (like a slice of pizza,) increasing what you have by an equal amount (another slice of pizza) won't be worth as much to you. In ever crueler twists of fate, the marginal utility of most things continues to decrease as you go on. Not only is the third slice of pizza not as good as the first, it's not even as good as the second one. The fourth is even less enjoyable, and so on....

At some point while eating pizza, having another slice just isn't worth it. You're pretty full and the pizza has cooled down a bit. You could eat an eighth slice, but you'll just feel like a bloated cow. You probably even regret having eaten slice #7. Your life would have been better if you didn't eat it at all.

So, when eating pizza, each of us has to ask a fundamental question: how much is enough?

The same goes for money. If you only make enough money to barely cover your bills, earning an extra $100 feels amazing! However, if you earn several thousand dollars more than what you spend each month, does a measly $100 make that much difference in your life?

We've arbitrarily decided that the average American family should be able to live pretty happily by only spending $57,758 each year. If you earn that much money, I feel like you're capable of having a pretty fantastic life. Now, would spending an extra $10,000 each year make your life better? Yes, it might. I can think of a lot of fun things I could do with that much money.

Marginal utility says that you'll get more overall life value from the first thousand of that $10,000 than you will from the last thousand. This effect continues no matter how much you increase your spending.

Psychologists have studied the marginal utility of money and determined that most people are happiest when their income is ~$75,000 per year. Any more than that doesn't have a significant effect on happiness.[25]

We're about to see how easy it is for a professional pilot to amass a Treasure Bath capable of providing passive income in this range...in record time. Once your passive income reaches that level, I want you to deliberately stop and ask yourself: will increasing my passive

---

[25] https://www.pnas.org/content/107/38/16489.full

income above this level make me happier? If not, then why would you keep working full-time after that point? Yes, you can continue working if you so desire. Maybe the work itself is fulfilling. Maybe you decide you want to buy a toy or a vacation, and a few months of full-time work can make that happen. However, continuing to work full-time every year from that point until you turn 65 just doesn't make sense once you understand Pilot Math.

Once you reach this level of understanding, it almost makes it tough to imagine not amassing this amount of wealth. So let's do it. It's time to take a look at some very specific Pilot Math.

CHAPTER FIVE
Major Airline Pilot Math

We're about to run the Pilot Math for a major airline pilot. We're going to assume that you start here with zero savings, although I sincerely hope that isn't the case. In later chapters, we'll look at how applying Pilot Math as a military or regional airline pilot can accelerate this process for you. It'll be useful to have these numbers as a baseline though.

When we asked "How much is enough?" we came up with $57,758 per year in annual spending to live like the average American from the $50,000-$69,999 annual earnings group (with a few adjustments for reality.)

Please take one moment to think about what that means. Pilot Math Treasure Bath draws some of its philosophy from the FIRE movement. That movement is known for embracing frugality. They put significant energy into finding ways to enjoy life while living an increasingly frugal life. Although I believe that a person can live a happier life by adhering to those ideas, I'm not even asking you to embrace much of what the FIRE community teaches.

I'm not asking you to enact draconian austerity measures. I'm not asking you to stop enjoying your life today, so that you can live a life you won't enjoy tomorrow. I'm not even asking you to kick your daily Starbucks habit.

All I'm asking is that you don't spend any more money each year than most upper-middle-class Americans. You still get to buy new cars. You get to eat at restaurants. You get to take vacations. You still get to drink good beer.

If the average American family can live a good life only spending (an adjusted value of) $57,758 per year, then I believe you can too.

Your current spending may be higher than that, requiring you to adopt some measure of frugality in your life. However, I believe that this level of spending is easily attainable for any airline pilot's family.

More importantly, when you see how quickly you can reach a level of wealth that provides enough passive income to cover all your family's needs, you won't be able to resist applying Pilot Math in your life.

However, I know that nobody is perfect. Just for grins, the calculations we look at in this book will focus on scenarios where you double your family's spending when you upgrade to Captain at a major airline. Pay for a Captain at the majors is so high today, that spending an *extra* $57,758 each year won't significantly delay your wealth accumulation. I'm not saying you must (or even should) double your spending, but I want you to see that all this is possible even if you do.

In either case, I think you'll be happily shocked to find out how rapidly you can reach true financial freedom as an airline pilot.

Let's look at what a first officer makes during his or her first year at my company. We'll assume that he or she only flies the reserve guarantee of 75 hours per month...a very conservative estimate that most pilots exceed by at least 5-10 hours per month. (A smart pilot living in base could pretty easily earn an average of 100 hours of pay, or more, every month. We'll consider that possibility a little later.) We'll use numbers from the 2019 pay charts for the lowest-paying aircraft at my company, the Boeing 717. These charts also assume that you never receive profit sharing. (At my company, profit sharing has ranged from 14% to over 21% for the past four years. Most airlines aren't that lucky.)

When calculating taxable income, we assume this first officer gets the new standard deduction for a married couple: $24,400. We'll also assume that this pilot contributes the maximum amount allowed into his Traditional 401K plan: $19,000. (We'll discuss 401K plans and contributions in great detail in the next chapter, taking a look at why you need to maximize your investments in that account.) When we consider those tax deductions, along with non-taxable per diem and company 401K contributions (additional earnings equal to 16% of the pilot's pay in my company's case,) our first officer's taxable income is pleasantly low. We'll discuss other ways to reduce his tax burden in later chapters.

Year 1 Pay	Amount
Position	B717 FO
Reserve Guarantee	75
Hourly Rate	$91.81
Monthly Flight Pay	$6,886
Company 401k	$1,102
Per Diem	$500
Monthly Total	$8,487
Annual Total	$101,850
Standard Tax Deduction	- $24,400
Traditional IRA Tax Deduction	- $19,000
Taxable Income	$39,229
After Tax Income	$97,523
Annual Spending	$57,236
Annual Savings	$40,287
Savings Rate	41%

This is some pretty decent pay, and 41% savings rate is actually quite respectable. It's nowhere near our ultimate goal, but it's a whole lot better than the 10% that many financial advisors suggest you use.

Now, let's project out a pilot's wealth, assuming he or she continues to only spend this much money each year. These charts assume that our investments earn 5% interest. This is well below the long-term average for the S&P 500 (just over 11%.) For our purposes, this means our numbers represent a very conservative estimate with some wiggle room for inflation and weak markets. The column for "Passive Income Available" assumes spending only 4% of the "Cumulative Savings" number. This is based on the "4% Rule" we discussed earlier.

These charts include federal income tax. We accounted for social security and medicare tax under our annual spending. We assume that you aren't taxed on your company's 401k contributions or per diem. A later chapter in this book will discuss some strategies for reducing the sting of the taxes you do have to pay.

These charts assume you don't pay any state income tax, because why would you intentionally live in a state that does that?

Seriously though, choosing where to live is an important

undertaking with a plethora of considerations. States with income tax may not charge as much in sales, property, or other taxes, resulting in a lower overall tax burden. Also, if living in a state with income tax allows you to live at a major airline domicile, rather than commuting, it's easy for you to more than make up the difference with increased earnings. A friend and I wrote an article exploring this concept on The Pilot Network.[26]

I've come to the conclusion that living at your airline base can easily equal a $50,000 per year increase in your earnings, or more. That's almost enough to cover the total annual spending we're aiming for! Any of the numbers in these spreadsheets may need adjustment for your own personal situation. That's why they're available for anyone to download, for free.[27]

The pay rates I used for these calculations can be found on airlinepilotcentral.com.[28] That site maintains pay charts for every airline in the US, so you can use it to calculate potential earnings at your company of choice.

Assuming what will be a slower-than-average career progression for the next several years, this pilot's first 12 years of income and savings will look something like this:

Year	Position	Annual Total Compensation	After Tax Earnings	Annual Spending	Annual Savings Total	Savings Rate	Cumulative Savings	Passive Income
1	B717 FO	$ 101,850	$ 97,523	$ 57,758	$ 39,765	41%	$ 39,765	$ 1,591
2	B717 FO	$ 138,014	$ 129,946	$ 57,758	$ 72,188	56%	$ 113,942	$ 4,558
3	A320 FO	$ 171,599	$ 157,862	$ 57,758	$ 100,104	63%	$ 219,743	$ 8,790
4	A320 FO	$ 175,608	$ 161,111	$ 57,758	$ 103,353	64%	$ 334,082	$ 13,363
5	B757 FO	$ 192,270	$ 174,613	$ 57,758	$ 116,855	67%	$ 467,641	$ 18,706
6	B757 FO	$ 196,937	$ 178,394	$ 57,758	$ 120,636	68%	$ 611,660	$ 24,466
7	B757 FO	$ 202,199	$ 182,658	$ 57,758	$ 124,900	68%	$ 767,143	$ 30,686
8	B757 FO	$ 206,803	$ 186,389	$ 57,758	$ 128,631	69%	$ 934,131	$ 37,365
9	A320 CA	$ 288,594	$ 252,584	$ 115,516	$ 137,068	54%	$ 1,117,906	$ 44,716
10	A320 CA	$ 290,765	$ 254,307	$ 115,516	$ 138,791	55%	$ 1,312,591	$ 52,504
11	A320 CA	$ 292,947	$ 256,037	$ 115,516	$ 140,521	55%	$ 1,518,742	$ 60,750
12	A320 CA	$ 295,119	$ 257,759	$ 115,516	$ 142,243	55%	$ 1,736,922	$ 69,477

---

[26] This is a must-read if you want to understand the full earning potential of a major airline pilot: https://community.thepilotnetwork.org/posts/careful-what-you-ass-u-mehttps://community.thepilotnetwork.org/posts/careful-what-you-ass-u-me. You can also read this post for free in the TPN-Go app: https://pilotmathtreasurebath.com/tpn-go-and-tpnq-free-access-to-my-other-writing/
[27] https://pilotmathtreasurebath.com/calculators/
[28] APC is the best website I know to get specific information about airlines: http://www.airlinepilotcentral.com/.

After that first year, our pilot's paltry $39,765 in savings was only enough to provide $1,591 in annual passive income. However, by holding his spending down to the national average level, we see that it only takes a little over eight years to accumulate more than a million dollars in total savings! In about 10.5 years, our pilot has enough money saved that the passive income from his investments can cover his annual spending forever. He has, for all intents and purposes, achieved financial freedom.

This is the first point where each of us needs to go back to the question of "How much is enough?" With all his needs (and many wants) covered, how much happier will this pilot become by working longer to increase his annual spending ability?

Working longer will make it possible to buy more toys or take more trips, but if he's lived happily for the last ten years at this spending level, why wouldn't he be able to live happily at that spending level indefinitely?

Maybe he's like me and he has a wife who would simply say, "It's not enough. End of discussion." Here's what things look like if this pilot continues working:

Year	Position	Annual Total Compensation	After Tax Earnings	Annual Spending	Annual Savings Total	Savings Rate	Cumulative Savings	Passive Income
1	B717 FO	$ 101,850	$ 97,523	$ 57,758	$ 39,765	41%	$ 39,765	$ 1,591
2	B717 FO	$ 138,014	$ 129,946	$ 57,758	$ 72,188	56%	$ 113,942	$ 4,558
3	A320 FO	$ 171,599	$ 157,862	$ 57,758	$ 100,104	63%	$ 219,743	$ 8,790
4	A320 FO	$ 175,608	$ 161,111	$ 57,758	$ 103,353	64%	$ 334,082	$ 13,363
5	B757 FO	$ 192,270	$ 174,613	$ 57,758	$ 116,855	67%	$ 467,641	$ 18,706
6	B757 FO	$ 196,937	$ 178,394	$ 57,758	$ 120,636	68%	$ 611,660	$ 24,466
7	B757 FO	$ 202,199	$ 182,658	$ 57,758	$ 124,900	68%	$ 767,143	$ 30,686
8	B757 FO	$ 206,803	$ 186,389	$ 57,758	$ 128,631	69%	$ 934,131	$ 37,365
9	A320 CA	$ 288,594	$ 252,584	$ 57,758	$ 194,826	77%	$ 1,175,664	$ 47,027
10	A320 CA	$ 290,765	$ 254,307	$ 57,758	$ 196,549	77%	$ 1,430,995	$ 57,240
11	A320 CA	$ 292,947	$ 256,037	$ 57,758	$ 198,279	77%	$ 1,700,824	$ 68,033
12	A320 CA	$ 295,119	$ 257,759	$ 57,758	$ 200,001	78%	$ 1,985,867	$ 79,435
13	A320 CA	$ 295,119	$ 257,759	$ 57,758	$ 200,001	78%	$ 2,285,161	$ 91,406
14	A320 CA	$ 295,119	$ 257,759	$ 57,758	$ 200,001	78%	$ 2,599,420	$ 103,977
15	B757 CA	$ 318,222	$ 276,083	$ 57,758	$ 218,325	79%	$ 2,947,716	$ 117,909
16	B757 CA	$ 318,222	$ 276,083	$ 57,758	$ 218,325	79%	$ 3,313,427	$ 132,537
17	B767-300 CA	$ 325,008	$ 281,465	$ 57,758	$ 223,707	79%	$ 3,702,805	$ 148,112
18	B767-300 CA	$ 325,008	$ 281,465	$ 57,758	$ 223,707	79%	$ 4,111,652	$ 164,466
19	B767-300 CA	$ 325,008	$ 281,465	$ 57,758	$ 223,707	79%	$ 4,540,942	$ 181,638
20	B767-300 CA	$ 325,008	$ 281,465	$ 57,758	$ 223,707	79%	$ 4,991,696	$ 199,668
21	A330-200 CA	$ 364,743	$ 312,979	$ 57,758	$ 255,221	82%	$ 5,496,501	$ 219,860
22	A330-200 CA	$ 364,743	$ 312,979	$ 57,758	$ 255,221	82%	$ 6,026,547	$ 241,062
23	A330-200 CA	$ 364,743	$ 312,979	$ 57,758	$ 255,221	82%	$ 6,583,095	$ 263,324
24	A330-200 CA	$ 364,743	$ 312,979	$ 57,758	$ 255,221	82%	$ 7,167,470	$ 286,699
25	A330-900 CA	$ 369,692	$ 316,903	$ 57,758	$ 259,145	82%	$ 7,784,989	$ 311,400
26	A330-900 CA	$ 369,692	$ 316,903	$ 57,758	$ 259,145	82%	$ 8,433,384	$ 337,335
27	A330-900 CA	$ 369,692	$ 316,903	$ 57,758	$ 259,145	82%	$ 9,114,198	$ 364,568
28	A330-900 CA	$ 369,692	$ 316,903	$ 57,758	$ 259,145	82%	$ 9,829,054	$ 393,162
29	A350 CA	$ 385,205	$ 329,207	$ 57,758	$ 271,449	82%	$ 10,591,956	$ 423,678
30	A350 CA	$ 385,205	$ 329,207	$ 57,758	$ 271,449	82%	$ 11,393,003	$ 455,720

Most of us don't get to the major air lines with 30 years before mandatory retirement, but is it really necessary to work that long? Sure, it'd be great to have $11.39M in the bank that produces $455K per year in passive income, but what would you spend all that on?

We've already talked about the marginal utility of money - asking "how much is enough?" The beauty of pursuing this path is that you've already trained yourself to live happily while only spending an average amount...our $57,758 per year. If you can live happily at that spending level, you can certainly live happily spending more.

As you look at the far right column in this chart, there should be some point at which you say, "Okay already! There is no way I couldn't live happily on this amount of passive income. I gain nothing by continuing to work full-time."

If $57K per year isn't enough spending money, you could work for a total of 15 years at your major airline and double your passive income. That's enough to buy a new boat, airplane, or Tesla Model 3 every year...for the rest of your life...in addition to spending your regular $57K per year...without ever putting in another day at work. How much more do you need?

There's even a point (around 26 years) where the passive income produced by your investments each year is more than you'll ever make from actively working for the rest of your career. You make more money from not working than you do at work.

No matter which line of this chart you pick as your "I'm good" point, it doesn't mean that you're morally obligated to actually stop working. If you enjoy your job, you're free to continue working part-time. The beauty of the situation is that you now only do the trips you want. Why not bid for one or two trips a month with layovers that you enjoy? Let your company pay to put you in fancy hotels for a few days. You can either get a few days of luxury away from it all, or bring your spouse/family with you and enjoy the trip together. If you live at one of your company's bases, you can bid reserve on a widebody aircraft. Chances are you'll only have to work a few days a month, but you'll get a full 75 hours of pay for it. Not that you need the money....

At that point you're not technically "retired," but you have essentially as much time as you could ever want to pursue the things you want. You'd be working 4-8 days a month, leaving you as many as 27 days to spend as you choose. You can't help but enjoy that kind of life!

At this point you may be thinking that $57K of spending per year just won't cut it. You want things a little nicer in life. You want to have some toys now. You want to give your kids a fancier wedding or cover college at a more expensive school. I'm not going to blithely suggest that it's $57,758 or nothing. Let's look at another scenario. Let's say you hold yourself to our average spending level as long as you're a first officer at your major airline. Then, once you upgrade to captain, you double your spending to $115,516.

I assert that you'd actually have to try hard to spend that much money on toys once you realize the power of Pilot Math. As pilots, we're good at optimizing. You probably already optimize a lot in your life. If you fit this description, you can make $115,516 per year go a long way. (We'll discuss why we're allowing ourselves to spend this much money and what to do with it at the end of the book when we look at The Way Forward.) Let's look at this scenario anyway though:

Year	Position	Annual Total Compensation	After Tax Earnings	Annual Spending	Annual Savings Total	Savings Rate	Cumulative Savings	Passive Income
1	B717 FO	$ 101,850	$ 97,523	$ 57,758	$ 39,765	41%	$ 39,765	$ 1,591
2	B717 FO	$ 138,014	$ 129,946	$ 57,758	$ 72,188	56%	$ 113,942	$ 4,558
3	A320 FO	$ 171,599	$ 157,862	$ 57,758	$ 100,104	63%	$ 219,743	$ 8,790
4	A320 FO	$ 175,608	$ 161,111	$ 57,758	$ 103,353	64%	$ 334,082	$ 13,363
5	B757 FO	$ 192,270	$ 174,613	$ 57,758	$ 116,855	67%	$ 467,641	$ 18,706
6	B757 FO	$ 196,937	$ 178,394	$ 57,758	$ 120,636	68%	$ 611,660	$ 24,466
7	B757 FO	$ 202,199	$ 182,658	$ 57,758	$ 124,900	68%	$ 767,143	$ 30,686
8	B757 FO	$ 206,803	$ 186,389	$ 57,758	$ 128,631	69%	$ 934,131	$ 37,365
9	A320 CA	$ 288,594	$ 252,584	$ 115,516	$ 137,068	54%	$ 1,117,906	$ 44,716
10	A320 CA	$ 290,765	$ 254,307	$ 115,516	$ 138,791	55%	$ 1,312,591	$ 52,504
11	A320 CA	$ 292,947	$ 256,037	$ 115,516	$ 140,521	55%	$ 1,518,742	$ 60,750
12	A320 CA	$ 295,119	$ 257,759	$ 115,516	$ 142,243	55%	$ 1,736,922	$ 69,477
13	A320 CA	$ 295,119	$ 257,759	$ 115,516	$ 142,243	55%	$ 1,966,012	$ 78,640
14	A320 CA	$ 295,119	$ 257,759	$ 115,516	$ 142,243	55%	$ 2,206,556	$ 88,262
15	B757 CA	$ 318,222	$ 276,083	$ 115,516	$ 160,567	58%	$ 2,477,450	$ 99,098
16	B757 CA	$ 318,222	$ 276,083	$ 115,516	$ 160,567	58%	$ 2,761,890	$ 110,476
17	B767-300 CA	$ 325,008	$ 281,465	$ 115,516	$ 165,949	59%	$ 3,065,933	$ 122,637
18	B767-300 CA	$ 325,008	$ 281,465	$ 115,516	$ 165,949	59%	$ 3,385,179	$ 135,407
19	B767-300 CA	$ 325,008	$ 281,465	$ 115,516	$ 165,949	59%	$ 3,720,386	$ 148,815
20	B767-300 CA	$ 325,008	$ 281,465	$ 115,516	$ 165,949	59%	$ 4,072,355	$ 162,894
21	A330-200 CA	$ 364,743	$ 312,979	$ 115,516	$ 197,463	63%	$ 4,473,435	$ 178,937
22	A330-200 CA	$ 364,743	$ 312,979	$ 115,516	$ 197,463	63%	$ 4,894,569	$ 195,783
23	A330-200 CA	$ 364,743	$ 312,979	$ 115,516	$ 197,463	63%	$ 5,336,760	$ 213,470
24	A330-200 CA	$ 364,743	$ 312,979	$ 115,516	$ 197,463	63%	$ 5,801,061	$ 232,042
25	A330-900 CA	$ 369,692	$ 316,903	$ 115,516	$ 201,387	64%	$ 6,292,501	$ 251,700
26	A330-900 CA	$ 369,692	$ 316,903	$ 115,516	$ 201,387	64%	$ 6,808,514	$ 272,341
27	A330-900 CA	$ 369,692	$ 316,903	$ 115,516	$ 201,387	64%	$ 7,350,327	$ 294,013
28	A330-900 CA	$ 369,692	$ 316,903	$ 115,516	$ 201,387	64%	$ 7,919,230	$ 316,769
29	A350 CA	$ 385,205	$ 329,207	$ 115,516	$ 213,691	65%	$ 8,528,883	$ 341,155
30	A350 CA	$ 385,205	$ 329,207	$ 115,516	$ 213,691	65%	$ 9,169,019	$ 366,761

We see that doubling your spending has a big impact, but it's not the end of the world. Since we assumed you didn't upgrade to captain (and simultaneously upgrade your spending) until Year 9, you still reach the $1,000,000 mark before that point. However, if you want your passive income to completely cover your $115,516 in annual spending you'll have to work for just under 17 years. It's also worth noting that this spending level will cost you more than $2.2M in total earnings over a 30-year major airline career. (Assuming you wanted to work full-time for that long.)

If you want to maintain higher spending levels, you'll have to work at least a little harder to support them. We've assumed thus far that you wait until your 9th year at your airline to upgrade to captain.
Depending on the company you work for, you could feasibly upgrade much sooner than this.

I've only been with my company a few years, but I've seen pilots successfully bid for captain seats as quickly as four months after being hired. My company has started phasing out the older aircraft that made this possible, but between increasing numbers of retirements and an insatiable demand for air travel, there are still a lot of impressive opportunities in our industry. I won a bid to become an A220 captain after just 3 years and 2 months at my company.

Surprisingly, it turns out that upgrading early doesn't actually help if you also increase your spending. The spending happens early enough in your career to mitigate any long-term gains from increased pay...and then some. Here are the numbers to prove it:

Year	Position	Annual Total Compensation	After Tax Earnings	Annual Spending	Annual Savings Total	Savings Rate	Cumulative Savings	Passive Income
1	B717 FO	$ 101,850	$ 91,793	$ 57,758	$ 34,035	37%	$ 34,035	$ 1,361
2	B717 FO	$ 138,014	$ 121,098	$ 57,758	$ 63,340	52%	$ 99,076	$ 3,963
3	B717 CA	$ 257,817	$ 217,759	$ 115,516	$ 102,243	47%	$ 206,273	$ 8,251
4	B717 CA	$ 259,831	$ 219,357	$ 115,516	$ 103,841	47%	$ 320,428	$ 12,817
5	A220-100 CA	$ 265,928	$ 224,192	$ 115,516	$ 108,676	48%	$ 445,125	$ 17,805
6	A220-100 CA	$ 268,006	$ 225,840	$ 115,516	$ 110,324	49%	$ 577,706	$ 23,108
7	A220-100 CA	$ 270,136	$ 227,529	$ 115,516	$ 112,013	49%	$ 718,604	$ 28,744
8	A220-100 CA	$ 272,349	$ 229,285	$ 115,516	$ 113,769	50%	$ 868,303	$ 34,732
9	A320 CA	$ 288,594	$ 242,168	$ 115,516	$ 126,652	52%	$ 1,038,370	$ 41,535
10	A320 CA	$ 290,765	$ 243,891	$ 115,516	$ 128,375	53%	$ 1,218,663	$ 48,747
11	A320 CA	$ 292,947	$ 245,621	$ 115,516	$ 130,105	53%	$ 1,409,702	$ 56,388
12	A320 CA	$ 295,119	$ 247,343	$ 115,516	$ 131,827	53%	$ 1,612,014	$ 64,481
13	A320 CA	$ 295,119	$ 247,343	$ 115,516	$ 131,827	53%	$ 1,824,442	$ 72,978
14	A320 CA	$ 295,119	$ 247,343	$ 115,516	$ 131,827	53%	$ 2,047,491	$ 81,900
15	B757 CA	$ 318,222	$ 265,667	$ 115,516	$ 150,151	57%	$ 2,300,017	$ 92,001
16	B757 CA	$ 318,222	$ 265,667	$ 115,516	$ 150,151	57%	$ 2,565,168	$ 102,607
17	B767-300 CA	$ 325,008	$ 271,049	$ 115,516	$ 155,533	57%	$ 2,848,960	$ 113,958
18	B767-300 CA	$ 325,008	$ 271,049	$ 115,516	$ 155,533	57%	$ 3,146,941	$ 125,878
19	B767-300 CA	$ 325,008	$ 271,049	$ 115,516	$ 155,533	57%	$ 3,459,821	$ 138,393
20	B767-300 CA	$ 325,008	$ 271,049	$ 115,516	$ 155,533	57%	$ 3,788,344	$ 151,534
21	A330-200 CA	$ 364,743	$ 302,563	$ 115,516	$ 187,047	62%	$ 4,164,808	$ 166,592
22	A330-200 CA	$ 364,743	$ 302,563	$ 115,516	$ 187,047	62%	$ 4,560,095	$ 182,404
23	A330-200 CA	$ 364,743	$ 302,563	$ 115,516	$ 187,047	62%	$ 4,975,147	$ 199,006
24	A330-200 CA	$ 364,743	$ 302,563	$ 115,516	$ 187,047	62%	$ 5,410,950	$ 216,438
25	A330-900 CA	$ 369,692	$ 306,487	$ 115,516	$ 190,971	62%	$ 5,872,469	$ 234,899
26	A330-900 CA	$ 369,692	$ 306,487	$ 115,516	$ 190,971	62%	$ 6,357,064	$ 254,283
27	A330-900 CA	$ 369,692	$ 306,487	$ 115,516	$ 190,971	62%	$ 6,865,889	$ 274,636
28	A330-900 CA	$ 369,692	$ 306,487	$ 115,516	$ 190,971	62%	$ 7,400,154	$ 296,006
29	A350 CA	$ 385,205	$ 318,047	$ 115,516	$ 202,531	64%	$ 7,972,693	$ 318,908
30	A350 CA	$ 385,205	$ 318,047	$ 115,516	$ 202,531	64%	$ 8,573,858	$ 342,954

You could do a little better with an early captain upgrade by choosing to not double your spending at the same time. Unfortunately, it doesn't really put you very far ahead of a pilot who waits until Year 9 to upgrade. It would make more difference if you were spending significantly less than our arbitrary $57K figure, but I'm not going to run these scenarios. I'll let you try them out yourself.

Early upgrade or not, I hope you're as amazed by these numbers as I was when I first discovered Pilot Math. If you're willing to limit yourself to just average spending and save the rest, you can achieve total financial freedom in just a few years.

Do you want even better news? These numbers are the absolute low-end of what a pilot makes at my company. Only the bottom 10%, or so, of the seniority list is forced to fly on reserve. The rest of the the pilots on the seniority list are "line holders"…they get an assigned schedule each month. In almost every case, that line includes 5-10 hours above the reserve guarantee. This means that even the laziest line holder gets 7-13% more pay than what you've seen so far.

I don't do a lot of extra flying because I have to commute to work and I choose to pass up on some money to have more time with my family. (We also have a fairly healthy Treasure Bath, so we're not afraid of going hungry.) However, a friend at my company who lives within driving distance of his base has a completely different strategy.

When an airline pilot gets sick, or delayed at one destination long enough that she can't make her next flight in time, the company has to assign another pilot to cover that next flight in her place. That's what reserves are for. My company has long call reserve, where they have to give you at least 12 hours of notice if they're going to assign you to a trip.

Those rules make long call reserve pilots useless for last minute drop-outs, so we also have short call reserve. Our contract doesn't specify how much time a short call reserve pilot has to show up at the airport after getting a phone call, but the company would prefer we be less than two hours away. Ideally (for the company) they can use a short call reserve pilot to cover the late notice flight. Thankfully though, sometimes the company runs out of options. Either they use up all the short call reserve pilots available for the day, or the next flight leaves so soon that they want to try to find someone who is available immediately. This is where my friend, Steve, makes his money.

Steve uses our airline's system to let the company know that he's available for last-minute trips. If the company finds itself in a bind, they call him to offer some extra flying. If the situation is dire enough, they award him premium (double) pay for the trip.

Why would an airline do this? They're pretty good at staffing things to meet their needs, but pilots are very expensive. Hiring, training, health care, and pay cost a lot more than you might think. It's far cheaper for them to pay double for some last-minute trips every day than to hire more bodies that end up sitting around a lot while still receiving the 75-hour reserve guarantee.

Premium pay doesn't always happen, but with some strategy and careful exploitation of some good deals in our contract, Steve averages 85-120 hours of pay every month while only working as many days as I do. This is the power of living in domicile at your airline. As a rule of thumb, I say that living in base pays at least an extra $50,000 per year. However, let's run some actual numbers so you can see what the upper end of pay possibilities looks like.

We'll assume that Steve averages 100 hours of pay per month (while only working 12-16 days.) Otherwise, we'll assume nothing else changes.

Year	Position	Annual Total Compensation	After Tax Earnings	Annual Spending	Annual Savings Total	Savings Rate	Cumulative Savings	Passive Income
1	B717 FO	$ 133,800	$ 126,168	$ 57,758	$ 68,410	54%	$ 68,410	$ 2,736
2	B717 FO	$ 182,018	$ 166,305	$ 57,758	$ 108,547	65%	$ 180,377	$ 7,215
3	A320 FO	$ 226,799	$ 202,593	$ 57,758	$ 144,835	71%	$ 334,231	$ 13,369
4	A320 FO	$ 232,144	$ 206,924	$ 57,758	$ 149,166	72%	$ 500,109	$ 20,004
5	B757 FO	$ 254,361	$ 224,813	$ 57,758	$ 167,055	74%	$ 692,169	$ 27,687
6	B757 FO	$ 260,583	$ 229,748	$ 57,758	$ 171,990	75%	$ 898,768	$ 35,951
7	B757 FO	$ 267,599	$ 235,312	$ 57,758	$ 177,554	75%	$ 1,121,261	$ 44,850
8	B757 FO	$ 273,737	$ 240,181	$ 57,758	$ 182,423	76%	$ 1,359,747	$ 54,390
9	A320 CA	$ 381,792	$ 326,500	$ 115,516	$ 210,984	65%	$ 1,638,718	$ 65,549
10	A320 CA	$ 384,687	$ 328,796	$ 115,516	$ 213,280	65%	$ 1,933,934	$ 77,357
11	A320 CA	$ 387,596	$ 331,104	$ 115,516	$ 215,588	65%	$ 2,246,218	$ 89,849
12	A320 CA	$ 390,492	$ 333,400	$ 115,516	$ 217,884	65%	$ 2,576,413	$ 103,057
13	A320 CA	$ 390,492	$ 333,400	$ 115,516	$ 217,884	65%	$ 2,923,117	$ 116,925
14	A320 CA	$ 390,492	$ 333,400	$ 115,516	$ 217,884	65%	$ 3,287,157	$ 131,486
15	B757 CA	$ 421,296	$ 357,831	$ 115,516	$ 242,315	68%	$ 3,693,830	$ 147,753
16	B757 CA	$ 421,296	$ 357,831	$ 115,516	$ 242,315	68%	$ 4,120,837	$ 164,833
17	B767-300 CA	$ 430,344	$ 364,621	$ 115,516	$ 249,105	68%	$ 4,575,984	$ 183,039
18	B767-300 CA	$ 430,344	$ 364,621	$ 115,516	$ 249,105	68%	$ 5,053,889	$ 202,156
19	B767-300 CA	$ 430,344	$ 364,621	$ 115,516	$ 249,105	68%	$ 5,555,689	$ 222,228
20	B767-300 CA	$ 430,344	$ 364,621	$ 115,516	$ 249,105	68%	$ 6,082,579	$ 243,303
21	A330-200 CA	$ 483,324	$ 402,986	$ 115,516	$ 287,470	71%	$ 6,674,178	$ 266,967
22	A330-200 CA	$ 483,324	$ 402,986	$ 115,516	$ 287,470	71%	$ 7,295,356	$ 291,814
23	A330-200 CA	$ 483,324	$ 402,986	$ 115,516	$ 287,470	71%	$ 7,947,594	$ 317,904
24	A330-200 CA	$ 483,324	$ 402,986	$ 115,516	$ 287,470	71%	$ 8,632,444	$ 345,298
25	A330-900 CA	$ 489,922	$ 407,764	$ 115,516	$ 292,248	72%	$ 9,356,314	$ 374,253
26	A330-900 CA	$ 489,922	$ 407,764	$ 115,516	$ 292,248	72%	$ 10,116,377	$ 404,655
27	A330-900 CA	$ 489,922	$ 407,764	$ 115,516	$ 292,248	72%	$ 10,914,444	$ 436,578
28	A330-900 CA	$ 489,922	$ 407,764	$ 115,516	$ 292,248	72%	$ 11,752,414	$ 470,097
29	A350 CA	$ 510,607	$ 422,743	$ 115,516	$ 307,227	73%	$ 12,647,261	$ 505,890
30	A350 CA	$ 510,607	$ 422,743	$ 115,516	$ 307,227	73%	$ 13,586,851	$ 543,474

If I've failed to impress you so far, this should do the trick. If he applies Pilot Math, Steve's Treasure Bath should surpass the $1M mark with under seven years at the company. The passive income from his investments is large enough to match his annual spending level before the end of Year 8, right before he upgrades to captain. His passive income exceeds his doubled spending at Year 13. If this isn't a case for living in base, then I don't know what is.

You might think that only a pilot with perfect career timing could make this work, but that's not the case. It's true that you need to be as senior as possible to maximize your access to extra trips and premium pay. However, what matters is seniority in your category, rather than your overall seniority at the company.

When it comes to your schedule and picking up extra flying, you only have to compete with the pilots in your seat (FO vs Captain,) on your aircraft, at your base. You will always have a better schedule and make more money by bidding to an unpopular category where you can be more senior. Don't bid for a bigger, fancier airplane just because the hourly pay rate is higher or the jet seems cool. If you want to make money as an FO, choose the oldest narrowbody at the least popular base where you can stand to live.

I hesitated to present this last scenario here because I don't want to be guilty of making things seem too rosy. I don't want families to assume they can make this much money while commuting, or doing a full-time Guard or Reserve flying job, or other time-consuming projects. For this to work you need to be available for last-minute trips. My friend still works less than 15 days per month on average, but flexibility is essential.

And although I'm trying hard to temper my enthusiasm, I have to mention one more fact: This isn't the true top-end of a major airline pilot's earning potential.

Our Pilot Working Agreement (PWA) has all kinds of other good deals that you learn to take advantage of as time goes on. The scenario we just looked at would put a Year 12 A320 Captain's pre-tax income at $390K. I met a senior MD88 FO in New York who made $380K in a year. I got the impression that he spent far more time at work than I would ever care to, but if I were single I'd absolutely consider spending a copule years bombarding my savings like him before settling back down to a more sane schedule.

The point is that the numbers we'll focus on for most of this book are extremely low-end estimates of your earnings as a major airline pilot. From here on out, we're going to assume that you only ever get the reserve guarantee of 75 hours per month. Realize that if you want to live in base like my buddy Steve, you'll beat the numbers you see by up to 33%. That's not even being unrealistically rosy.

I hope you're excited. If I were you I'd also be a little skeptical. The math doesn't lie, but it's a lot of money. In our society, it seems like this level of income is reserved for some chosen few. When I think about average Joes and Janes making this kind of money, I immediately think scam. That's not the case here.

This isn't some crazy scheme reserved for a chosen few. This level of wealth is achievable for every pilot at my company. Other major airlines have different pay scales, meaning the specific amounts and overall timeline will vary a little. Overall though, the scenario is the same no matter what major airline you join.

As much as these numbers impress me, they only tell part of the story. In order to get to a major airline, you have to do some flying elsewhere. Whether you go through the military or take an all-civilian route, you have the opportunity to build a rock-solid foundation before you even reach the majors. We'll look at those scenarios in the later chapters.

Before we do that, let's look at the specifics of where you're going to put all this money you're accumulating.

CHAPTER SIX

Nuts & Bolts - Getting Started

We've just seen how impressive our earning potential really is. We have the opportunity to earn as much as $8-10 Million over a 30 year major airline career, using assumptions so conservative that they're borderline unrealistic.

A full 30 years of major airline pilot earnings could easily be enough money to set your progeny up with the kind of generational wealth that used to be reserved for European aristocrats and the trust fund babies of American robber barrons. Not bad for a bunch of glorified bus drivers like us, huh?

We've gone from general to specific in this book. We know exactly how much money we can expect to earn. Now it's time to talk about exactly what we're going to do with all that cash. Here's the overview of our strategy:

- Find out how much money you spend each month/year.
- Optimize your expenses to maximize the value you get from them.
- Debt is only allowed when it makes sense.
- Invest every dollar above our average spending figure of $57,758 per year.
  - This starts by maximizing contributions to "tax-advantaged" accounts, because we don't want to pay any more in taxes than we have to. We'll discuss each one in detail.
  - After reaching the IRS limits on tax-advantaged accounts, the rest of your money goes into what's called a brokerage account. We'll go into great detail

on what that looks like, and what you'll invest in.

Tracking Your Spending

First off, you need to know how much money you spend on a regular basis, and where that money goes. Pilot Math doesn't work if you're spending thousands of unplanned dollars on hookers and blow...or Starbucks and unused gym memberships. Thankfully, there is some really great software in our world designed to help you.

Some people like to use a budget to help track and manage spending. Personally, I hate living on a budget and end up quitting every time I try. If you are good at budgeting, then I highly recommend sticking with it. If not, my strategy has always been trying to optimize all my spending to get the most utility and/or life happiness possible out of each dollar. I'm sure I would love eating steak and lobster every day, owning a brand-new/top-of-the-line MacBook, and driving a Tesla Model S P100D. However, I realize that these things would cost a lot in terms of future freedom. I'm very happy eating simpler food, working on older/cheaper computers, and driving my 8 year old car. Although the more expensive options might improve my happiness somewhat, I don't think it would be enough to justify the additional cost.

Whether you budget or not, it's very useful to take a look at where your money's going from time to time. I try to optimize, but I still find waste in my spending. Three of my favorite flight instructor techniques are: fear, sarcasm, and ridicule. I've employed them against myself very successfully over the years to decrease my wasteful spending.

I recommend you choose one of three fantastic software tools for tracking your spending. You can set up a budget to keep you on track, or use them to ridicule yourself into cutting waste out of your life. (Whatever works is fine as far as I'm concerned.)

The first resource is called Personal Capital.[29] It's a system that gathers information from all of your banking, investment, and credit card accounts and shows you how you're doing. You can use it to track spending, and see your net worth. It's an outstanding tool, and it's free! (They'll call you and try to offer you financial advisor services.

---

[29] https://www.personalcapital.com/

You're welcome to decline those services and keep using their online product.)

The next resource is Mint.com.[30] It's run by Intuit, the people who do the Quicken line of products and TurboTax. It functions a lot like Personal Capital, and it's the same kind of free. I don't care which one you use as long as it helps you stay within budget or optimize spending to maximize the benefit you get from each dollar.

I've heard of some people using both Personal Capital and Mint. They prefer the way the the former presents your net worth, and say the later works better for tracking spending. Running two similar systems sounds like a lot of work to me, but if you benefit from it then more power to you!

If you're not a crazy spender, either of these programs should do everything you need. However, if you aren't yet as disciplined as you need to be, there's another great resource. It's called You Need a Budget, or YNAB for short.[31] You can also set it up to track your spending, but it has more robust budgeting tools. It isn't free, but I believe it's worth the money for someone who needs budgeting help.

You need to go, right now, and sign up for at least one of these three options. You don't need to check the app on your phone obsessively and agonize over every little fluctuation in your accounts. However, you do need to check periodically to make sure that you aren't going wild in some area.

And yes, I'm serious. Put down your book, Kindle, iPad, Kobo, phone, or whatever and go sign up for one of these apps. I'll wait.

Debt

Debt is a trap. When you incur debt, you're giving other people permission to control your life. They're essentially forcing you to work for their benefit. You also agree to let them take your property away from you if you stop doing what they want (making your payments.) If someone were to put you in this position without your permission you'd call it slavery or theft and call the cops. Worse, this is completely voluntary slavery. Sadly, almost every human being in the

---

[30] https://www.mint.com/
[31] https://www.youneedabudget.com/

"developed" world has willingly signed up for a set of gilded shackles. Don't be stupid enough to volunteer for this just to buy consumer goods!

There are a few things in this world worth incurring debt to fund: a reasonable home, an education that will actually lead to meaningful employment, and maybe a car. Business ventures, especially real estate, can also successfully employ debt, but this requires careful planning based on a realistic expectation of monetary returns. Beyond that, there is nothing in this world worth enslaving yourself over.

If you've made bad decisions in your past and are now trapped in debt, do everything you can to get out. I won't even judge you if you're honestly working hard to escape. How to make that happen is beyond the scope of this book. If you feel overwhelmed or completely clueless, start reading and watching Dave Ramsey.[32] His book, The Total Money Makeover[33] can absolutely help you fix your finances. It has literally saved the financial future of tens of thousands of people.

Dave Ramsey is a great resource for people with weak financial skills or self-discipline. However, once you've completed most of his baby steps, or you've otherwise learned to stop moronically spending money you don't have, you need to leave Dave behind! His philosophies are great for getting out of debt, but terrible for building long-term wealth. There are better resources available to you. A great place to start is a website/podcast/community called ChooseFI.[34] (The FI stands for Financial Independence.)

You can find a much longer list of great resources at: pilotmathtreasurebath.com/bible.[35]

Investing

---

[32] Dave Ramsey is possibly the best resource on the planet for getting yourself out of debt and setting you up for a future of financial success: https://www.daveramsey.com/.

[33] Here's an affiliate link to his book: https://amzn.to/301n2JR. However, you can probably find a copy at your local library. If your debt is out of control, don't use a credit card to buy a book about debt!

[34] I found ChooseFI through their podcast, but they have all kinds of other great resources. Dave Ramsey can only get you so far. Once you've completed his baby steps, you'll find yourself at a loss for what to do next. ChooseFI is the easiest next step: https://www.choosefi.com/.

[35] This website should grow and update to make sure you have access to the best resources available: http://www.pilotmathtreasurebath.com/bible.

Now that you're tracking spending and destroying debt, we need to set up your investments. The first and best step to making sure you invest like you should is to automate! You should go, right now, to the employee portal on your company's website and set things up so that money gets transferred automatically from your paycheck to your investment accounts each month.

If you can't do this online, or you can't figure out how, your company should have a Human Resources office that can help you set this up. Worst case, most banks and online brokerages like Vanguard have websites that allow you to set up automatic transfers from your checking account that happen each month after your paycheck gets deposited.

For investing, anybody can set up what's called a "brokerage account." You can go to any major investment company's website like Vanguard, Fidelity, Charles Schwab, etc. and probably get started without having to speak to a human being. I also recommend looking into Betterment.com.[36] They're a new type of brokerage firm that offers some benefits you won't get at more traditional companies.

You'll be able to use a brokerage account at any of these companies to buy stocks, bonds, mutual funds, ETFs, and other investment "products."

If you do nothing else, this brokerage account will be subject to a wide variety of tax laws. In the United States, it's not enough that the government taxes your income, your spending, your property, and even your death. If your investments earn money, those earnings get taxed as well. We'll do our best to legally mitigate these taxes, but they exist as an unfortunate reality for us.

Thankfully, the government does make some exceptions. There are several types of accounts that offer us tax advantages. (The idea is to motivate individuals to save for retirement instead of relying on the Ponzi Scheme also known as Social Security to support them in old age.) Some of these types of accounts are set up through your

---

[36] Betterment is what's being called a "robo-advisor." They charge much lower fees than traditional financial advisors, and have some unique benefits that you won't get anywhere else. I recommend looking in to what they offer. This is not an affiliate link: http://www.betterment.com.

employer (the most common ones for pilots are the 401K and TSP.) You're also allowed to set up Individual Retirement Accounts, or IRAs. There is no limit on the number of accounts you can set up and designate as an IRA. However, you are limited on the total amount of money you're allowed to contribute to IRA accounts each year.

The government makes sure you save this money for retirement by penalizing you if you spend it early. In most cases, if you withdraw money from a tax-advantaged retirement account before age 59 1/2, you'll have to pay a 10% penalty to the IRS. Don't worry, we'll figure out how to survive until you reach that point. There are also ways to get access to the money, if necessary, with a little planning. If you think you're going to need access to some retirement money in the next few years, Google "Roth IRA Conversion Ladder."

We're going to take a look at each of these accounts. We'll discuss how much you're allowed to contribute to each one, and what the tax advantages are. Given these advantages, you should be investing as much as possible each year in these accounts before you invest in a regular, taxable brokerage account. We'll be looking at:

- TSP
- 401k
- IRA
- HSA
- Other Retirement Accounts
- 529 Plans

TSP

The TSP, or Thrift Savings Plan, is the fundamental tax-advantaged investment account for military aviators and other federal employees. You need to go to myPay[37] and make sure that some money is going to your TSP every month.

For 2019, you're allowed to contribute up to $19,000 per year into the TSP. That might be a lot for a young warrant officer or lieutenant, but it's important for you to do everything you can to hit that number.

Since my wife and I had two incomes while we were on active duty, and no problem maintaining healthy savings, we'd always take turns

---

[37] You should already know what myPay is, but here's the link to get you there quickly: https://mypay.dfas.mil/.

setting our TSP contributions to 90% of our paycheck, as early as possible each year. We'd quickly reach our (then) $18,000 limit for the year, at which point the government just stopped pulling that money out of our paychecks. If that won't work for you, then divide the amount of money you want to put into the TSP for the year (hopefully you can choose the maximum of $19,000 for 2019) by 12 and put that much in each month. The stupid website will make you specify a percentage of your pay instead of a dollar amount, so you'll have to do some non-pilot math. (Sorry…the system was developed by the lowest bidder. Your tax dollars at work, huh?)

In years when you deploy to a combat zone, you get an even better deal with the TSP: your contribution limit goes up to $56,000 per year! Not only that, but since all your pay earned in a combat zone is tax-free, you have some unique advantages. To explain these advantages we need to introduce one more piece of information about tax-advantaged retirement accounts:

Many of these accounts come in two flavors: traditional and Roth. In a "traditional" TSP (also traditional 401K and traditional IRA) you contribute pre-tax money into the account. This is a good deal. The IRS doesn't count this money as part of your income, so they don't make you pay taxes on that portion of your earnings. This also has the effect of decreasing the overall earnings that count against you for a given year, meaning you'll pay less overall in taxes on the remaining income that the IRS does count against you.

In most cases, you don't get to ride that tax-free good deal train forever though. You get to pay taxes on this money (and any investment gains) when you withdraw and spend it later in life. Paying taxes is never fun, but giving your money a few decades to grow leaves you way better off than if the money had been taxed on the way into a regular brokerage account, then taxed *again* when you withdrew it.

Most people assume that their income will be lower in retirement than during the heart of their working years, so it doesn't hurt as much to pay your taxes later when you're in a lower tax bracket. We'll see that this may or may not be the case, depending on how much you decide to fill up your Treasure Bath.

The Roth TSP (also Roth 401K and Roth IRA) works the other way around. You contribute after-tax money into the account. The good news is that the IRS only taxes you on that money once. Since you paid taxes before depositing that money, they'll never charge you taxes on that money (or the investment gains you get from it) again!

If you think you'll have a large income in retirement, you're better off paying taxes on this money when you're a poor junior/first officer with a low tax rate. However, if you're an airline captain making $350,000 or more per year, you're better off trying to reduce your taxable income now and pay taxes later when your income probably won't be quite as high.

The financial independence community has been debating the specific strategies for traditional versus Roth retirement accounts as long as such things have existed. I'm not so concerned about which one you do right now as long as you're contributing the maximum number of dollars allowed each year. Once you've started doing that, you'll have plenty of time to read the various opinions on the internet.

Better yet, contact a professional advisor and ask her what she thinks you should do. For starters, look for a fee-only Certified Financial Planner (CFP) and pay for an hour or two of her time. We'll discuss later whether you might want to continue working with a CFP as time goes on.

Now that we know the difference between traditional and Roth retirement accounts, we can look at the other good deal that deployments have to offer.

Normally, you'd have to pay taxes on the money you put into a Roth retirement account like the Roth TSP, but when you're deployed you get to take advantage of the Combat Zone Tax Exclusion (CZTE.) This means that you pay zero taxes on any money you earn while you're deployed, and that any money contributed to your Roth TSP is untaxed. That tax-free money will grow in your Roth TSP, and you'll be able to withdraw it later without paying any tax on it. That money will never be taxed. As a great man once said, "Dude, you just scored."

Your Roth TSP contributions are limited to that $19,000 figure, no matter whether you're in a combat zone or not. Once you've dumped that amount in, you'll have to contribute your next $37,000 as traditional TSP. If you can schedule your saving and spending properly, you can save those $37,000 of contributions for months when you won't be deployed and eligible for the CZTE. This will further reduce your overall taxable income for the year and save you thousands of dollars. One year during my military service I earned more than $80,000, but thanks to deployments and strategic traditional TSP contributions, my taxable income was only $24,000. This was even a pretty ham-fisted attempt at optimizing that situation. I challenge you to do better!

Although military officer pay (like Air Force pilot morale) is pretty darn good, it's nowhere near what you'll make as an airline pilot. If you employ the strategies we cover in this book, it's also nowhere near the amount of annual income you'll have in retirement. For this reason, I advocate prioritizing Roth TSP (and Roth IRA) contributions, over traditional TSP/IRA, while in the military.

One of the problems with some types of investments is that the people running the program charge you a lot for their services. In theory, they're good enough at investing your money to more than make up for their fees. In reality, this almost never happens for "actively managed" funds. (Author JL Collins has an outstanding discussion of this principle in *The Simple Path to Wealth*, the 5th Book of the Pilot Math Bible.)[38]

Thankfully, the TSP does not have this problem. Since the program is run with taxpayer-funded subsidies, the fees charged by the funds in the TSP are miniscule. The government also simplifies the program by only offering you limited number of investment options. I recommend you consider investing everything in the C Fund. It's designed to track/match the performance of the S&P 500 and has a respectable expense ratio of 0.04%. I'll be recommending that you consider investing in similar funds in your other accounts.

A low-fee index fund designed to match the performance of the S&P 500, or the stock market as a whole, is almost guaranteed to outperform most actively-managed investments over the long run. However, the stock market is also subject to volatility. If you can't handle watching your account balance jump up and down from time to time, you might consider investing in one of the TSP's Lifecycle funds. They automatically shift your investments among the five major TSP funds over time. Their goal is to maximize returns early on, then gradually prioritize stability over gains as they approach a targeted retirement year. If I was going to start investing in one of the Lifecycle

---

[38] Here's an Amazon Affiliate link to Mr. Collins' masterpiece: https://amzn.to/2PHkNrJ

funds I'd consider the L2050 fund for now. When they start the L2060, I'd consider it instead.

Bottom line: Contribute the maximum of $19,000 per year to your TSP. ($56,000 in years that you deploy.) Consider putting everything into the C Fund, or the L2050 Fund.

401K

Non-military pilots should have a 401K plan through your employer. (If not, you have some other options beyond the scope of this book. A quick search through the online Financial Independence community will show you everything you need to know a SEP IRA or Solo 401K.) My company uses Fidelity for our 401K plans, and I simply log into my accounts at Fidelity.com.[39] You also need to go, right now, and make sure that you're automatically contributing as much as you can stand directly from your paycheck to your 401k each month. (The 2019 annual limit is $19,000, the same as the TSP for military pilots.) You'll probably also have Roth vs Traditional options here.

Most US airlines went through bankruptcies at some point in the last couple decades that allowed them to shed the burden of funding huge pilot pensions. They replaced that retirement benefit with these 401K "Defined Contribution" (DC) plans. Your employer probably "matches" any contributions you make to your 401K, up to a certain percentage. If nothing else, you need to at least contribute enough to get the full match from your employer. Otherwise, you're voluntarily letting your company pay you less than you've earned...like a moron.

Other employers (like mine) will contribute a fixed percentage of your pay each month, whether you contribute or not. (I get 16%.) The IRS allows a maximum of $56,000 per year in total contributions to my 401K for 2019 (just like a deployed military pilot's TSP.) After that, my company pays my 16% directly to me as taxable cash. Some companies automatically contribute the excess to special health care accounts called VEBAs, or other places.

Unless you work for a major airline or have a really great corporate flying job, you probably have a smaller income right now than you will in the future. Knowing that, I recommend you prioritize

---

[39] Fidelity.com

contributions to your Roth 401K for now. There are caveats to this, but we'll save them for later.

As with the TSP, I recommend investing your 401K in a low-fee index fund that tracks the whole stock market, or at least the S&P 500. My company's plan at Fidelity gives me access to their S&P 500 Index fund with an expense ratio of just 0.01%. (Google ticker symbol FXAIX for it's stats.) If you invest through Vanguard, I recommend you consider VTSAX, their total stock market index fund. Charles Schwab also has a total stock market index fund, SWTSX, with an expense ratio of 0.03%. If your company's 401K is run through another company, look for a similar index fund with fees in this range.

Bottom line: Contribute the maximum of $19,000 per year to your 401K. Choose a low-fee index fund like FXAIX, VTSAX, or SWTSX.

IRA

An IRA, or Individual Retirement Account, is a catch-all for people who don't have access to a 401K, TSP, or other employer-sponsored plan. However, since the US is obsessed with and has a warped view of fairness, you may still be able to contribute to an IRA, even if you have access to these other types of accounts. In 2019, any individual is allowed to contribute to a Roth IRA as long as his or her total annual income is less than $122,000. (For a family filing jointly, the maximum annual income limit is $193,000.) In 2019, each individual is limited to contributing only $6,000 into a Roth IRA.

You can only contribute earned income to an IRA. You don't have to deduct it automatically from your paycheck (you can just write a check or do a balance transfer to your retirement account,) but you do have to earn money from some sort of job. If your spouse doesn't work, it might be worth finding him or her a side-hustle that generates at least $6,000 per year in income.

Though not mandatory, it's a good idea to automate this process as well. You should be able to set up an allotment from your paycheck through your company's HR department, or set up an automatic transfer through your bank. $6,000 per year doesn't seem like much when we just talked about a career that pays upwards of $10M, but even this small amount adds up to a lot of money over time with interest. The other side of that coin suggests that the average pilot should have no trouble coming up with $6,000 per year to put into a Roth IRA. When we were able to contribute to Roth IRAs, my wife and I deposited the maximum amount in a single lump-sum right after the holidays. You should feel extremely uncomfortable until you've contributed the maximum allowed to your Roth IRA each year.

Most major airline pilots will make too much money to contribute to a Roth IRA. However, junior military and regional airline pilots should be under the limits, unless your spouse also has a high-paying job. It's worth noting that the $122,000/$193,000 limits are based on your taxable income. That's calculated after accounting for all of your tax deductions. It's possible to earn more than these limits, but still contribute to a Roth IRA because your taxable income ends up being low enough. If you're close to the limit, get a tax pro to help you figure out if you qualify. He or she may also be able to help you find some additional, legal ways to reduce your taxable income and stay eligible to contribute to a Roth IRA.

You can also have traditional IRA accounts. The contribution and income limits are different, but it works much like the other traditional tax-advantaged retirement accounts. However, since most pilots will have access to a 401K or TSP, I feel like a traditional IRA probably won't be useful to you in most cases. This type of account can be a tool for certain strategies, but we'll discuss those later.

Bottom line: Contribute the maximum of $6,000 per year to your Roth IRA. If you set up your account at Vanguard, Fidelity, or Schwab, you'll be able to invest in VTSAX, FXAIX, or SWTSX, respectively.

HSA

If you're a military pilot who has always had Tricare, you've probably never heard of an HSA, or Health Savings Account. Tricare is a great deal, at least for now. It covers almost any medical expense you could imagine and costs you almost nothing while on active duty. If you earn a military retirement, the retired flavor of Tricare will cost you some money out-of-pocket, but it's still a pretty amazing deal.

However, for pilots without access to Tricare, or military pilots who chose not to join the check-of-the-month club, you should be very excited about having access to an HSA! A blogger known as the Mad Fientist has an outstanding post explaining why the HSA is the

Ultimate Retirement Account.[40] To summarize:

You get to put pre-tax money into your HSA, just like you do with a traditional TSP/401K/IRA. That money can be invested and earn interest, just like those other accounts as well. However, as long as you use the money from your HSA to pay for authorized health care expenses, it doesn't get taxed when you withdraw it either. That's right, it's money on which you will *never pay tax*. It's like the best parts of traditional and Roth accounts all rolled into one.

But wait, there's more!

There is no requirement to pay for your health care expenses directly from your HSA at the time of service. You're allowed to pay for those expenses using your regular old bank account, a credit card, or money you had stashed under your mattress. Then, you can reimburse yourself for that expense from your HSA, and you still don't have to pay taxes on it. There's also no limit on the timeframe for this reimbursement. You could pay $100 for a doctor's visit today, but wait 40 years to reimburse yourself. If that $100 earns you 8% per year for 40 years, it will have grown to more than $2100 by the time you finally get around to reimbursing yourself. You can transfer the $100 to cover that one reimbursement, and save the other $2000 to reimburse yourself for something else later.

As the Mad Fientist suggests, all you have to do is keep a ledger of all your authorized health care expenses throughout your life. I'd do it electronically and make backups. I'd include scans or photos of all receipts in case the IRS asks. The bank that runs my HSA has an app that allows me to track all of my medical expenses and even take pictures of the receipts with my phone. My HSA is linked to my family's regular checking account, and I can transfer funds to reimburse myself from the app at any time. I won't be doing this for a long time though, because I want all this tax-free money to grow for as long as possible.

Your plan will be to maximize contributions to your HSA every year, but pay for all your expenses out-of-pocket. Then, many years in your future, you can start reimbursing yourself for these expenses any

---

[40] This may be one of the most important personal finance articles ever written: https://www.madfientist.com/ultimate-retirement-account/.

time you need cash. This truly is the Ultimate Retirement Account.

It's important to note that there are other types of tax-advantaged healthcare-related savings accounts. Most of them do *not* give you the same advantages of the HSA. Many of them don't allow you to keep a balance in the account from year to year...they're use-it-or-lose-it. These are much less advantageous than an HSA and should only be used if your healthcare plan doesn't offer any HSA options. Don't accidentally dump a bunch of money into one of these accounts thinking it's an HSA because you'll lose it. Do your homework first!

In 2019 an individual can contribute up to $3,500 to an HSA, and a family can put in $7,000. This doesn't seem like much now, but if you plan to contribute this much every year and let your money grow for at least 2-3 decades before you reimburse yourself for any of your medical expenses, we're suddenly talking about a lot of money that the IRS will never, ever touch!

My company will contribute about 25% of the annual maximum to my HSA, in addition to all my other pay and benefits, as part of my overall compensation package. Some companies choose to fully fund your HSA for you each year.

Like any of these accounts, there are rules on who gets to have an HSA. The biggest limitation is that you must have a "high deductible" health insurance plan. Most insurance providers offer several types of qualifying plans. For a family with major health issues, a high-deductible plan may not be the right answer. If you're healthy, getting access to an HSA is a great advantage of these plans.

Bottom line: Contribute the maximum of $3,500 (individual) or $7,000 (family) per year to your HSA. I recommend you consider putting all your HSA funds into a low-fee total stock market index fund like VTSAX, FXAIX, SWTSX, or something similar. (You should be sensing a theme by now.)

Summary: Tax-Advantaged Accounts

I've just told you to maximize contributions to your TSP or 401K, your Roth IRA, and your HSA. When we add these up, we're looking at a pretty hefty contribution to your overall savings:

$19,000-$56000   TSP/401K

$6000	Roth IRA
$3500-$7000	HSA
$28,500-$69,000	Annual Total

That's a lot of money to be able to invest in tax-advantaged accounts. I cannot emphasize enough how important it is that you automate your contributions to these accounts and try to maximize them every year. As a young pilot, you probably won't make enough to do this. My Pilot Math assumptions allow you to spend either $57,758, or every penny you make each year, whichever is lower. If that level of spending leaves less than $28,500 available for investments, I recommend you maximize your HSA or Roth IRA first, then your TSP/401K.

Although saving $28,500-$69,000 may seem like a lot at first, you'll find yourself saving more than this before you know it. Year 2 pay for a lazy 717 FO at my company puts you well past that mark. If you stay in the military until retirement you'll be hitting this level of savings for much of the last half of your career. We'll discuss in a moment what to do with the rest of that money once you've maximized your tax advantages.

Other Retirement Accounts

If you have a side job, or your spouse has a job, one or both of you may have access to other types of tax-advantaged retirement accounts. Some common ones are a 403b, 457, and a traditional pension (aka: Defined Benefit) plan. The specifics of these types of accounts are beyond the scope of our discussion here. For our purposes I'll just say this: I recommend investing as much as you can into any type of tax-advantaged account to which you have access.

It's also worth mentioning that there is a way to take after-tax money you've contributed to retirement accounts and convert it into a Roth IRA. Nicknames like the Super-Mega Roth and Backdoor Roth make this sound shady, but it's 100% legal and widely used. My 401K provider, Fidelity, refers to this trick as an "in-service withdrawal." I used to have to call them on the phone every month to do it, but they recently automated the process on their website.

We'll briefly go into more detail on this next chapter. I plan to further expand on this topic at pilotmathtreasurebath.com, or I'll at least make sure to post links to someone who has.

529 Plans

Once you've maximized your contributions to these retirement accounts, you could consider contributing to a tax-advantaged educational savings account, commonly called a 529 plan, for each of your kids. You generally have to contribute after-tax money to these plans. However, as long as the money taken out of the plan is used to cover authorized educational expenses (tuition, books, fees, even room & board...the law is pretty liberal in what it allows) that money doesn't ever get taxed again.

You don't necessarily want to end up with millions of dollars in a 529 plan because it'll go unused. However, if you "over-fund" it you can transfer it to other family members. The list of eligible transfer recipients includes yourself, your spouse, other kids, siblings, cousins, and more. You can probably find someone close to you who could put your money to good use.

These funds can also be used to cover vocational education expenses. You could use any excess funds to educate yourself by getting your Commercial Blimp Pilot Certificate, or a B-29 type rating ($40,000 last time I checked.) I'm confident that I can can find *very* educational uses for every penny in my kids' plans, if necessary.

The authorized educational expense of housing is another convenient catch-all (or magnificent loophole) to alleviate any worry of over-funding a 529 plan. There's no reason you couldn't use the money in your child's 529 plan to subsidize the expense of buying a house, or even an apartment complex. Your purchase is technically covering your child's housing costs. However, you can also rent extra rooms/ units to other college students. There's a limit on what you're allowed to charge your kid for rent, and it's different for each school. If you want to try this, you need to do your research and talk to a financial professional with experience in this area. Part of that process will involve talking to the finance office at your kid's school to find out their figure for total cost per year. That number will play in to the equation you use to calculate how much of your kid's 529 money you can pay yourself for his or her rent.

We'll talk later about how real estate can be a great investment alternative to the stock market. Using funds from a 529 plan to acquire some of that real estate is a nice benefit of our country's ridiculous tax code. There's absolutely nothing wrong with obeying the laws...especially when they benefit you this much!

It's also worth noting that education costs have far outpaced inflation for many years. If your kids choose to go to graduate school, or possibly go to an aviation university where expenses for flight training quickly hit the tens of thousands of dollars, it might be a challenge to over-fund a 529.

My wife and I started putting $6,000 per year per child into a 529 plan when each of our kids was born. My daughter is 9 and my son is 8 and their 529 plans have a combined value of $180,000, including investment gains. We have another 9-10 years before they'll need this money, during which time I'd expect that figure to at least double again, even without any additional contributions. That will cover a lot of college!

It would feel pretty painful to shell out $180K right now (or $360K in 10 years,) but it was not difficult at all to invest $6K-12K each year. This is one example where automating our investments and taking a slow-and-steady approach to saving has really paid off for my family. If you've maximized your other tax-advantaged accounts, you can probably manage $6,000 per year into a 529 plan for your kid.

The rules for 529 plans vary because they're administered at the state level. You do NOT have to use your state's plan though. You're free to sign up for any plan sponsored by any state. The contribution limits and other rules will vary, but they're all somewhat similar.

My wife and I also transferred our Post 9/11 GI Bill benefits to our kids. This isn't money for you to invest, per se, but it's a very valuable benefit that comes from serving in the military. Remember that you incur a 4-year service commitment after you designate a transfer beneficiary. Unless you plan to retire in the military, you need to transfer your GI Bill the moment you are eligible to do so, to avoid getting trapped on active duty longer than necessary.

This may also play into your family planning. It's okay to have a kid less than four years before you separate from military service, but the GI Bill may not be an option for that particular rugrat. If things work out this way, I'd consider letting your firstborn use the GI Bill benefit and establishing 529 plans for any subsequent children. There are also ways to fulfill GI Bill transfer obligations with service in the Guard or Reserves. You can skin this cat many ways, but do it intentionally.

No matter whether you plan to use the GI Bill or a 529 plan, you and your spouse need to openly discuss whether you want to fund your kids' college in the first place...and if so, then how much? Our society seems to be convinced that parents are obligated to fund college for their children at any cost. While this is noble in many ways, it has some undesirable side-effects. Would college cost so much these days if the only way students could fund it was scholarships and part-time work? Would a kid choose a useless degree at an ultra-expensive school if he or she had to pay for it out of pocket? College should be a fun time, but wouldn't kids probably focus a little more on learning and a little less on partying if they were costing themselves money anytime they failed?

My wife rejects most of these arguments. She worked incredibly hard in college and had a good time anyway. As you can see, we'll probably end up with enough to fund undergrad and grad school for our kids. However, I hope we can find ways to challenge them to value their educations and sweat just a little bit in exchange for our funding.

None of this accounts for kids shortening college by taking AP/IB classes, dual-enrollment college courses, or CLEP tests during high school. It also assumes that your kids get zero scholarships. There are a lot of ways to fund school without having a full-on Treasure Bath filled up just for that purpose. We'll look specifically at some of those in our chapter on Baby Pilot Math. I also plan to write more on this topic at pilotmathtreasurebath.com.

Overall, I think of money for college much like I think of altitude, fuel and runways. I'd rather have altitude below me than above me, fuel in my tanks instead of in the truck, and runway in front of me instead of behind. I'd rather have more money saved for my kids' college than not enough. A 529 plan is a way to do that with with major tax advantages.

Taxable Investing

Until now, we've concentrated on getting $28,500-$69,000 into tax-advantaged accounts each year. Hopefully, every major airline pilot will still have money that needs to go into savings, even after doing all of the above. We're out of tax-advantaged places to stash it, so you'll have to put it into a regular old taxable brokerage account. The easiest way to do this is to go to Vanguard.com[41] and set up an account online. You don't even have to even talk to a human being to do it. If you want a newer company with some interesting benefits, check out Betterment. (Do your research and pick the one you like. Or, invest some money with each and decide which is better after a couple years.)

Wall Street and others offer us a seemingly unlimited number of investment options. There are more stock-based mutual funds than there are stocks. That only scratches the surface on the thousands of other "opportunities" or "investment vehicles" where you can stash your cash. If you ask around, I guarantee you can find someone interested in doing your investing for you. They'll pick stocks, bonds, mutual funds, ETFs, and other securities with the intention of using your money to make themselves rich.

Wait, what?

Yes, you heard me right.

You can't fault these people. Financial advisors and stockbrokers don't exist to make you rich. They work for their own good. Yes, in some ways they only make money when you make money. However, they also get to charge you a commission or a fee for their services. They also work under a system of constraints that has fascinating, and distressing, consequences for you as an individual. In some cases, investment broker fees are outrageous. Best case, hiring someone to do your investing for you will cost 1% of your account's value each year. It gets worse from there.

In full disclosure, my wife and I use a financial planner. We use them because her parents used them. (Emet's Marriage Success Rule #1: Happy wife, happy life. Emet's Marriage Success Rule #2: If she insists on a given course of action because her daddy taught her to do it that way, don't bother arguing. You will lose.) Our financial planners have produced great returns for us (though the market overall has

---

[41] Vanguard is the most popular brokerage among members of the Financial Independence community. It was founded by Jack Bogle, the inventor of the index fund. It's also 100% owned by its investors...suggesting that there should be less conflict of interest between customers and owners. http://www.vanguard.com/

been on a tear for nearly a decade.) They spend a lot of time answering our questions, they know us and our kids by name, they've helped us set up parts of our financial life well beyond just "where should we stick our money?" However, they cost us 1%. I'm happy working with them as long as my wife is. If you want, I'll even be happy to refer you to them. However, I recommend you consider another option.

As I mentioned, a brilliant man named Jim Collins wrote a book called *The Simple Path to Wealth*.[42] He wrote it for his daughter. Collins hit financial independence and quit full-time work year ago, but he used to work in finance and loves studying stocks and investing. His daughter once told him that she had no interest in that stuff and wished she could invest her money without having to be bored by all the details. *The Simple Path to Wealth* is his advice to her.

Collins does an outstanding job explaining and justifying a very simple investing strategy. He recommends putting 100% of your funds into Vanguard's Total Stock Market Index Fund, VTSAX. This fund essentially buys one share of stock from each publicly traded company in the US at a time. Once it's bought one share of each, it goes and buys another. They've done this with more than $203,000,000,000!

By owning the entire stock market, the value of this fund's shares is all but guaranteed to increase in the long run. Over that run, this has resulted in a very impressive average return of more than 11%. You might think that you could beat this performance by identifying the bad companies that will underperform and instead investing money in those that will beat the average. There are a few people in the world who have successfully done this, but most of the "active management" funds that try this fall short of the market average in the long run. If thousands of highly-paid analysts who spend all day every day doing market research can't beat the average, what chances do we have of doing better? In most cases, you're far better off just buying VTSAX.

Collins does understand that it's tough to stomach the short-term volatility of the US stock market. If you're susceptible to panic, he suggests that a portion of your investment portfolio include bonds. He also recommends Vanguard's Total Bond Market Fund, VBTLX.

Bonds are more stable, but they don't pay very well right now. Stocks have a lot of short-term volatility, but they pay the most over

---

[42] Here's that affiliate link again, just in case you didn't use it the last time I mentioned this book: https://amzn.to/2PHkNrJ.

time. Collins recommends having anywhere from 50-100% of your investment funds in stocks (VTSAX) and the rest in VBTLX. The amount in bonds will depend on your tolerance for volatility, and he explains reasons that you may want to regularly adjust that balance over time.

That's the shortest summary you're likely to find of his advice. I cannot recommend highly enough that you go read his book itself. The investing principles in this book are so fundamental to our goals that I've made it the 5th Book of The Pilot Math Bible.

So, for taxable investments, our plan is to open a regular old brokerage account and use it to buy shares of VTSAX (and possibly VBTLX.) And that's it.

See, it really is simple!

If you're a pilot like me, you may not necessarily love putting all your eggs in one basket...or all your fuel in one tank. You like the redundancy that comes from having multiple, independent systems. I won't say that one type of investment is "better" than the other. I just like the fact that they carry different types or risk, influenced by different factors in the real world. My wife and I are invested primarily in stocks, but we also have some other investments. We'll discuss some options in the next chapter.

For now, here's where we are:

$57,758	Annual Spending
$28,500-$69,000	Tax Advantaged Investments
$86,258-$126,758	Total Money Spoken For Each Year

For military and regional airline pilots, you won't even reach the lower-end of that limit for the first few years of your career, and that's okay. Limit your spending, invest every spare dollar in those tax-advantaged accounts for now, and look forward to the point when you'll start exceeding the minimums.

Major airline pilots are well above that minimum in year one. Once you've maximized your tax-advantaged accounts, every spare dollar goes into your brokerage account.

You'll be tempted to spend some of this money on luxuries, but if you're smart you won't! You're already spending a lot of money every year - just as much as any other family in the $50K-$70K income bracket. Remember that you started with Why. You have bigger and better things to do in life than owning some more Chinese-manufactured electronic gadgets, or transferring overpriced lattes to the nearest airport toilet.

Once you start saving this much, it'll become addictive. You'll see your Treasure Bath filling up rapidly and you'll want to keep it going. Instead of useless junk you're buying yourself freedom to live your life exactly how you want to, completely on your own terms. The more you save now, the sooner you'll reach that point.

Emergency Fund

Dave Ramsey and many other financial gurus will tell you that you need an emergency fund. Most will recommend having a savings account with a balance large enough to cover anywhere from 3-12 months of your average expenses. This isn't terrible advice, but I think the more important point is that you need to have a plan for dealing with unexpected expenses.

Anecdotally, the average American consumer can't even cover an unexpected expense of $400. For them, building up an emergency fund is a critical early step. As pilots, you and I make enough money that this shouldn't be an issue for us. There's nothing wrong with keeping some money in a regular bank account to cover these types of expenses on short notice, but those accounts pay almost zero interest. Leaving too much money in a savings account is just wasteful.

I recommend having about one month's worth of spending available in a checking or savings account at all times. Beyond that, I recommend using credit cards, backed up by your taxable brokerage accounts as your emergency fund. Let's look briefly at this idea:

Credit Cards

One of the reasons that people put too much money into emergency fund accounts is that Dave Ramsey is extremely anti-credit card. In the context of what he does and the people he serves, this is absolutely the correct stance for him to take. A person who lacks the self-discipline to not spend every available dime should not have access to a credit card. Hopefully, you and I are not those people.

Credit cards are convenient. Many of them offer useful fraud protection and other useful services, and they can be a great resource for a hobby called "travel hacking" in the hands of a disciplined person. I'm not going to dive into travel hacking in this book, but I think it's such an outstanding tool that it's worth mentioning the basics here.

My wife and I have started doing travel hacking. We took a trip to California for spring break this year and covered all our hotel expenses with points. My wife and I also got to take a kid-free trip to Las Vegas this summer. We traveled for free through a combination of airline employee standby benefits and travel hacking, and stayed in a gorgeous room in the Mandalay Bay for free thanks to travel hacking. Our goal for next year is to pay absolutely nothing for a family trip to Costa Rica for spring break next year.

For people like you and me, who are smart enough to make good decisions with our money, it doesn't quite make sense that banks would just give away free flights, hotel stays, and cash in exchange for using their credit cards. I once heard it put like this: A credit card signup bonus is a bank betting that you aren't responsible enough with money to pay off your card balance every month. It's a sad statement on American consumerism that banks continue offering these bonuses because they win this bet far more often than they lose. Don't let that keep you from taking advantage of it though!

If you want to learn about travel hacking, I recommend all of the following resources:

- Episode 9 of the ChooseFI podcast is an outstanding introduction to this topic.[43]
- My friend and fellow pilot, Anthony "El Gato" Felix, has travel hacked all over the world with his family. He's written about it on Invest in Travel.[44]
- The Points Guy has a well put-together site with great information and reviews. (His site is very commercialized.

---

[43] Listen to this. You will rarely get a better Return on Investment for an hour of your life: https://www.choosefi.com/009-travel-rewards-travel-world-free-ultimate-guide/.
[44] Shameless plug for a friend's blog. It's actually very well written and informative: http://www.investintravel.com/.

Avoid it if that offends you.)[45]

- A Facebook group called Award Travel 101 is an outstanding community for getting educated and asking questions.[46]
- The Mad Fientist's CardRatings Tool is the best way to decide which cards to use for travel hacking.[47] I'm a Mad Fientist fan for many reasons and I recommend you use his links to get new cards because he gets a kickback when you do. If you don't want to use his links, use El Gato's website instead.
- Travel Miles 101 is a website dedicated to educating you about travel hacking.[48] They have free online courses that walk you through the entire process of getting started. One of the ChooseFI hosts co-founded it.

Taxable Brokerage Accounts as Emergency Funds

Another reason that people keep too much money in savings accounts is that they don't understand how our financial system works. They think that if a sudden expense pops up, they must have money to cover it that instant. For someone living paycheck-to-paycheck, this is terrifying and problematic. Again, we're not those people.

If your car breaks down and you have to pay $1,800 for a new transmission, you do not have to shell out all that money that instant. Worst case, you'll have to pay part of it up front, and cover the balance after the repairs are done. Chances are the shop doesn't stock transmissions for every make and model of vehicle on the road. They're going to have to order one and it'll take a few days to arrive. Then, it'll take at least a day to swap it out. This gives you several days to come up with the cash.

As long as you're disciplined and you have a plan, there's nothing

---

[45] https://www.thepointsguy.com/

[46] https://www.facebook.com/groups/awardtravel101/

[47] A fantastic example of what you can accomplish with a little programming knowledge and some time to put them to use. This is a truly awesome site for choosing your next rewards credit card. If you use the links he provides, he'll make money every time you sign up for a card (and I won't.) It doesn't cost you anything, so please reward him for his excellent work: http://madfientist.cardratings.com/.

[48] https://www.travelmiles101.com/

wrong with using a credit card to cover this expense. As an added bonus, you'll get at least 1,800 hotel points or frequent flier miles by paying this way. When you use a credit card to pay for something, you have 30 days to pay off that expense without having to pay any interest to your credit card company.

If you have a full month's worth of expenses sitting in a checking or savings account, you can quickly use an app on your phone to transfer some cash to pay off your credit card bill the same day. Easy peasy! If not, either of these cases still gives you enough time to tap into your brokerage account. Instead of having your emergency fund lying around as cash in a savings account, you can be storing it as shares of VTSAX. You just sell a few shares of your mutual fund and use the proceeds to pay off your credit card.

Years ago, converting those shares back into to cash would have been a chore. You would have had to pick up a telephone (attached to the wall by a cord,) dial a 10-digit number by hand, and call your stock broker. He (probably not a she back then) would have had to call someone else and sell your shares. Then, he would write you a check and mail it to you. You would have to then drive to your bank, and wait in line, sign the check, and hand it to a person called a bank teller. Your bank would write some information in their ledger, bundle your check with thousands of others, and drive it to the local airport. From there, a small army of snot-nosed 20-year-old pilots would use a fleet of Piper Navajos to fly your check back to your stock broker's bank... probably in the town from which he sent it. Once the stock broker's bank got the signed check, they'd finally transfer the funds to your bank.

You should bow your head right now and thank Our Loving God in Heaven that those days are over!

Instead, you'll be able to access your brokerage account from any computer in the world (including your phone) by going to Vanguard, Schwab, Fidelity, or your company of choice. With a few clicks, you'll be able to sell as many shares of VTSAX as you need, all by yourself. Worst case, you'll have to wait until the end of the day before you see cash show up in your brokerage account. You will have your regular bank account linked to your brokerage account and you'll be able to immediately set up an electronic transfer from your brokerage account to checking.

This gives you more than enough time to have the money ready by the time the repairs are completed later this week, or to pay off your credit card by the end of the month. Thanks to modern technology, money stored as shares of VTSAX is as good as liquid for anyone disciplined enough to properly use a credit card.

Many people don't even consider the possibility of running their emergency fund like this because they're scared of investments. They don't understand the difference between tax-advantaged accounts and brokerage accounts. They don't understand how easy it is to convert shares of stock into cash using modern technology. Aren't you glad that you read this book and that you no longer have to be one of those people?

There is one other valid concern about having your emergency fund in stocks. We've mentioned that the stock market experiences short-term volatility. It's entirely possible that the day you really need to sell a bunch of your VTSAX shares is a day the market dropped a few hundred points and you'll lose some money.

I don't want to blithely ignore this loss, but I'm too much of an optimist to let it rule my life. Yes, the market will fluctuate from day to day and you may lose some money if an unexpected expense forces you to sell when the market is own. However, the alternative is a checking or savings account that pays, at best, 2% interest.

Historically, inflation has been 2.5-3%. This means that every dollar in a savings account is actually losing at least 1% of its value every year that it sits there. (Most savings accounts pay closer to 0.5%, or less, meaning you're losing 2.5% or more every year.) When you let that compounding interest work *against* you for several years, you start losing a lot of money. As Jim Collins writes in his book, the market always goes up over the long run. Even if it's down a little today, I feel like it will have been up enough overall that you'll lose less than if your money had been eroding in a savings account instead.

Bottom line: I recommend no more than a month or two of expenses in a savings account emergency fund. The rest of your "emergency fund" is held in the form of credit cards and your taxable brokerage accounts. If market volatility scares you, then you can keep a few more months of expenses in a cash emergency fund.

—

And with this, we have our fundamental nuts and bolts in place. We've identified the basic, specific things we're going to do to fill up our Treasure Bath from here on out.

- You're going to sign up for Personal Capital, Mint, or YNAB. (Pick at least one) You're going to use those tools look for ways to optimize spending to achieve maximum value per dollar.
- You're going to eliminate bad debt from your life. If necessary, use Dave Ramsey's *The Simple Money Makeover* to help you do it.
- You're going to invest $28,500-$69,000 in tax-advantaged investment accounts each and every year. You will use those accounts to buy VTSAX/VBTLX if available, or the lowest-fee total market index fund available if they aren't. Your IRA, 401K, and HSA will all be invested in these mutual funds. If you have a TSP, you'll invest that money in the C or the L2050 Fund.
- You're going to consider contributing money to a 529 plan for each of your children every year.
- You're going to open a regular brokerage account at Vanguard, Betterment, or another brokerage of your choice. You'll pour every dollar you make into this account, above the $57,758 you spend each year and the $28,500-$69,000 you put into tax-advantaged accounts.

Once you've invested these funds, do your absolute best to forget about them. I like checking from time-to-time, but it is critical that you hold on to your shares and don't sell, even if the market drops.

Jack Bogle, the inventor of the index fund and founder of Vanguard was famous for giving this same advice. He said that you should completely ignore your investments and let them grow for 40 years. When you do finally look to see how much money you have, you'll need to make sure there's a cardiologist in the room because you'll have a heart attack when you see how big the number is.

For us pilots, this will be a beautiful clawfoot bathtub overflowing with gold and jewels. You'll be able to dive on in and start luxuriating without a care in the world. Thanks to the power of Pilot Math, you won't even have to wait as long as the average schmuck to enjoy this either. We have the income potential to enjoy an overflowing Treasure Bath after a relatively short career.

We've covered the basics here, but there are potentially other ways for us to optimize. We'll look at some of those in the next chapter.

CHAPTER SEVEN
Nuts & Bolts - Advanced Topics

If you want a Treasure Bath deep enough to cover all your needs (or more) with passive income, your money must be put into something that generates high amounts of interest. Even with years to let your investments earn interest, you can't afford to put your cash into things that pay low interest rates. The best savings accounts, bonds, and certificates of deposit all return less than 3% interest annually. They're all considered relatively secure investments, but I believe that most of your money is better invested in other things. Inflation averages 2.5-3% per year, meaning these types of low-yield investments can, at best, only ever mitigate your losses. It's just not enough.

Over the very long term, the average return of the stock market is above 11%. Many stocks appreciate from year-to-year while also paying 2-5% in dividends. The stock market is your primary vehicle for building actual wealth in our world. Last chapter, I echoed Jim Collins' advice that the simplest path to this is buying the entire market in the form of a total stock market index fund, like Vanguard's VTSAX, Fidelity's FXAIX, or Schwab's SWTSX.

I have faith that the market will continue to rise overall. Each dollar you put into stocks buys a small piece of an actual company. That company owns physical and/or intellectual property with real value. Its clients buy products or services. That company has (and is supposed to care about) employees. The owners of the company are frequently compensated with stock or stock options. Every company has a myriad of powerful incentives to be better than the competition, to innovate, and to continue making money in the long run.

I guarantee the market will experience drops, corrections, and recessions in the future. However, every time that happens it bounces back and reaches new heights. The only way the market would lose money in the very long-term is if our entire economy collapsed. If that happened, it wouldn't matter how much money anyone had because it would all be worthless. (For reference see: Venezuela.)

All that said, the market does experience short-term volatility. In some cases, my idea of "short-term" could mean as long as several years. There are risks associated with this volatility, and some people have a tough time stomaching them. Although I believe that stocks are the best vehicle for long-term wealth building, I believe it's important to identify other investment opportunities capable of producing high returns.

I don't say that these opportunities are better or worse than stocks, only that they are different. What's most important for me is that some of the *risks* associated with these opportunities are different than the risks associated with stocks. I invest in some of these alternatives in hopes that if the stock market is down, these other investments will be up, or at least not drop as much. Let's look at a few.

Individual Stocks

I'm a fan of JL Collins' *Simple Path to Wealth* because it really is simple. It offers a very high mathematical likelihood of excellent investment gains in exchange for almost no effort on my part. What's more, the average long-term performance of most actively managed funds is worse than most low-cost total market index funds. This is despite the work of "experts" who put in hundreds of thousands of hours of research every year, trade actively every day, and charge you extra for their efforts.

For pilots, I recommend buying index funds and then forgetting about them for as long as possible. However, I realize that most of us have a lot of time on our hands. If someone has a hot stock tip, the flight deck is a perfect place to convey it. You may feel compelled to buy individual stocks. I feel like it's worth discussing that possibility here, but I saved it for the section on alternative investments. Unless you're willing to dedicate a lot of time and energy into taking this seriously, investing in individual stocks probably isn't worth your time.

There are a chosen few people in the world who are really good at picking stocks and getting rich. Warren Buffett and Charlie Monger are perhaps the most famous examples. I was also inspired when I read *Beating the Street* by Peter Lynch.[49] He ran mutual funds for Fidelity that performed far better in than the overall market and is now so rich that he works full-time figuring out how to give away his millions. If you read his book, you'll be tempted to think that you could replicate, or at least approximate, his results.

I recently listened to Episode 75 of the ChooseFI podcast.[50] The guest, Brian Feroldi, identified some interesting reasons why actively managed investment funds might underperform the market, and made a strong case for why an individual investor is free from many of those constraints. He also suggests that an individual investor choosing individual stocks could beat the market average.

I like Feroldi's points, and it's tough to argue with the success of investors like Peter Lynch, Warren Buffet, and Charlie Monger. However, I feel like their success comes with a cost. Specifically: they have to put a lot of time into education, tracking corporate performance, and managing their investments. I'm not a stock broker, I'm a pilot. I have a lot of hobbies more interesting than reading financial statements. If I can get performance more than good enough to fill up my Treasure Bath using index funds, I'm happy to use my spare time for other pursuits. If nothing else, a few hours spent flying a trip for premium pay is likely grant me a far better return than I could get from an equal amount of time spent researching individual stocks.

And yet, I can't help myself.

Every once in a while I note that a company's stock is way down and, feeling like I know something important about that industry that the general public doesn't, so I buy some. Instead of risking my family's entire future on this, I've given myself a little sandbox to play in. I set aside a few hundred dollars in an online brokerage account, and about 0.5% of my current 401K balance into a self-directed stock portfolio, and decided that I can invest those funds in whatever I want. I'm not allowed to put any more in though. If I want to expand those investing operations, I have to invest well enough for my funds to support it. I'm down a couple hundred dollars so far in my regular brokerage account, and up several thousand with my 401K money. No, I'm not telling you what I bought.

---

[49] Here's an affiliate link to *Beating the Street* by Peter Lynch: https://amzn.to/2oilKx5

[50] https://www.choosefi.com/075-unfair-advantage-brian-feroldi/

I recommend you start like that. Put everything into a total stock market index fund, like VTSAX, for now. Once your investment balance gets above $100,000 you can feel free to move a couple thousand dollars into a brokerage account and pick individual stocks. If you're as good as you think you are, that portion of your portfolio will perform very well. If you double your money you're allowed to put more in there. If you do worse than the market, you'll know that Warren Buffett isn't your spirit animal after all. You can cut your losses, take advantage of the tax loss harvesting we'll discuss later in this chapter, and buy some more shares of your favorite total stock market index fund.

Real Estate

In my opinion, the most obvious of the "alternative" investments we'll look at is real estate. At its most basic level, this has the potential to be a great investment. Everybody needs a place to live, and there will always be someone who can't afford a down payment on a house or apartment. If you buy the right property, at the right price, in the right location, it can give you a significant return. If you choose to rent it out, you'll also be building equity that can be tapped in a variety of ways later. There can also be significant tax advantages to owning real estate.

The stock market has returned a long-term average of 11%. That's a very nice return, and I don't expect it to ever get much better than that, on average. (For this book, I assume a long-term average stock market return of 8% and use 5% in my calculations to allow for 3% inflation.) However, if done right, real estate can return well beyond 11% in the long run.

So, if real estate is so wonderful, then, why isn't everyone doing it?

Sadly, it has its own problems.

First off, real estate can be a lot of work. Unlike buying VTSAX which can be done with your phone while laying by the pool sipping a margarita, real estate requires conscious action on your part. You have to shop for properties. You have to evaluate potential deals. You have to refurbish them, or at least manage contractors to do that work for you. You have to find, manage, and sometimes kick-out tenants. You have to deal with the aftermath of bad tenants. You have to deal with complex tax situations.

You can hire a property management company to deal with most of these headaches for you, but they charge 10% of your monthly rent. That's enough to destroy any profit margin on a lot of properties.

You also have to pay dearly for the privilege of buying into all that trouble. Unlike VTSAX where you can buy into the whole stock market a few bucks at a time, you have to come up with tens, if not hundreds of thousands of dollars to buy even one property, let alone remodel it. (This isn't completely true, as we'll see in a moment. Bear with me for now though.) It takes some form of work (and savings) to come up with enough cash to even get a loan...which can be a lot of work in and of itself. Closing that deal requires a real estate agent, to whom you pay a 6% commission. You could get your own real estate license, but that's some work too. If the average American can't even come up with $400 for an unexpected expense, how could he or she possibly afford to invest in real estate?

And yet, for all its problems, I still think real estate is a great investment option for the right person. If you know your area and you're willing to educate yourself and put in the work, this can be a great way to build your long-term wealth.

If you're interested in using real estate as an investment, go look up a site called BiggerPockets.com.[51] It's a community of people passionate about every type of real estate from flippers to buy-and-holders, from full time agents to side-hustlers. If nothing else, they have a podcast that can get you excited about the prospects of real estate investing while you're commuting to work or working out at the gym.

The central question for real estate investing is: how much time and attention do you want to spend on your investments? If you enjoy the process of finding, refurbishing, and managing properties, then by all means do it! Mr. Money Mustache and Vanilla Ice both like doing carpentry. Why not be like them - using your skills to fix up old houses and sell them at a profit? However, if that sounds like way too much hard work, then don't do real estate!

If you have other worthwhile ways of using your time, why not just

---

[51] BiggerPockets.com

pick the most passive possible investments and use your time for other things? It doesn't get any more passive than VTSAX.

REIT - Real Estate Lite

As I just alluded, there are ways to buy into big real estate holdings without having to own the whole thing yourself. They're called Real Estate Investment Trusts, or REITs. (REIT is pronounced: "I'll REIT you like a red-headed step-child!") They are corporate entities who raise lots of money from investors (us) and use that whole pool of money to buy big properties. If you've ever lived in a large apartment complex or been to a major shopping center, chances are you were at a property owned by a REIT of some kind.

Most REITs are set up for a specific term, all mine have been 5 years so far. They spend those years collecting rent and occasionally selling some of their properties at a profit. They pay us, the shareholders, a dividend during those years. At the end of the term there are a few options. 1) They can sell everything for a big pile of cash, divvy it up among the shareholders, and everyone walks away richer. 2) They'll offer to keep things going as they are, with regular dividend payments and continued ownership of shares that represent a real value backed by property. You're free to sell these shares to other investors at any time to cash-out. 3) They'll start a new business structure to hold the same portfolio. That new structure will offer to buy your shares just like #1, or they might also offer to convert your old holdings to shares in the new venture.

No matter how you slice it, the goal of a REIT is to produce an overall shareholder return at least as high as a targeted amount. (Mine have all cited 6% as their goal.) There's no guarantee they'll hit that mark, though mine have all exceeded it so far.

A return of 6% is far below what the stock market is capable of, but it's also a whole lot better than you can do with bonds or a savings account. The risks associated with REITs are more like those associated with holding individual real estate properties than owning shares of stock, which is something I like a lot about them. I feel like they also have different overall failure risks than regular stocks. If a company like Enron fails, your money is just plain gone. If a REIT were to completely fail, they'd still have to sell off all their properties and distribute the money evenly.

I feel like it's a significant mitigation of the downside, won by a likely reduction of the upside.

You can buy shares of many REITs directly on sites like Vanguard or Charles Schwab. I recommend speaking to a professional financial advisor before you do so.

Qualified Investors

As a major airline pilot, your annual investments will rapidly exceed the $69,000 maximum for tax-advantaged accounts that we calculated in the last chapter. In a way this is great news - more money to invest means your Treasure Bath fills up faster. Unfortunately, you're going to pay a lot of taxes for the privilege of earning this kind of money.

While those taxes are a frustrating fact of life, there are some ways beyond tax-advantaged retirement accounts to minimize your tax burdens. These opportunities are the illegitimate offspring of a tax code so convoluted and corrupt that should be thrown into a dumpster and set on fire...and yet they're 100% legal. Whether you like the tax code or not, I believe we might as well take advantage of any legal loopholes we can find.

I've noticed that many of these loopholes are associated with risky pet projects located in the districts of influential Congressional representatives. Since they're associated with higher risks, the US Government tries to keep the uninformed proletariats away by restricting access to "Qualified Investors." This term means people who have a net worth over $1M, or an income of at least $200K per year for two of the past three years. This automatically eliminates much of America, but includes most major airlines pilots.

Since these investments are risky enough that even an institution as financially reckless as the US Government considers them exceptional, you should absolutely get a professional financial advisor's help before investing in anything like this. This advisor can probably find dozens of opportunities for you to invest your money, but I'll give you one example:

The US Energy Development Corporation raises funds to drill oil and natural gas wells.[52] When they identify and obtain the rights to drill on a particular oil field, they offer qualified investors the

---

[52] http://usedc.com/

opportunity to help fund the project. They raise funds through private investors, use those funds to buy drilling equipment and hire people, then start drilling.

Thanks to Federal pork-barrel politics, most of the money you invest in these projects is tax-deductible in the first year of your investment. (I wonder what Congressional cronies invest in....) That means you're immediately realizing a return of 20-35% on your money invested through tax savings. That alone could make these investments meaningful for the right pilot.

From that point, you get part of the profit from every barrel of oil or cubic meter of gas pulled out of that project until the well runs dry. They don't bother going to the trouble of setting up projects like this unless their professional geologists convince them that there's plenty of money to be made. The returns each year are proportional to the price of oil. The USEDC has investment opportunities that promise profitability at today's oil prices. Imagine owning shares of an operation like this when oils was selling for $150 per barrell!

As an added benefit, investors also get tax breaks for "depletion" each year during the life of the project. (Similar to taking deductions for depreciation of the value of some real estate, or an airliner.) These breaks reduce your taxes and represent increased returns. In one fund I considered investing in, the combined tax deductions over the course of the project exceeded 100% of the money you invested. This seems too illogical to be true, until you remember that it's designed and regulated by the government with the largest debt in human history.

Your shares in these projects don't hold value like shares of stock or shares of a REIT. You're probably not going to resell them and they're worthless at the conclusion of the project. The "shares" are really just a tool for calculating your slice of the profits. However, for a good project you're looking at a healthy overall return on your investment, in addition to those ridiculous tax breaks.

If you don't care about the scientific or ethical concerns with fracking, or oil drilling in general, this could be an extremely profitable investment for you. I ended up not investing in this fund, though I was very tempted.

For every opportunity like the USEDC funds, there are dozens of others open only to qualified investors. Each one carries its own unique risks and requires some due diligence. They could provide you with higher returns or different risks.

Tim Ferris, a notable author and podcaster, chose to spend $120,000 on a "Real World MBA" by searching out unique investment opportunities instead of spending two years at a traditional business school. His thoughts on this approach make for an interesting read.[53]

If you're interested in opportunities restricted to qualified investors, go talk to a financial professional.

Creative (Legitimate) Real Estate

I've mentioned that I'm a fan of Robert Kiyosaki's book *Rich Dad, Poor Dad*. One of the most important achievements of that book is redefining the idea of assets vs liabilities for our society. According to him, an asset is something that produces passive income. Everything else is a liability. That one idea has redefined my relationship with money and stuff, and it will someday make me a rich man.

Kiyosaki is adamant that your primary home is (in almost every case) *not* an asset. You have to pay money toward a mortgage every month. You also have to pay taxes and insurance on it. You have to maintain it. If you lost the ability to make your payments, you would lose your house. That has the potential to become an extremely precarious situation very quickly.

There are a few exceptions to this rule. The idea of "house hacking" can be very useful, especially if you're young, single, and creative. Formerly known as just "having a roommate," you get someone else to live in part of your house and pay you for the trouble. If your house has enough rooms, or you own a duplex/triplex/etc., it's possible for your tenants to cover all your costs and even be net-positive every month.

Bigger Pockets is replete with examples of people employing this strategy. Unfortunately, many of us airline pilots were brought up in a mindset that makes house hacking difficult for us to consider. If you can overcome that upbringing, you can use this strategy to make a lot of money.

One of my pilot friends did exactly this while assigned to an Air Force base where most people chose to rent rather than buy. He purchased a triplex, lived in one unit, and rented the other two out to Airmen from base. The rent from the other two units covered his entire mortgage, meaning he lived there for free and got to keep his full

---

[53] https://tim.blog/tag/mba/

Housing Allowance to himself each month. This worked out so well that he bought another triplex in the same area and rented out all three units...producing significant income.

Another way to make your house an asset is the live-in flip. You buy a (discounted) house that needs a bunch of work and live in it while fixing it up. If you've lived in a house for at least 2 of the last 5 years, you don't have to pay any capital gains tax when you sell it. Many people make great profits flipping houses this way. As a major airline pilot, you will absolutely have enough capital to fund projects like this, and enough time to do the work yourself.

In both of these cases, I think it's potentially acceptable to think of your house as an asset, even if Mr. Kiyosaki is standing right next to you. However, for most of us houses are generally losing propositions.

Emergency Funds, Again

I'd like to present one more case where you can potentially use your house to enact a sort of alternative investment strategy. Specifically, you could make extra payments toward principal and try to pay it off quickly.

Unless you're house hacking this won't return you any sort of passive income. However, most homes hold their value and even appreciate over the long run. If nothing else, home appreciation is probably about the same as inflation...meaning it could be about as good as bonds, or better than a regular savings account.

Having equity in your home can also be useful in other ways. Most banks are more than happy to give you what's called a Home Equity Line of Credit, or HELOC. They'll loan you cash equal to the value of any equity you have in your home. You'd have to be a moron to spend this money arbitrarily, but it can be a good way to generate the cash needed for real estate investments. Again, go to Bigger Pockets and you can find hundreds of examples of people who use equity from one property to buy the next. As long as you buy good properties in good locations this can be an investment with reasonable risk. (Of course, there's danger if you're renting to people in shaky financial situations when a recession strikes. This investment has its pitfalls.)

However, a good investment property will hold value and even appreciate in most markets. It also gives you a great option for what MMM calls "springy debt." Many people think they need 3-12 months of cash sitting around as an emergency fund. Establishing that emergency fund is a large part of Dave Ramsey's program. I think having a month or two of expenses in cash savings is a good idea, but having too much is wasteful. Cash sitting around is constantly eroded by inflation. You're losing money.

Instead, set up a HELOC on your house, but never use it. This is now your emergency fund. If you have a sudden, major expense, you can immediately tap your HELOC (for potentially hundreds of thousands of dollars.) Then, you'll pay yourself back at a reasonable interest rate.

I also advocate using credit cards in a similar way. However, CC interest rates are high enough that you absolutely must, without question, pay them off completely at the end of each month. If you're having to deal with a major expense that will take more than a month to pay off, the low interest available with a HELOC is probably a better option.

While I feel like this is a pretty brilliant way to manage an emergency fund, I could understand feeling some angst over using your home as collateral to pay off unexpected expenses. Thankfully, anyone using Pilot Math to establish savings will have options. You'd only consider making extra payments to principal on your mortgage if you're earning more than our arbitrary figure of \$86,258-\$126,758 per year and need somewhere to stash the rest of your cash. You could also choose to split any excess between a taxable brokerage account and accelerated mortgage payments.

When you encounter an unexpected expense, you'd then have two easily accessible ways to cover it. You could pull the money from your HELOC, or sell some shares of VTSAX and cover the expense from your brokerage account. Either way, you can access the money quickly enough to keep things afloat. A credit card can help bridge the gap by giving you up to 30 days of wiggle room.

The flexibility of this strategy lets you minimize the impact of drawing from an emergency fund. If the stock market happens to be down on the day you need money, draw from the HELOC and let the market bring the value of your stocks back up later. If the market is way up you'll be able to sell fewer shares of stock to cover the same expense, without having to tap into your home's equity. Flexibility is the key to Air Power, right?

Not-Investments

There are all kinds of "opportunities" in this world that aren't investments. The problem is that all kinds of people, news outlets, and scam artists will try to convince you otherwise.

The most poignant example of this in recent past is cryptocurrency. Don't get me wrong, I love cryptocurrency. It has the potential to transform the way human beings interact with money and taxes. It has the potential to make financial transactions secure and anonymous in ways that our current financial systems never could.

As people have recognized this, the value of cryptocurrencies like Bitcoin has started to rise. Unfortunately, some people saw this rise and decided to gamble on it. As with any gamble, the lucky ones made incredible fortunes. You don't hear about them very much because Bitcoin is relatively anonymous and they're so rich that they don't need your approbation to know how well they've done.

Eventually though, people realized that the assumed value of Bitcoin (topping out at over $19,000 each!) was stupid. There wasn't anything meaningful backing that price…it was 100% hype. The price immediately crashed and billions of dollars were lost.

Cryptocurrency has the potential to do much good in our world, but not as an investment. You wouldn't plan to fund your retirement with a few rolls of the dice in Vegas, and you shouldn't plan to fund your retirement on Bitcoin either.

My rule is that anyone who wants to speculate in cryptocurrency must be able to read and comprehend Satoshi Nakamoto's original white paper on Bitcoin.[54] If you can do this, then you should be able to evaluate the advantages and vulnerabilities of any given cryptocurrency token (and realize that it holds no underlying investment value.) If after reading his paper you really can't help yourself, then limit your speculation to a maximum of $1,000 and do it just for fun.

There are plenty of other "opportunities" like this in our world. If you time things just right, and get very lucky, you stand the chance of winning big. However, most of these schemes are a lot closer to gambling than investing. I'm not even going to discuss other examples

---

[54] This is the actual source document that started Bitcoin. If you want to have anything to do with cryptocurrency you need to read it: https://bitcoin.org/bitcoin.pdf.

because I truly believe they aren't worth our time.

Don't be tricked into chasing fast or easy money. If it's too good to be true, then it probably is. Invest in something real, accept the lower returns, and let time work for you.

Advanced Topics (or Tax Mitigation)

Once you start down the Pilot Math rabbit hole, you'll find far more ways to optimize your finances than I could ever cover in this book. I absolutely recommend educating yourself on these topics, but not until you've covered the basics in the last chapter. Once you're ready to move on to more advanced strategies, here are a couple pieces of low-hanging fruit to start your research with: Tax loss/gain harvesting, and the mega-backdoor Roth IRA.

Tax loss harvesting is a great deal. If you sell stock while the market is down, the IRS allows you to claim that loss on your taxes and use it to reduce your taxable income. Unfortunately, they'll only allow you to apply a maximum of $3,000 of loss per year using this rule. However, you're allowed to take a loss one year and claim it at any time in the future. This means you could suffer one $9,000 loss this year, and claim it in $3,000 chunks over the next 3 years. For a pilot with a Treasure Bath $3,000 per year isn't much, but it's better than nothing, isn't it?

One other gotcha with this strategy is that you can't sell shares of a stock or mutual fund and then immediately buy back the same types of shares. The IRS calls this a "wash sale" and it's illegal. If you want to sell your shares and immediately put your money back in the market, you're required to invest in something that is different from what you were holding. Thankfully, the IRS's definitions of what "different" means are pretty liberal. Also, the wash sale rule only limits you for a couple months. After that you're welcome to move your money back into shares of the stock or fund that you were holding in the first place.

If you choose to use Betterment for your investments you'll be happy to note that they do tax loss harvesting automatically for you. They promise to save you far more through this strategy than you'll ever pay them in fees. If nothing else, I regard that as a pretty strong case for using them.

Tax gain harvesting is a similar idea that can be useful. Every time you sell a stock in a regular, taxable brokerage account it's a "taxable event." You have to pay capital gains tax on the money you made. If you bought very low and sold very high, this can trigger a pretty big tax bill. You're still only losing a portion of your gains, but if your income is high enough (B777 Captain at a major airline,) you won't like paying capital gains at such a high tax rate.

Capital gains harvesting is a strategy where you sell shares that have appreciated at a time when it makes a lot of sense for your tax situation. Maybe you're a 3-year FO about to upgrade to a 4-year Captain and your tax rate will be much higher next year. Maybe you expect your spouse's job or your side-hustle to pick up next year, increasing your tax rate. You'll save money overall by selling your shares now and taking the hit while your taxes are low. Then, you immediately buy shares of the same security again. The IRS wash sale rules don't apply here - they're getting their pound of flesh, so they're happy.

From now on, the "basis price" for those shares of that stock is the higher value at which you just re-purchased them. They'll continue to appreciate, but the next time you sell your capital gains will be calculated based on the more recent basis price, rather than the much lower price at which you bought the shares a long time ago.

If the market is on a steady climb, you could consider repeating this process every year to make sure your basis is at tight as possible. I don't know of a service that does this automatically, and if it sounds like a lot of work it may not be worth your time. I recommend more study, and talking to a financial professional before you make any tax-related decisions.

One final topic worth addressing here is the mega-backdoor Roth IRA. In the last chapter we mentioned that the contribution limit for a Roth IRA is a measly $6,000 per year. What's worse, most airline pilots will quickly reach an income level so high that they're not even eligible to contribute to a Roth IRA. However, thanks to some shady politics, or something, there's a loophole that we can all use.

The IRS allows investors to "reclassify" traditional IRA investments as Roth investments. There is no limit to the amount of money you can reclassify in a given year. The catch is that although you were able to put the money into a Traditional IRA before tax, you must pay tax on that money (and any gains) when you reclassify. It won't be fun paying that tax bill, but this strategy lets you strategically use two different tax advantages allowed by the US tax code. In the end, you're far better off with this money in a Roth account because it will grow significantly before you need to use it again.

The financial institution that manages your company's 401K plan may also be able to help you use a similar process with your defined contribution plan funds. They may be able to reclassify money from your Traditional 401K directly into a Roth 401K. Some airlines have plans that allow this, while others don't. (Call your airline's retirement plan provider and ask about doing an "in-service withdrawal" and/or "backdoor Roth." Either they'll understand what you want, or it will quickly become obvious this isn't on the menu for you.) If your company doesn't include this option in your 401K plan, you may be able to do a "roll-over" from you Traditional 401K to a Traditional IRA without incurring any tax bill. From there, you can do your reclassification to a Roth IRA, pay your taxes, and you're set.

There is a lot of strategy involved in deciding when to do these kinds of reclassification and how much money to reclassify each year. You definitely need to get more education and some help from a financial planner before you pull the trigger here.

These strategies might sound like a pain and a lot of work. For some people they will be. However, once you're doing everything else right you'll notice how quickly your Treasure Bath is filling up. It will excite you, and you'll naturally wonder if there are ways to further accelerate things. These are just a few of the many ways you can do that. All it takes is a little education, some planning, and probably a little help from a pro.

If you haven't implemented everything we discussed in the last chapter, go and take care of those things first. However, once you've done that don't be afraid to dig into these other options!

CHAPTER EIGHT

Military Officer Pilot Math

We've looked at the Pilot Math for your potential career earnings at a major airline. They're amazing, right? If you're smart enough and apply Pilot Math early in your life, those numbers are also very inaccurate. They're a ridiculously low estimate of your lifetime wealth accumulation.

Anyone who aspires to work at a major airline knows they don't just hire pedestrians. A pilot has to accumulate 750-1500 hours to earn an Airline Transport Pilot (ATP) rating, then spend 5-10 years flying professionally somewhere before a a major will hire her. Many of us choose to gain that flight experience while serving in the military. It has unique rewards and challenges, but it definitely pays well. It turns out that you can use Pilot Math during your time in the military to jump-start your wealth building and reach financial freedom even sooner after you start your dream job at a major airline.

I also assert that if you apply Pilot Math for a full 20-year military career, your Treasure Bath will be so full that it almost won't be financially justifiable to start a second career at the airlines. I'm going to show you the math for both cases.

We're going to look at the earnings for a military pilot and consider how much wealth she's capable of building if she chooses to hold her spending to the same average level we've used elsewhere in this book. This means that as a new Lieutenant or Ensign she won't be saving very much. However, we'll see that those savings can quickly build to impressive levels. (Since we allow airline pilots to increase spending when they upgrade to captain, we're going to allow for some lifestyle inflation for military officers too. The spreadsheets below show that once our theoretical officer takes the pilot retention bonus, she increases her annual spending by half of the bonus value.)

We'll assume that this pilot's savings earn interest at the same 5% and that she only gets to spend 4% of het nest egg per year if she decides to quit full-time work and live on passive income alone. For this book, I arbitrarily chose BAH values for Hurlburt Field, FL, because it was my favorite assignment, and they seem like a conservative/average value. I also use the no-dependents values.

It's beyond the scope of this book, but there are many ways to find a great place to live without spending all of your BAH. A pilot who can do that in a high BAH area can pour a lot of tax-free Treasure into her Bath over a military career. A great place to read about some of those strategies is Bigger Pockets.

To keep things simple, we're going to assume that this pilot invests as much as possible in her Roth TSP and Roth IRA each year, meaning that she pays taxes on that money in the year she earns it. We'll assume that any other investments go into regular old brokerage accounts that offer no special tax advantages. As we discussed earlier, this isn't the best solution for everyone. You may be better off reducing your taxable income and paying lower taxes now. However, I think you'll see how much lower military officer pay is than airline pilot pay and agree that it may be worth maximizing Roth contributions while in the military as both airline pilot income and eventual retirement income are likely to dwarf Active Duty military officer pay.

The military recently altered its pension system. Instead of paying 50% of a pilot's base pay in retirement, the military now pays 40%. The guaranteed payout might seem bad by itself, but there's another catch here. The government also contributes to a pilot's TSP. Under this new Blended Retirement System, or BRS, the government automatically contributes 1% of a pilot's base pay into her TSP each month. It will also match her contributions up to a total of 5% of base pay.

The charts here will assume the newer 40% retirement pension. You may need to adjust if you were grandfathered under the old scheme.

For someone who was going to stay in the military for a full 20 years and retire no matter what, this BRS probably isn't that great a deal. Is an ongoing 5% TSP contribution from the government enough to make up for decreasing the fixed pension payout from 50% to 40%? It depends on market performance and definitely isn't a sure thing.

However, the BRS is outstanding news for the vast majority of military service members who separate with fewer than 20 years of service. Under the old system, leaving early meant you got zero retirement benefits. Now, the BRS at least lets you keep the government's 5% TSP match contributions when you walk away. For the most of us, the BRS is a 5% raise.

We'll assume that our hypothetical pilot contributes at least enough to her TSP to get the government's 5% match, because only a moron would choose not to.

Let's start again by looking at what a brand-new butter bar makes:

Year 1 Pay	Amount
Rank	O-1
Base Pay	$3,107.70
BAS	$254.39
BAH	$1,137.00
Flight Pay	$150.00
TSP Match	$155.39
Monthly Total	$4,804.48
Annual Total	$57,653.76
Taxable Income	$14,692.40
Tax Rate	3%
After Tax Income	$56,184,00
Annual Spending	$52,455.00
Annual Savings	$3,729.00
Savings Rate	6.5%

Wow, this isn't a very impressive year, is it? A first-year military pilot makes so little after taxes that she doesn't even have as much money as the average family in our target income bracket spends. (And that's for an officer. We'll look at Pilot Math for Warrant Officers later.)

Tragically, the average American family in this pilot's income bracket ($40,000-49,999) spends more money than they earn every year. Our Lieutenant isn't going to be quite that stupid. Instead, she's just going to spend almost every penny she earns. The only money she puts into savings is 5% of her base pay: $155 per month. This gets her the 5% TSP contribution match from the federal government (another $155 per month.)

I present this as a hopefully unrealistic scenario to make our math easy. This is our young pilot's first year out of college and she's attending a military pilot training course. I assert that she can spend a lot more than she ever did in college without getting anywhere near blowing the full $52K this year. (She should be busy studying and chair flying anyway, right?) At the very least, this pilot should try to fill up her TSP and Roth IRA for the year. If she decides to contribute to the Traditional side of her TSP instead of making Roth contributions, she might even reduce her taxable income enough that she'll pay little (or zero) income tax for the year.

It's also worth noting that we didn't assume the lieutenant graduated from college debt-free or that she isn't going to incur some more debt to buy a house or a new car in the first few years of her career. Since the BLS statistics we used for spending include the average family servicing debt for both a home and cars, our arbitrary annual spending figure of $57,758 can include paying off some debt. If you can manage to avoid college and consumer debt, you'll be far better off, and the shiny golden pool starting to accumulate at the bottom of your new Treasure Bath will reflect your good decision making.

Based on my own past mistakes, I recommend military members not buy houses while on active duty. You just move too often and you won't be able to afford selling it after only 2-4 years. The exception here would be buying something specifically intended to be an investment property. In my opinion, the best possible option for this is a multi-family unit within walking distance of your base. If you can live in one of those units and rent out the other(s) during your assignment, you should at least be able to cover your mortgage, if not be cash-flow positive. (Run the numbers before you buy any real estate, and walk away from any deal that doesn't meet this criteria!) Then, when you PCS to another base, adding a(nother) tenant in your old unit will just improve your cashflow. This strategy will be increasingly difficult to do if you get married and have kids, but if your family is focused on a big enough Why, you can find a way to make it happen. It should be a no-brainer for a young, single officer.

For now, we'll assume that a brand-new military pilot is only going to save enough to get the TSP match until her income is greater than our arbitrary $57,758 spending threshold. Don't worry, she hits that point during her third year of service. Here is what a military pilot's earnings look like during the first 11 years of her career:

Year	Rank	Annual Total Income	After Tax Earnings	Annual Savings		Cumulative Savings	Passive Income
1	O-1	$ 57,654	$ 56,184	$ 3,729	$	3,729	$ 149
2	O-1	$ 57,654	$ 56,184	$ 3,729	$	7,645	$ 306
3	O-2	$ 71,078	$ 68,155	$ 10,397	$	18,424	$ 737
4	O-2	$ 78,869	$ 75,055	$ 17,297	$	36,643	$ 1,466
5	O-3	$ 89,347	$ 84,336	$ 26,578	$	65,053	$ 2,602
6	O-3	$ 89,347	$ 84,336	$ 26,578	$	94,884	$ 3,795
7	O-3	$ 99,288	$ 93,104	$ 35,346	$	134,974	$ 5,399
8	O-3	$ 99,288	$ 93,104	$ 35,346	$	177,068	$ 7,083
9	O-3	$ 102,948	$ 96,345	$ 38,587	$	224,508	$ 8,980
10	O-3	$ 102,948	$ 96,345	$ 38,587	$	274,320	$ 10,973
11	O-4	$ 117,561	$ 109,274	$ 51,516	$	339,552	$ 13,582

While this isn't quite as impressive as major airline pilot pay, it's still not bad. A brand-new lieutenant's pay puts her in the 67th percentile for annual income in America. Her Year 11 pay puts her all the way up at the 89th percentile. A Treasure Bath containing $345K may not seem like a lot, but it's worth remembering that she accumulated all that Treasure while also spending a total of $620K during these 11 years. What's really impressive, though, is what those $345,308 dollars do for her if she now decides to leave the military and start flying at a major airline.

This next chart continues to show our military pilot's career, assuming she starts Year 1 at a major airline with that $339,552 in her Treasure Bath:

Year	Aircraft	Position	Annual Total Compensation	After Tax Earnings	Savings Total	Cumulative Savings	Passive Income
1	717	FO	$ 101,850	$ 97,523	$ 39,765	$ 396,295	$ 15,852
2	717	FO	$ 138,014	$ 129,946	$ 72,188	$ 488,298	$ 19,532
3	320	FO	$ 171,599	$ 157,862	$ 100,104	$ 612,817	$ 24,513
4	320	FO	$ 175,608	$ 161,111	$ 103,353	$ 746,810	$ 29,872
5	757	FO	$ 192,270	$ 174,613	$ 116,855	$ 901,005	$ 36,040
6	757	FO	$ 196,937	$ 178,394	$ 120,636	$ 1,066,692	$ 42,668
7	757	FO	$ 202,199	$ 182,658	$ 124,900	$ 1,244,926	$ 49,797
8	757	FO	$ 206,803	$ 186,389	$ 128,631	$ 1,435,804	$ 57,432
9	320	CA	$ 288,594	$ 252,584	$ 137,068	$ 1,644,662	$ 65,786
10	320	CA	$ 290,765	$ 254,307	$ 138,791	$ 1,865,686	$ 74,627
11	320	CA	$ 292,947	$ 256,037	$ 140,521	$ 2,099,491	$ 83,980
12	320	CA	$ 295,119	$ 257,759	$ 142,243	$ 2,346,709	$ 93,868
13	320	CA	$ 295,119	$ 257,759	$ 142,243	$ 2,606,288	$ 104,252
14	320	CA	$ 295,119	$ 257,759	$ 142,243	$ 2,878,845	$ 115,154
15	757	CA	$ 318,222	$ 276,083	$ 160,567	$ 3,183,354	$ 127,334
16	757	CA	$ 318,222	$ 276,083	$ 160,567	$ 3,503,089	$ 140,124
17	763	CA	$ 325,008	$ 281,465	$ 165,949	$ 3,844,192	$ 153,768
18	763	CA	$ 325,008	$ 281,465	$ 165,949	$ 4,202,351	$ 168,094
19	763	CA	$ 325,008	$ 281,465	$ 165,949	$ 4,578,417	$ 183,137
20	763	CA	$ 325,008	$ 281,465	$ 165,949	$ 4,973,287	$ 198,931
21	332	CA	$ 364,743	$ 312,979	$ 197,463	$ 5,419,414	$ 216,777
22	332	CA	$ 364,743	$ 312,979	$ 197,463	$ 5,887,847	$ 235,514
23	332	CA	$ 364,743	$ 312,979	$ 197,463	$ 6,379,702	$ 255,188
24	332	CA	$ 364,743	$ 312,979	$ 197,463	$ 6,896,150	$ 275,846
25	339	CA	$ 369,692	$ 316,903	$ 201,387	$ 7,442,345	$ 297,694
26	339	CA	$ 369,692	$ 316,903	$ 201,387	$ 8,015,849	$ 320,634
27	339	CA	$ 369,692	$ 316,903	$ 201,387	$ 8,618,029	$ 344,721
28	339	CA	$ 369,692	$ 316,903	$ 201,387	$ 9,250,318	$ 370,013
29	350	CA	$ 385,205	$ 329,207	$ 213,691	$ 9,926,525	$ 397,061
30	350	CA	$ 385,205	$ 329,207	$ 213,691	$ 10,636,543	$ 425,462

This is basically the path that I'm on and I'm extremely happy with it. This chart suggests that after just 8 years at a major airline, I should have enough money saved that the passive income from my investments can cover my family's spending forever. However, some families will decide that it's better for their pilot to serve a full 20 years on active duty to earn a pension, plus Tricare for life.

Let's start looking at this case by first only considering the total compensation and savings that a military pilot will earn over a career. We'll assume that this pilot signs a pilot retention bonus for $35,000 per year, for Years 12-20, and that he or she receives the maximum monthly flight pay allowed by law. (Inexplicably, even though the USAF is authorized to pay $1,000 per month in flight pay to experienced aviators, they aren't! They're at least 10% short on pilots and they're not even paying their pilots the money authorized by Congress. Why? Beats me! I guess they're using their military intelligence.) Here are the 20-year earnings for a military pilot:

Year	Rank	After Tax Earnings	Annual Spending	Cumulative Savings	Passive Income
1	O-1	$ 56,184	$52,455	$ 3,729	$ 149
2	O-1	$ 56,184	$52,455	$ 7,645	$ 306
3	O-2	$ 68,155	$57,758	$ 18,424	$ 737
4	O-2	$ 75,055	$57,758	$ 36,643	$ 1,466
5	O-3	$ 84,336	$57,758	$ 65,053	$ 2,602
6	O-3	$ 84,336	$57,758	$ 94,884	$ 3,795
7	O-3	$ 93,104	$57,758	$ 134,974	$ 5,399
8	O-3	$ 93,104	$57,758	$ 177,068	$ 7,083
9	O-3	$ 96,345	$57,758	$ 224,508	$ 8,980
10	O-3	$ 96,345	$57,758	$ 274,320	$ 10,973
11	O-4	$ 109,274	$57,758	$ 339,552	$ 13,582
12	O-4	$ 137,091	$75,258	$ 418,362	$ 16,734
13	O-4	$ 140,587	$75,258	$ 504,609	$ 20,184
14	O-4	$ 140,587	$75,258	$ 595,169	$ 23,807
15	O-4	$ 143,016	$75,258	$ 692,685	$ 27,707
16	O-4	$ 143,016	$75,258	$ 795,078	$ 31,803
17	O-5	$ 151,801	$75,258	$ 911,374	$ 36,455
18	O-5	$ 151,801	$75,258	$1,033,486	$ 41,339
19	O-5	$ 154,200	$75,258	$1,164,102	$ 46,564
20	O-5	$ 154,200	$75,258	$1,301,250	$ 52,050
				Retirement	$ 41,713
				Total	$ 93,763

Impressive, isn't it? If an officer can hold herself to only spending $57,758 per year (plus half her bonus starting in Year 12) and invest the rest, she will retire with more than $1.3M in the bank, assuming rather conservative investment returns. That Treasure Bath is capable of producing $52,637 per year in passive income for the rest of her life, even if she never spends another day at work.

Her situation looks even better when you add her military pension to that number. Our military retiree will receive 40% of her base pay, $41,713, per year. Add that to $52,637 of annual passive investment income and she has a guaranteed annual income of $94,350.

She's just spent the last 20 years enjoying life while only spending our average amount of $57,758, with an increase to $74,736 once she hit the bonus. If she was able to live happily on $74,736 of spending per year, we can only assume she'd be even happier at $94,350 of spending. The amazing thing is that she can spend like this until the day she dies and likely not deplete the principle in her Treasure Bath at all. In an overwhelming majority of cases, her $1.3M will more than double before she dies.

This begs the question: if you retire from the military, do you need to pursue a second career at all?

I hope you'll agree that, financially speaking, the answer is a solid "No!" The pilot in this example can already increase her spending by another $20K the day she retires and not even deplete the principle in her investment accounts. Even if she wants to start buying fancy things and traveling the world, she should be covered.

Unfortunately, I feel like most military pilots are clueless about Pilot Math. Though they might be smart enough to not spend all of their money each month, they tend to increase spending in pace with their income. I know many military pilots who were spending 80-100% of their Final Average Earnings (FAE) in the years leading up to retirement. When they left active duty, their pension was only ever going to provide 40-50% FAE, meaning that they couldn't afford *not* to pursue a second career.

This illustrates the importance of having a driving Why and choosing to live a good life on less spending early in life when implementing Pilot Math. Saving a lot of your income helps build up your nest egg, which is important. (The pilot in our charts above will receive more from her passive investment income than she does from her military pension!) However, it's equally important that you learn how to enjoy life at those lower spending levels. The lower your spending, the smaller the nest egg that will cover your costs using the 4% Rule.

It's not all about the money though, right? If you don't have a military job anymore, what do you want to do with your time instead? I know pilots who have embarked on a complete career change after leaving active duty...moving on to med school, real estate, nursing, and even Hollywood.

Thanks to my wife being smarter, more talented, and better looking than me, I feel like my Treasure Bath is already quite full. I've adopted an attitude that I think could work for most military retirees: I consider my major airline job to be an enjoyable side-hustle. I regard my work here as part-time and only work as much as makes sense for my family. I love the flying, I enjoy free stays in swanky hotels and getting to see the world. I enjoy access to a decent health care plan (though military retirees will have Tricare anyway.) On top of all this, my company insists on paying me better to enjoy this gig than I'd be making if I were still on active duty.

Maybe I don't *necessarily* need the money, but I figure I'll eventually find a way to put it to good use. I have a long list of airplanes I'd like to own and operate. I'd like to get rated to fly some classic warbirds. I also have some ideas for big-picture, change-the-world kinds of projects that will require funding from somewhere. I'm looking forward to trading some of the gold coins in my Bath for these other types of Treasure.

I also love the flexibility that the airline pilot job offers. Yes, I'm working part-time now and it's absolutely perfect for my family. However, I may someday think to myself, "I'd really like a new Tesla Model 3." I have the option of deciding to work full-time for a few months, stacking up a bunch of cash, buying myself that new toy, and then going back to only working part-time so that I have plenty of opportunity to enjoy driving my new car. I challenge you to find another job in the world that offers these levels of scheduling and income flexibility.

(I could also apply this strategy if my daughter were to suddenly announce that she'd been accepted to Harvard Law...without any scholarships. It might not be as fun as buying a new Tesla, but I suppose it would also be an acceptable application for some of my Treasure.)

The bottom line here is that Pilot Math works for military pilots. It can give you a huge head-start on filling up your Treasure Bath before you hit the airlines. Or, you can do 20 years in the military and have more than enough money to live without working for the rest of your life. If a retiree does decide to pursue an airline career, she could immediately turn it into a fun side-gig and live a life of easy, free travel. I'd have a tough time finding fault with someone who made either choice.

CHAPTER NINE

Reserve Officer Pilot Math

We just saw how amazing Pilot Math can be for a full-time military officer. Unfortunately, serving on active duty comes with a lot of costs. Deployments, toxic leaders, unwanted assignments in bad places, and hours upon hours of meaningless queep (busywork) for every hour you spend flying are just some of the hazards of active duty military service.

Despite these hazards, military flying can offer fun and fulfillment that just don't exist in other professions. If you ever pull more than about 1.41 Gs in an airliner, something has gone very, very wrong. Not everyone wants to rush to that job and give up fun flying forever.

Thankfully, there's a way to get the best of both worlds. I've written extensively about what I consider to be The Ideal Career Path for a Military Pilot.[55] It goes like this:

---

[55] I wrote a 3-part series on this idea. You can read those posts at these links:

https://community.thepilotnetwork.org/posts/ideal-military-pilot-career-path-spelling-it-out-part-1

https://community.thepilotnetwork.org/posts/ideal-military-pilot-career-path-making-it-happen-part-2

https://community.thepilotnetwork.org/posts/ideal-military-pilot-career-path-making-it-happen-part-3

or access them for free on the TPN-Go app: https://pilotmathtreasurebath.com/tpn-go/.

1. Do the minimum 11 or 12 years on active duty in the military
2. Start working for a major airline. Give them at least one full year, ideally two, while continuing part-time military service in the Guard or Reserves.
3. Continue serving part-time in the Guard/Reserves until accumulating 20 total years of military service. If during these 8-9 years you get the opportunity to do something special, you can apply the provisions of the Uniformed Services Employment and Reemployment Rights Act (USERRA) to take up to 5 years of military leave.[56]
4. At 20 years of total service, retire from military service and go full-time airlines.
5. At age 60, start collecting a military pension.

If you haven't already made the mistake of selling your soul to the Active Duty military, you may even be able to take the **Ultimate Military Pilot Career Path**[57] by replacing Step 1 above with applying directly to a Guard/Reserve unit and having them send you to military pilot training. This gets you to a Restricted ATP rating, and able to start down the airline pilot career path years before your Active Duty peers.

I feel like service in the Guard or Reserves has the potential to give you almost everything you love about the military while reducing or eliminating many of the headaches associated with Active Duty.

In addition to giving you the opportunity for fulfilling flying, part-time military service pays a salary, earns you points toward retirement, and gives you access to some of the cheapest health care in the world. These are all compelling reasons to continue your military service after leaving Active Duty (or instead of signing up for Active Duty in the first place.)

We're going to look at the potential earnings and savings associated with this career path. As with airline work (and unlike Active Duty service) a Guard or Reserve pilot gets paid for the amount of time he or she spends at work. If you choose to work more, you get paid more.

In theory, it's possible to work a full airline schedule and squeeze

---

[56] https://bogidope.com/military-to-airlines/userra-for-pilots/
[57] https://bogidope.com/civilian-to-guard-or-reserve/the-ultimate-military-pilot-career-path-part-2/

your military flying in around it. Personally, I feel like this is just too much in most cases, especially if you want to obtain (or retain) a family.

Instead, we're going to assume that you replace 1/4 of your airline flying with one full week of military service each month. We'll assume that you're able to get credit for two drills periods per day, every day that you're working for the military. (In most cases, your unit should schedule you for two drill periods any day you show up. There would need to be a very good reason to only be scheduled for one drill period.)

We'll assume that you put in five days of regular flying, at two drill periods per day, for a total of 10 drill periods. In addition, we'll assume you attend your unit's "drill weekend" each month, a 2-day event worth another 4 points. This means we'll assume you complete a total of 14 drill periods per month in our calculations.

For the sake of simplicity, we're also going to assume that you don't deploy at all. Deployments complicate this math to the point where it just doesn't fit book format very well. All of the spreadsheets used in this book are available on pilotmathtreasurebath.com, and and I encourage you to adapt them for your specific situation. It's just too much for me to try and examine every possible career path, and this book is long enough already.

In Chapter 8 we examined the lifetime earnings a major airline pilot could potentially look forward to after completing 11 years of Active Duty military service. Here is a chart showing how those earnings change if that pilot continues serving in the Guard or Reserve by replacing one week of airline flying per month with military duty for the next 9 years:

Year	Reserve Rank	Aircraft	Position	Annual Airline Subtotal	75% Airline Pay	Annual Reserve Pay	Combined Total Income	Difference	Cumulative Savings	Passive Income
1	O-4	717	FO	$ 101,850	$ 76,387	$ 47,070	$ 123,457	$21,607	$ 414,733	$ 16,589
2	O-4	717	FO	$ 138,014	$ 103,510	$ 49,134	$ 152,644	$14,630	$ 518,438	$ 20,738
3	O-4	320	FO	$ 171,599	$ 128,699	$ 49,134	$ 177,833	$6,234	$ 647,740	$ 25,910
4	O-4	320	FO	$ 175,608	$ 131,706	$ 50,568	$ 182,274	$6,666	$ 787,062	$ 31,482
5	O-4	757	FO	$ 192,270	$ 144,203	$ 50,568	$ 194,771	$2,500	$ 943,477	$ 37,739
6	O-5	757	FO	$ 196,937	$ 147,703	$ 54,579	$ 202,282	$5,345	$ 1,113,677	$ 44,547
7	O-5	757	FO	$ 202,199	$ 151,649	$ 54,579	$ 206,228	$4,029	$ 1,295,586	$ 51,823
8	O-5	757	FO	$ 206,803	$ 155,102	$ 55,962	$ 211,064	$4,261	$ 1,490,467	$ 59,619
9	O-5	320	CA	$ 288,594	$ 216,445	$ 55,962	$ 272,407	-$16,186	$ 1,686,903	$ 67,476
10		320	CA	$ 290,765			$ 290,765		$ 1,910,038	$ 76,402
11		320	CA	$ 292,947			$ 292,947		$ 2,146,061	$ 85,842
12		320	CA	$ 295,119			$ 295,119		$ 2,395,608	$ 95,824
13		320	CA	$ 295,119			$ 295,119		$ 2,657,631	$ 106,305
14		320	CA	$ 295,119			$ 295,119		$ 2,932,756	$ 117,310
15		757	CA	$ 318,222			$ 318,222		$ 3,239,961	$ 129,598
16		757	CA	$ 318,222			$ 318,222		$ 3,562,526	$ 142,501
17		763	CA	$ 325,008			$ 325,008		$ 3,906,601	$ 156,264
18		763	CA	$ 325,008			$ 325,008		$ 4,267,880	$ 170,715
19		763	CA	$ 325,008			$ 325,008		$ 4,647,223	$ 185,889
20		763	CA	$ 325,008			$ 325,008		$ 5,045,533	$ 201,821
21		332	CA	$ 364,743			$ 364,743		$ 5,495,272	$ 219,811
22		332	CA	$ 364,743			$ 364,743		$ 5,967,498	$ 238,700
23		332	CA	$ 364,743			$ 364,743		$ 6,463,336	$ 258,533
24		332	CA	$ 364,743			$ 364,743		$ 6,983,965	$ 279,359
25		339	CA	$ 369,692			$ 369,692		$ 7,534,551	$ 301,382
26		339	CA	$ 369,692			$ 369,692		$ 8,112,666	$ 324,507
27		339	CA	$ 369,692			$ 369,692		$ 8,719,686	$ 348,787
28		339	CA	$ 369,692			$ 369,692		$ 9,357,058	$ 374,282
29		350	CA	$ 385,205			$ 385,205		$ 10,038,602	$ 401,544
30		350	CA	$ 385,205			$ 385,205		$ 10,754,224	$ 430,169

Total Pay Difference	$49,087
Cumulative Savings Difference	$117,681

It turns out that trading a week of airline pay for a week of Guard or Reserve service each month earns you more money overall until you upgrade to Captain (given our assumptions.) The raw increase in pay is just over $49,000 over the 9 years, and you end up with a grand total of $117,681 more in your Treasure Bath than if you hadn't served in the Guard or Reserves, thanks to the power of compounding interest.

(I didn't account for adding a Guard or Reserve retirement at or just before age 60 in these numbers. There are too many variables for deciding how much that pension is and when it kicks in. Also, we'll see shortly that five years of those pension payments are that impressive anyway.)

The pay bonus here is nothing to sneeze at, especially given that your part-time military service can ease your financial transition to civilian life early in your major airline pilot career when that pay is the lowest. Whether an additional nine years of service is worth that extra $117,681 depends on how much you like your Guard or Reserve job, whether commuting is involved, how much you'll have to deploy, and a few other factors.

Although I didn't account for a military pension in this chart, creating it made me wonder what the pension is worth overall. I was even more surprised by what I found when I dove down that rabbit hole, and I want you to see the results too.

We're going to run through a series of calculations to determine the lifetime total amount of money a Guard or Reserve pilot earns for each hour of his or her service. It turns out this math is pretty straightforward.

As a part-time military pilot, you earn base pay, flight pay, and a government TSP match (if you fall under the new Blended Retirement System, or BRS.) We'll assume that the pilot in these calculations starts collecting his or her pension at age 60 and lives to be 100 years old. (I think the life expectancy for most pilots is well short of 100 years, but using the round figure of 40 years is convenient. This will provide us with an overly-generous estimate of lifetime earnings, and that will help make my point later.)

In theory, the Reserve retirement isn't all that different from the active duty one. It pays 2% of your base pay (under the BRS) or 2.5% (under the legacy retirement system) for each year of your military service. You must serve for a total of 20 calendar years to earn this pension. For an Active Duty pilot, 20 years of service times 2.5% equates to 50% of base pay for a full retirement. Under the new BRS, 20 years of service times 2.0% yields 40% of base pay.

The Reserve retirement pays these same rates, but it requires you to convert the total number of days you spent at work into a value for equivalent years of service. As we mentioned, a Guard or Reserve pilot earns credit for one "pay period" for each four hours that he or she works. These credits are counted as points toward retirement. For a pilot who transitions from Active Duty, each year of service is converted to 356 retirement points. (Partial years are credited at one point per day.)

I left Active Duty with roughly 11 years and 77 days of service. Multiplying 11 years by 365 and adding 77 yielded roughly 4092 retirement points. I'm in a non-flying job now, so I don't earn as many points as the average pilot. If I continue to earn at least 50 points per year for my last 9 years, I'll accumulate another 450 points for a total of 4542.

These points would be divided by 360 to arrive at an equivalent of 12.6 years.

4542 total points ÷ 360 points per year = 12.6 years (equivalent)

I wasn't able to opt into the BRS, so my "service multiplier" will be:

12.6 years x 2.5% per year = 31.5%

This is the percentage of my base pay that I would expect to receive in retirement if I earned exactly 50 points per year as a Reservist.

Before we go on, let's note that although it's possible (and probable) to earn two points per day of Guard or Reserve service, you're not allowed to accrue more than 360 points in any given calendar year of part-time service. If a Guard or Reserve pilot were to accumulate the maximum number of points per year, he or she would reach the ultimate number of 7200 retirement points. Using the same mathematical steps we see that:

7200 points ÷ 360 = 20 equivalent years of service

20 equivalent years x 2% (or 2.5%) = 40% (or 50%)

If you achieve this magic number, you're considered to have given the equivalent of 20 full years of Active Duty service and you get to immediately start collecting your pension like an Active Duty officer. This is a great deal because the average Reservist has to wait until about age 60 before collecting anything. We're going to ignore this fact for the following set of calculations, just for the sake of the demonstration.

(When we run our numbers in a moment we'll eventually divide by 7200, meaning the dollars per hour figure we come up with applies to any pilot, no matter how many total points he or she earns.)

Although the Reserves offer opportunities to promote to O-6 and above, I feel like the majority of pilots there retire as an O-4 or an O-5. For 2019, the monthly base pay for an O-4 is $8,073.90, and the monthly base pay for an O-5 is $9,243.60.

This means an O-4 who retires under the old system with 7200 points will receive $4,036.95 per month, while an O-5 will get $4,621.80. Under the new BRS these numbers become $3,229.56 and $3,697.44, respectively. Let's summarize that in a table:

	O-4 Monthly Retirement Pay	O-5 Monthly Retirement Pay
Legacy Retirement System (50%)	$4,036.95	$4,621.80
New Blended Retirement System (40%)	$3,229.56	$3,697.44

We're assuming that our pilot receives a retirement check every month from ages 60 to 100. This span of 40 years means that he or she receives 480 of those checks. Multiplying the values in the table above shows us the lifetime total retirement pay that this pilot receives.

Lifetime Retirement Pay = Monthly Retirement Pay x 480 months

	O-4 Lifetime Retirement Pay	O-5 Lifetime Retirement Pay
Legacy Retirement System (50%)	$1,937,736	$2,218,464
New Blended Retirement System (40%)	$1,550,189	$1,774,771

At first glance, these numbers look pretty impressive. A reserve retirement could be worth *millions* of dollars! However, let's divide by the total number of points earned to find out the lifetime retirement money paid to our pilot per pay period (point) that he or she worked. (In this example, it was 7200 points, but you'll get the same answer no matter how many points you earned.)

Retirement Pay Per Point = Lifetime Retirement Pay ÷ Total Points Earned

	O-4 Retirement Pay Per Point	O-5 Retirement Pay Per Point
Legacy Retirement System (50%)	$269.13	$308.12
New Blended Retirement System (40%)	$215.30	$246.50

This should be a more telling number. This is essentially a half-day rate for your work. We can take the next step in our exercise by remembering that each pay period represents four hours of a pilot's life.

Dollars Per Hour = Dollars Per Point ÷ 4 Hours Per Point

	O-4 Retirement Pay Per Hour	O-5 Retirement Pay Per Hour
Legacy Retirement System (50%)	$67.28	$77.03
New Blended Retirement System (40%)	$53.83	$61.62

I hope these numbers impress you a lot less than the millions we just saw. The values in this table represent the total retirement pay dollars you will receive for every hour that your spend serving in the Guard or Reserves (at home station.) While it'd be fun to conclude things here and head to the bar to complain about how poorly the military pays, it wouldn't be fair.

Since we also have charts for a pilot's regular pay, we can calculate how much he or she makes in immediate pay per hour at any given point in his or her career. We'll look at three specific points for illustration purposes:

- A 3-Year Guard or Reserve O-2 who has just completed seasoning and is now serving part time
- A 12 Year O-4 who just fulfilled his or her Active Duty Service Commitment and started serving part-time with the Guard or Reserves while also working as an airline pilot
- An 18- or 19-Year Guard or ReserveO-5 who is nearing the 20-year point and preparing to retire

The next table takes the pay rates for each of these officers and shows how those equate to dollars per pay period, and dollars per hour. We assume that each officer contributes at least enough to the TSP to receive the government's full 5% match. We assume that the O-5 retires at that rank, and the O-2 will excel enough to retire at O-5. In order to show a low-end for the retirement portion of these numbers we'll assume the O-4 will retire as an O-4.

Rank	18+ Yr O-5	12 Yr O-4	3 Yr O-2
Monthly Base Pay	$8,998.50	$7,596.30	$4,818.30
Monthly Flight Pay	$1,000.00	$1,000.00	$250.00
Monthly TSP Match	$449.93	$379.82	$240.92
Monthly Subtotal	$10,448.43	$8,976.12	$5,309.22
Pay Per Point	$348.28	$299.20	$176.97
Pay Per Hour	$87.07	$74.80	$44.24

Having already calculated the lifetime retirement dollars received, we can now determine the lifetime total compensation that each of these pilots will earn for devoting an hour of his or her life to military service. We'll assume our O-5 retires under the legacy retirement system to get a upper limit value, and that our O-4 and O-2 will eventually retire under the BRS to get lower-end numbers.

Rank	18+ Yr O-5	12 Yr O-4	3 Yr O-2
Immediate Pay Per Hour	$87.07	$74.80	$44.24
Lifetime Retirement Pay	$77.03	$53.83	$61.62
Lifetime Total Compensation Per Hour	**$164.10**	**$128.63**	**$105.86**

The numbers on the bottom line of this chart show the exact value that the US military places on an hour of your life.

(Actually, these numbers are way too high. When you're deployed you're essentially working 24 hours per day. At the very least, you're likely to be on 12-hour shifts. Since you're on Active Duty orders while deployed, you only get one point per day. This means your compensation on deployment is probably closer to 1/2 to 1/3 of these values.)

If you compare these numbers with the $15 per hour minimum wage that is a topic of hot debate in our country, this Guard and Reserve pay is pretty impressive. Don't get too excited though.

When I calculated my total compensation during my third year at Delta[58] I came up with an average of $1,256 per day. Delta guarantees at least 5.25 hours of pay per day, so my average hourly rate was

---

[58] www.tpn-go.com/airline-pilot-third-year-in-review/

$239.24. This more than doubles the hourly rate of a junior Guard/Reserve officer, and still beats top O-5 pay by about $75 per hour.

Those calculations were based on me flying as a Year 3 B717 FO... the lowest paying seat on the lowest paying aircraft at my company. Delta's pay charts top out at 12 years. Captain's pay on the 717 reaches almost double what I made this year, and A350/B777 Captain's pay is nearly triple this figure. We're also in contract negotiations that should increase our hourly rates again.

These numbers all reflect flying for normal pay. When a pilot picks up trips for premium pay at Delta, each of these figures doubles again.

The 4th book of The Pilot Math Bible is *Your Money or Your Life* by Vicki Robin and Joe Dominguez.[59] The fundamental question of that book boils down to: "What is an hour of your life worth?"

Each of us has a limited number of hours on this Earth. We can spend them working for someone else's benefit. We can spend them on hobbies or things that have meaning to us. We can spend them with our loved ones.

We all have to spend some of those hours working, but what are you getting in exchange for that work? If you have the choice of spending an hour of your life working for $105-164, or working for $239+, which offers more long-term value for you and your family?

In case I haven't been clear enough about my position on this matter, I believe that he military doesn't pay you what you're worth. I don't believe that the Guard or Reserves offer a compelling financial reason to give them any more hours of your life than are absolutely necessary.

Sure, you might as well put in enough hours to get credit for a "Good Year" toward the 20 years required for retirement. However, anything beyond that is a financial loss.

That said, it's not all about the money.

Military flying is fun and fulfilling in ways that most airline jobs will never be.

I will never forget flying the B-1B at 540 KGS, 500' AGL, at night,

---

[59] Here's an affiliate link to *Your Money or Your Life* on Amazon: https://amzn.to/2LhwW7X.

through clouds and heavy rain, through a mountain range with peaks above 12,000' MSL, watching a thunderstorm through my night vision goggles, while dropping strings of 500 pound bombs.

I will never forget commanding the crew of a U-28A while supporting Special Operations Forces on missions that could come directly from the script of a Hollywood movie, and then landing at base and debriefing with the amazing men who had just risked their lives under my watch.

I will never forget chasing another T-6 around billowing cumulus clouds at hundreds of knots while pulling 5-6 Gs.

I'm happy with the course my life has taken, but that course no longer includes military aviation and I miss it! While there is zero financial justification for spending extra time on military flying, I will never fault a pilot who gives up extra airline flying to enjoy the types of adventures we can only get in the military if it provides him or her significant non-monetary value.

CHAPTER TEN
Warrant Officer Pilot Math

There was a time when being a military helicopter pilot was about as useful for pursuing an airline career as trying to operate a submarine with screen doors. When pilot supply is high, the first group the airlines will drop is helicopter pilots. Thankfully, that's not the case right now! The airlines are desperate for every pilot they can get and any regional airline worth joining has a program to help get helicopter pilots from the military to the majors.

I've met many pilots pursuing this career through The Pilot Network. I want you to know that, although your path isn't quite as straightforward or easy as the rest of us, Pilot Math still works for you! You can absolutely enjoy an overflowing Treasure Bath that includes both money and fulfillment in life. This isn't the longest chapter in this book, but I want to give you a very conservative glimpse of what the numbers can look like for you.

We're going to assume that you're a Warrant Officer because, frankly, there's no point in being an officer helicopter pilot in the Army. Officers spend a lot of time behind desks dealing with upper-level, non-pilot commanders who only think of a helicopter as: "very-fast-truck" or "very-fast-tank." Army officer helicopter pilots don't get the volume of flight hours or experience necessary for pursuing a professional flying career on this timeline. If your goal is a long flying career as a professional pilot, I recommend you not even consider an Army flying position as anything but a Warrant Officer. (The other branches do a little better with their helicopter pilot officers. I recommend those pilots base their Pilot Math on the numbers in the chapter for officers.)

As a rotary wing pilot, you're going to have to spend some time at a regional airline before you go to a major. This isn't a bad thing...you should be happy to get a warm-up for the transition from rotary- to fixed-wing aviation before your forever job depends on your successful completion of a major airline training course. We're going to assume that you have to do three years at a regional airline, and that you upgrade to captain at the end of Year 2.

In the past, three years would have been too little. The first helicopter pilots of the most recent era to make this transition have had to spend 6-10 years at the regionals before moving on. I don't believe this will be the case for military helicopter pilots moving forward. The major airlines have been growing (and hiring) like crazy, but they haven't even started hiring to replace the upcoming wave of mass retirements. When they do, they'll be forced to drain the regional airlines, including helicopter pilots who have only been there for a few years. I believe that the average amount of time that any pilot spends at the regionals will decrease significantly. If you think three years is too short, you're welcome to download this spreadsheet from pilotmathtreasurebath.com, and adapt it as you see fit.

For the sake of readability, I've displayed the chart in two sections. The first section covers an Active Duty WO's 11-year military career and three years at a regional airline.

Here are our numbers:

Year	Rank/ Position	Annual Total	Annual Spending	Cumulative Savings	Passive Income
1	W-1	$ 56,769	$ 55,384	$ 3,645	$ 146
2	W-1	$ 56,769	$ 55,384	$ 7,472	$ 299
3	W-2	$ 67,423	$ 57,758	$ 15,006	$ 600
4	W-2	$ 68,693	$ 57,758	$ 24,040	$ 962
5	W-2	$ 69,562	$ 57,758	$ 34,297	$ 1,372
6	W-2	$ 69,562	$ 57,758	$ 45,066	$ 1,803
7	W-2	$ 78,994	$ 57,758	$ 64,690	$ 2,588
8	W-2	$ 78,994	$ 57,758	$ 85,295	$ 3,412
9	W-3	$ 86,969	$ 57,758	$ 113,994	$ 4,560
10	W-3	$ 86,969	$ 57,758	$ 144,128	$ 5,765
11	W-3	$ 93,890	$ 57,758	$ 181,886	$ 7,275
Year	Position	Annual Total Compensation	Annual Spending	Cumulative Savings	Passive Income
1	Q400 FO	$ 66,160	$ 57,758	$ 195,370.94	$ 7,815
2	Q400 FO	$ 46,884	$ 45,184	$ 205,139.48	$ 8,206
3	Q400 CA	$ 75,996	$ 57,758	$ 228,951.58	$ 9,158

The second section of this chart repeats the regional airline section, then goes on to show the major airline portion of the WO's career:

Year	Position	Annual Total Compensation	Annual Spending	Cumulative Savings	Passive Income
1	Q400 FO	$ 66,160	$ 57,758	$ 195,370.94	$ 7,815
2	Q400 FO	$ 46,884	$ 45,184	$ 205,139.48	$ 8,206
3	Q400 CA	$ 75,996	$ 57,758	$ 228,951.58	$ 9,158
Year	Position	Annual Total Compensation	Annual Spending	Cumulative Savings	Passive Income
1	B717 FO	$ 101,850	$ 57,758	$ 280,164	$ 11,207
2	B717 FO	$ 138,014	$ 57,758	$ 366,361	$ 14,654
3	A320 FO	$ 171,599	$ 57,758	$ 484,783	$ 19,391
4	A320 FO	$ 175,608	$ 57,758	$ 612,375	$ 24,495
5	B757 FO	$ 192,270	$ 57,758	$ 759,848	$ 30,394
6	B757 FO	$ 196,937	$ 57,758	$ 918,477	$ 36,739
7	B757 FO	$ 202,199	$ 57,758	$ 1,089,301	$ 43,572
8	B757 FO	$ 206,803	$ 57,758	$ 1,272,397	$ 50,896
9	A320 CA	$ 288,594	$ 115,516	$ 1,473,085	$ 58,923
10	A320 CA	$ 290,765	$ 115,516	$ 1,685,529	$ 67,421
11	A320 CA	$ 292,947	$ 115,516	$ 1,910,327	$ 76,413
12	A320 CA	$ 295,119	$ 115,516	$ 2,148,086	$ 85,923
13	A320 CA	$ 295,119	$ 115,516	$ 2,397,734	$ 95,909
14	A320 CA	$ 295,119	$ 115,516	$ 2,659,864	$106,395
15	B757 CA	$ 318,222	$ 115,516	$ 2,953,424	$118,137
16	B757 CA	$ 318,222	$ 115,516	$ 3,261,662	$130,466
17	B767-300 CA	$ 325,008	$ 115,516	$ 3,590,694	$143,628
18	B767-300 CA	$ 325,008	$ 115,516	$ 3,936,178	$157,447
19	B767-300 CA	$ 325,008	$ 115,516	$ 4,298,936	$171,957
20	B767-300 CA	$ 325,008	$ 115,516	$ 4,679,831	$187,193
21	A330-200 CA	$ 364,743	$ 115,516	$ 5,111,285	$204,451
22	A330-200 CA	$ 364,743	$ 115,516	$ 5,564,312	$222,572
23	A330-200 CA	$ 364,743	$ 115,516	$ 6,039,991	$241,600
24	A330-200 CA	$ 364,743	$ 115,516	$ 6,539,453	$261,578
25	A330-900 CA	$ 369,692	$ 115,516	$ 7,067,813	$282,713
26	A330-900 CA	$ 369,692	$ 115,516	$ 7,622,590	$304,904
27	A330-900 CA	$ 369,692	$ 115,516	$ 8,205,107	$328,204
28	A330-900 CA	$ 369,692	$ 115,516	$ 8,816,750	$352,670
29	A350 CA	$ 385,205	$ 115,516	$ 9,471,279	$378,851
30	A350 CA	$ 385,205	$ 115,516	$ 10,158,534	$406,341

I guess you could say that these numbers aren't as overwhelmingly impressive as some snot-nosed kid who starts working at a major airline at age 25, or the snot-nosed lieutenant who started trying to tell you how to do your job the day he showed up with 100.1 total flight hours.

You could even let this make you bitter, but why? It's still a pretty amazing amount of money and you hit all the key milestones for financial freedom far earlier in life than most people. I assert that if you can't live an amazing life on the amount of Treasure in this Bath, you won't do any better than the pilots who end up with an extra couple million.

Plus, you have skills and experiences that most other pilots could only dream of. I intend on earning a helicopter rating some day, but I'll never have the street cred that you do. The world is chock-full of fun and interesting side-hustles that are only accessible to you. Find one you'll enjoy while luxuriating in your Treasure Bath, and go live the good life that you've earned!

For the sake of being thorough, here's a chart of the Treasure Bath a Warrant Officer could expect to accumulate by limiting spending to this level and staying in the military for a full 20 years. It assumes no retention bonus and no spending increase above our arbitrary average value.

Year	Rank	Annual Total	Annual Spending	Cumulative Savings	Passive Income
1	W-1	$ 56,769	$55,384	$ 3,645	$ 146
2	W-1	$ 56,769	$55,384	$ 7,472	$ 299
3	W-2	$ 67,423	$57,758	$ 15,006	$ 600
4	W-2	$ 68,693	$57,758	$ 24,040	$ 962
5	W-2	$ 69,562	$57,758	$ 34,297	$ 1,372
6	W-2	$ 69,562	$57,758	$ 45,066	$ 1,803
7	W-2	$ 78,994	$57,758	$ 64,690	$ 2,588
8	W-2	$ 78,994	$57,758	$ 85,295	$ 3,412
9	W-3	$ 86,969	$57,758	$ 113,994	$ 4,560
10	W-3	$ 86,969	$57,758	$ 144,128	$ 5,765
11	W-3	$ 93,890	$57,758	$ 181,886	$ 7,275
12	W-3	$ 93,890	$57,758	$ 221,531	$ 8,861
13	W-3	$ 96,022	$57,758	$ 265,046	$ 10,602
14	W-3	$ 96,022	$57,758	$ 310,737	$ 12,429
15	W-4	$ 106,470	$57,758	$ 367,967	$ 14,719
16	W-4	$ 106,470	$57,758	$ 428,059	$ 17,122
17	W-4	$ 110,020	$57,758	$ 494,298	$ 19,772
18	W-4	$ 110,020	$57,758	$ 563,850	$ 22,554
19	W-4	$ 112,926	$57,758	$ 639,453	$ 25,578
20	W-4	$ 112,926	$57,758	$ 718,837	$ 28,753
				Retirement	$ 31,718
				Total	$ 60,472

This is certainly nothing to sneeze at. Staying in until 20 years would provide enough passive income to continue spending as much as you have been, plus an excess of more than $3000 of spending money, forever. However, it pales in comparison to what you could make by spending those extra years in the airlines.

If your ultimate goal is to be an airline pilot, I highly recommend leaving Army active duty at the earliest possible opportunity. Thankfully, the Army has National Guard units flying most of our current helicopter variants all over the country. If you enjoy Army aviation and want to earn a retirement, it shouldn't be difficult to find a way to do that in the Guard while simultaneously pursuing your airline pilot career.

CHAPTER ELEVEN

Regional Airline Pilot Math

I freely admit that my writing is biased toward military pilots. It's where I came from and it's what I know best. That said, I'm not one of those people who looks down on civilian pilots. I believe that our industry is successful, in part, because we have such a wide variety of experience. A military pilot is good for many things, but sometimes past experience taxiing at Chicago O'Hare…at night…in a snowstorm is far more valuable than past experience dogfighting.

Recency goes a long way too. I just flew a trip with a Captain who has been at my airline for decades, but has somehow avoided operating at LaGuardia for years. He was downright apprehensive about going there and made some unnecessarily conservative decisions on those legs. I was based in New York when I started airline flying, and having flown trips to New York since being based there. I had more recent/applicable LaGuardia experience than he did. My experience was valuable that trip, and my captain would have benefitted even more if he'd been flying with a long-time regional airline pilot who knew LaGuardia better than I do.

As a regional pilot, you probably aren't going to make as much money in your lifetime as a pilot who went through the military. You also miss out on free healthcare and some pretty interesting flying. That said, Pilot Math works for you too! You can amass a Treasure Bath that puts your net worth in the tippy top of all Americans. It's enough money to live life however you want and still leave generational wealth for your progeny. Although the military does have some benefits, it also has its headaches. You get access to Pilot Math in your life without having to deploy to the Armpit of the Earth or endure a lot of eye-gouging wastes of time. You could do a lot worse!

We're going to assume that you have to spend 5 years at a regional airline before getting hired by a major (though our initial chart will go all the way to 15 years.) Like I just told the Warrant Officers in the last chapter, I think the majority of pilots won't have to stay at a regional airline that long. Current rules require you to have 1,000-1,500 flight hours before starting at a regional, meaning you should hold an unrestricted ATP within 12-18 months of flying at that regional. You should plan to upgrade to Captain the moment you hit 1,000 Part 121 hours, and from that point you'll be logging multi-engine turbojet PIC time.

From there, the amount of time you have to wait before moving up to a major airline will largely be under your control. If you go to the training department, take a job working a desk at company headquarters, or bid reserve and try not to fly, you'll accrue hours very slowly. This will directly translate into you spending more years at the regional, rather than the majors. You're competing against military pilots with thousands of hours in fancy airplanes and other attractive qualities. Unless taking a job that leads to less flying does something very important to fill a glaring hole in your resume, your best bet is to avoid those jobs like the plague and focus all your time and energy on flying as much as possible. (We'll talk about those resume gaps a little later.)

We're going to assume that you decide to work at Horizon Airlines for the regional airline portion of your career. I like their mentality as a company, I love their locations, and I think they have good aircraft. I think they'd make you competitive for any airline, but they also give you a significant competitive advantage if you want to end up at Alaska. Also, their pay is some of the best in the industry. You won't make this much money at every regional airline, but the differences in pay between companies are getting smaller. The bottom line is: the minimum market value of a regional airline pilot right now is $55,000-$60,000 per year in total compensation. Unless you absolutely can't get hired anywhere else, do not take a regional airline job that pays less. Let's take a look at how the numbers work out for you:

Year	Position	Profit Sharing / Profit	Annual Total Compensation	After Tax Earnings	Annual Spending	Cumulative Savings	Passive Income
1	Q400 FO	$ 25,000	$ 66,160	$ 62,149	$ 57,758	$ 4,391	$ 176
2	Q400 FO	$ -	$ 46,884	$ 45,184	$ 45,184	$ 4,611	$ 184
3	Q400 CA	$ -	$ 75,996	$ 71,313	$ 57,758	$ 18,396	$ 736
4	Q400 CA	$ -	$ 78,858	$ 73,851	$ 57,758	$ 35,409	$ 1,416
5	ERJ 175 CA	$ -	$ 80,766	$ 75,543	$ 57,758	$ 54,965	$ 2,199
6	ERJ 175 CA	$ -	$ 82,674	$ 77,235	$ 57,758	$ 77,190	$ 3,088
7	ERJ 175 CA	$ -	$ 85,536	$ 79,773	$ 57,758	$ 103,065	$ 4,123
8	ERJ 175 CA	$ -	$ 88,398	$ 82,311	$ 57,758	$ 132,771	$ 5,311
9	ERJ 175 CA	$ -	$ 91,260	$ 84,849	$ 57,758	$ 166,501	$ 6,660
10	ERJ 175 CA	$ -	$ 95,076	$ 88,233	$ 57,758	$ 205,301	$ 8,212
11	ERJ 175 CA	$ -	$ 97,938	$ 90,771	$ 57,758	$ 248,579	$ 9,943
12	ERJ 175 CA	$ -	$ 100,800	$ 93,309	$ 57,758	$ 296,559	$ 11,862
13	ERJ 175 CA	$ -	$ 103,662	$ 95,847	$ 57,758	$ 349,476	$ 13,979
14	ERJ 175 CA	$ -	$ 106,524	$ 98,385	$ 57,758	$ 407,577	$ 16,303
15	ERJ 175 CA	$ -	$ 109,386	$ 100,923	$ 57,758	$ 471,121	$ 18,845

There's no arguing the fact that regional airline pilots get paid less than their peers. However, now that these companies are realizing they have to at least pay a living wage to hope for any semblance of retention, they're doing a lot better. This shows that even a Horizon Airlines pilot can spend as much as any other pilot applying Pilot Math, except for Year 2, and still contribute lots of Treasure to his or her Bath. (Our theoretical Horizon pilot is actually better off than his or her military peers who can't afford this spending level for Year 1 *or* Year 2.)

I hope these numbers didn't get you down, but if they did you should feel a lot better when you see what happens when you consider what your full-career Treasure accumulation looks like after you get to a major airline. Here are those numbers:

Year	Position	Annual Total	After Tax Earnings	Annual Spending	Cumulative Savings	Passive Income
1	Q400 FO	$ 66,160	$ 62,149	$ 57,758	$4,391	$176
2	Q400 FO	$ 46,884	$ 45,184	$ 45,184	$4,611	$184
3	Q400 CA	$ 75,996	$ 71,313	$ 57,758	$18,396	$736
4	Q400 CA	$ 78,858	$ 73,851	$ 57,758	$35,409	$1,416
5	ERJ 175 CA	$ 80,766	$ 75,543	$ 57,758	$54,965	$2,199
Year	Position	Annual Total	After Tax Earnings	Annual Spending	Cumulative Savings	Passive Income
1	B717 FO	$ 101,850	$ 97,523	$ 57,758	$ 97,478	$3,899
2	B717 FO	$ 138,014	$ 129,946	$ 57,758	$ 174,541	$6,982
3	A320 FO	$ 171,599	$ 157,862	$ 57,758	$ 283,372	$11,335
4	A320 FO	$ 175,608	$ 161,111	$ 57,758	$ 400,893	$16,036
6	B757 FO	$ 196,937	$ 178,394	$ 57,758	$ 685,318	$27,413
7	B757 FO	$ 202,199	$ 182,658	$ 57,758	$ 844,484	$33,779
8	B757 FO	$ 206,803	$ 186,389	$ 57,758	$ 1,015,339	$40,614
9	A320 CA	$ 288,594	$ 252,584	$ 115,516	$ 1,203,174	$48,127
10	A320 CA	$ 290,765	$ 254,307	$ 115,516	$ 1,402,123	$56,085
11	A320 CA	$ 292,947	$ 256,037	$ 115,516	$ 1,612,751	$64,510
12	A320 CA	$ 295,119	$ 257,759	$ 115,516	$ 1,835,631	$73,425
13	A320 CA	$ 295,119	$ 257,759	$ 115,516	$ 2,069,656	$82,786
14	A320 CA	$ 295,119	$ 257,759	$ 115,516	$ 2,315,382	$92,615
15	B757 CA	$ 318,222	$ 276,083	$ 115,516	$ 2,591,718	$103,669
16	B757 CA	$ 318,222	$ 276,083	$ 115,516	$ 2,881,871	$115,275
17	B767-300 CA	$ 325,008	$ 281,465	$ 115,516	$ 3,191,913	$127,677
18	B767-300 CA	$ 325,008	$ 281,465	$ 115,516	$ 3,517,458	$140,698
19	B767-300 CA	$ 325,008	$ 281,465	$ 115,516	$ 3,859,280	$154,371
20	B767-300 CA	$ 325,008	$ 281,465	$ 115,516	$ 4,218,193	$168,728
21	A330-200 CA	$ 364,743	$ 312,979	$ 115,516	$ 4,626,565	$185,063
22	A330-200 CA	$ 364,743	$ 312,979	$ 115,516	$ 5,055,356	$202,214
23	A330-200 CA	$ 364,743	$ 312,979	$ 115,516	$ 5,505,586	$220,223
24	A330-200 CA	$ 364,743	$ 312,979	$ 115,516	$ 5,978,328	$239,133
25	A330-900 CA	$ 369,692	$ 316,903	$ 115,516	$ 6,478,632	$259,145
26	A330-900 CA	$ 369,692	$ 316,903	$ 115,516	$ 7,003,951	$280,158
27	A330-900 CA	$ 369,692	$ 316,903	$ 115,516	$ 7,555,535	$302,221
28	A330-900 CA	$ 369,692	$ 316,903	$ 115,516	$ 8,134,700	$325,388
29	A350 CA	$ 385,205	$ 329,207	$ 115,516	$ 8,755,126	$350,205
30	A350 CA	$ 385,205	$ 329,207	$ 115,516	$ 9,406,574	$376,263

Compared to the numbers from our chapter on Military Officer Pilot Math, this chart is slightly less impressive at first glance. After 30 years at a major airline, it appears that this regional airline pilot will have a total of roughly $1.2M less than a peer who started in the military. Don't forget, though, that the military pilot had to serve 11 years on Active Duty while the all-civilian pilot in our example only did five years at the regional before moving up. This means that at the point where he or she has $1.2M less in a Treasure Bath, there are still 6 years of work before ending up at the same age as the military pilot.

The best way to compare these numbers to those of a military pilot is to look at total work years since college. At 20 total years, the regional pilot here has $2.6M in her Treasure Bath, compared to the military pilot who only has $1.6M. In this way, Pilot Math actually works better for a non-military pilot.

The catch, of course, is that the civilian pilot has to accrue enough hours to at least get a Restricted ATP rating before she can start this clock. Most civilian pilots don't graduate college with enough hours for the RATP, though it's not impossible. There's no reason a college student can't give flight instruction on the side during college. In the right location, this could absolutely provide 50-100 hours per month.

It's also possible to accrue flight hours before you even show up at college. A friend of mine grew up in an aviation family. He showed up at college with 900 hours and an old C-140. We were glider flight instructors throughout college and he earned his instrument rating before going on to Air Force pilot training. He would have had more than enough hours for an RATP under today's rules, and could have started out as a regional airline pilot the day he graduated.

This path is absolutely available to any young pilot willing to work hard enough. We'll outline some ways to start down that path without breaking the bank in the next chapter.

Another benefit of flying at a regional airline so early in your career is that you'll be eligible for rapid upgrade to captain once you get to a major airline—an opportunity that military pilots just won't get. The FAA requires airline pilots to have 1000 Part 121 (airline) hours before upgrading to captain. If you accumulate these hours at a regional airline, you could theoretically accept a captain position the moment you start working at your major airline. Although some military pilots can get some credit for their experience, they'll still need 1-3 years before they get enough Part 121 hours to upgrade.

At the moment, it doesn't seem realistic that major airlines could hire "street captains," pilots who get a captain's seat as soon as they're hired. However, the tsunami of mandatory pilot retirements is only getting started at the major airlines. I predict that even the major airlines are going to start having to work harder to get the pilots they need and we will see some unprecedented opportunities for rapid upgrade to major airline captain. Even if you wait 6-12 months before bidding for an upgrade, the increased pay could have a significant impact on your career (especially if you can keep your spending in check.)

I believe that the most important thing a regional airline pilot can do to get hired by a major airline is to fly. The major airlines are hiring each and every pilot to fulfill one mission: commanding their aircraft in revenue flight operations. The most important way to develop yourself is to demonstrate your ability to do exactly this at your regional. That said, pilots face a lot of competition, even in the current environment of rampant hiring. The airlines recognize that some other types of experience are valuable for their flying operations, and having some of those items on your resume/application will be helpful.

Airlines don't hire first officers, they hire future captains. This means they need their pilots to be leaders. You can and should seek out opportunities to demonstrate your leadership ability by logging Pilot in Command hours. However, serving in non-flying leadership positions is also valuable. If you have enough hours to be otherwise competitive, taking a leadership position in your current company could be a plus.

You can also demonstrate leadership in other areas of your life. Are you involved at your church, in a community service organization, a club, a musical group, on a sports team? Serving as a leader in any of these organizations can be just as valuable as taking a desk job at the headquarters of Brand X Regional Airline. You can also show leadership by starting and running a company as a side-hustle while you're an airline pilot. The best part is that you can show your leadership in those kinds of organization while flying a full schedule and accumulating the flight hours that are most important.

Airlines also value education. We can argue all day about whether a pilot really needs a 4-year degree, but our opinions don't matter. Most major airlines require applicants to have completed college. Just do it.

In my opinion, once you have a 4-year college degree your next priority should be aviation-related learning. Look for courses on aviation safety, survival skills, weather, management, and logistics. There are also lots of fun types of flying to build breadth. Consider earning your CFI, CFII, and MEI. Consider adding a glider, seaplane, helicopter, or other rating. Go get a tailwheel endorsement, learn to fly on skis, do an upset recovery course, learn aerobatics, or do some work as a ferry or test pilot. Any of these educational opportunities translates directly to you being a more valuable resource for your future major airline.

Although I advocate flying-related education, it's also valuable to study other things. I attended a lecture with some of the top leaders at my airline and they mentioned a preference for pilots who hold a master's degree. Pursuing a graduate degree may seem daunting, but it's really not that difficult. I earned mine through 100% online courses with a young family while serving as a pilot in the Air Force, including several combat deployments to Afghanistan. I have never even set a foot on the University of Idaho campus. Whatever flying job you're doing, if getting a job at a major airline is a priority you can find a way to earn a master's degree while continuing to work at your current job...and still accrue flight hours.

Beyond grad school, there are plenty of other courses in the world worth listing on an application or resume that will catch the eye of your desired airline's hiring department. You could earn certifications managing computer networks and other IT systems, you could earn business-related certifications like a six-sigma green or black belt, you could work on medically-related certifications like paramedic or EMT, you could work toward an Airframe and Powerplant mechanic license. Not only do these give your future airline the option of eventually offering you a job at headquarters, they also give you a lot of options for side-hustles, if our industry has a bad day and you end up furloughed, or if you lose your medical.

You won't see most of these educational opportunities identified as required, or even desired, on most job listings, but they all make you more attractive to a major airline. Again, don't give up flying to pursue them, but if you have time on your hands anyway, working on something educational is a lot more valuable to a future employer than you sitting around watching TV.

One more benefit of educating yourself while you're young is that you'll be setting yourself up for unique and desirable opportunities in the future. Eventually, you'll find yourself working for a major airline and you will have a lot of extra time on your hands. You'll want a hobby or at least a side-hustle to put that time to good use (and just prevent boredom.) The more skills you've developed in the past, the more ideas and possibilities you'll be able to come up with. You'll also be more qualified than others if you decide to pursue side gigs that look like jobs and require you to get hired somewhere. I believe that hobbies/side-hustles are so fundamental to a Treasure Bath that I've devoted a whole chapter to them later in this book.

There's no denying that flying for a regional airline isn't as desirable as flying at a major. You'll work longer days, have a busier schedule, and have worse work-rules...all for less pay. That said, it can still be a fun and rewarding job. The more you study your contract, the more you'll learn to optimize your schedule to suit your family's needs. Don't let relatively low pay or increased challenges deter you from pursuing your longer-term goals. We've just seen that Pilot Math works as well for regional airline pilots as it does for people from the military, if not better. Keep your ultimate goal, your driving Why, in mind and the difficulties you face earlier in your career will seem manageable. Learn everything you can while you're there and you'll be rewarded later.

CHAPTER TWELVE
Baby Pilot Math

This chapter will be a little different from the others. This is for anyone considering a flying career who hasn't yet achieved that first big-time flying job. We're not going to look at your potential earnings before you hit 1,500 flight hours because there's just too much variety in flying jobs. (Also, unfortunately, most of those jobs pay pretty terribly. You'll be working hard just to stay afloat.) Instead, we're going to talk about how to accrue those 1,500 hours without simultaneously burying yourself in a mountain of debt that will take years to escape and significantly delay the filling of your Treasure Bath.

I won't lie to you, pursuing a career as a professional pilot is a long and difficult path. It requires a lot of hard work and sacrifice on your part. While you're on this path, you cannot match the "lifestyle" that your friends and peers have without going deeply into debt. If you (or your family) can't handle that, then don't pursue this path in the first place.

That said, you've already seen the numbers...you already know that Pilot Math eventually works out. If you stick with it and make sacrifices now, this career will not only set you up for life, it could potentially set up your future generations in perpetuity.

You'll have to scrape and work hard to get your first 1,500 hours, but you'll eventually pursue one of the paths that we've already discussed: becoming a regional airline pilot, an Army Warrant Officer flying helicopters, or a commissioned Officer.

Although I don't directly address it in here, you also have an alternate option of pursuing corporate aviation. Like your other options, I don't think this one is any better or worse...it's just different. I honestly don't have enough knowledge on that topic to write about it here. One thing I do know is: each job is so unique that it would be pointless to quantify an "average" corporate pilot's career earnings. It is definitely a viable way to get to the airlines, if that's your ultimate goal. For some, it's also a wonderful career in and of itself. Hopefully, I'll be able learn or find someone who does know more about corporate aviation and post some information on it at pilotmathtreasurebath.com.

At this point in your life, you may be tempted to look at the charts in this book that show lifetime earnings and choose the track that pays the most. Don't do that! Although it may not be obvious to you right now, life isn't all about the money. There are so many other important factors in life that deserve as much consideration as earnings, if not more.

The regionals don't pay as well as the military early on, and they generally come with difficult schedules, commutes, etc. All-civilian pilots tend to accrue a lot of debt to pay for their flight training, unlike military pilots. However, the military also has its pitfalls. The military tells you where to live, and this frequently involves 6-12 month stints away from your family, deployed in the Armpits of the Earth. The military fills your workdays, whether you have anything useful to do or not, and you'll spend several hours on unfulfilling office work for every hour that you get to enjoy flying.

If you don't already know which of these options you want to pursue, start talking to people and asking questions! I'm involved with The Pilot Network, a rapidly growing social network of more than 30,000 pilots from all types of aviation backgrounds. If nothing else, you can ask around TPN and find someone who will gladly tell you all about a particular kind of flying.

No matter which path you choose, you should start flying on your own. The quickest and (in some ways) easiest way to do this is to attend a university with a flying program. Though these programs charge you a lot of money in addition to tuition, fees, etc., you'll earn ratings through single- and multi-engine commercial and flight instructor, including an instrument rating. If you're interested, they'll gladly let you defray some of your costs by teaching for them the moment you've earned your CFI. Most programs are also happy for you to stay on after graduation and continue teaching while you build hours.

These programs have the added benefit of qualifying you to earn a Restricted ATP rating with as few as 1,000 or 1,250 hours, depending on the type of program you complete. That could get you hired by a regional airline at least a year sooner than many of your peers. That year could make a huge difference for your Treasure Bath...easily $500,000 or more!

The problem with these programs is the cost. College is expensive enough without adding $60,000-$100,000 in flight training expenses to it. If you start down this path without a plan, you'll end up so deep in debt that you won't finally dig yourself out until you've been at a major airline for a few years. This also means you'll have delayed getting a meaningful start on your Treasure Bath.

Aren't you glad you're learning Pilot Math right now?

What follows here are some of the options I'd consider if I were you, just starting my career as a pilot and anxious to avoid crippling debt in the process. You don't have to use any or all of these ideas, but I feel like they can't hurt.

We're going to cover a lot of ground here. Hopefully you've already noticed me mentioning that it won't be easy. When deciding whether or not to apply one of these strategies you have to ask yourself: what is my ultimate goal? Yes, you need to live your life and there's no point in being miserable for a decade just to land some job. However, if you really, truly want to be a pilot and enjoy all the fruits that career bears, the best path should be clear to you. You're welcome to choose a path that appears to require less sacrifice or work on your part, but you're not allowed to complain about the consequences.

First off, you need to work during high school and use that money to either pay for college or some flight training. You can get creative here, and I'm not saying you have to work full-time. You don't have to progress very far in your flight training, but you do need to start.

As long as you're still living at home, you may consider hitting up your parents for some assistance. Don't be the entitled brat who acts like they are obligated to pay for everything, but don't be afraid to ask for a little help.

I sold fireworks one summer and made $800. (Yes, it was an awesome job.) I told my mom that I was going to use my hard-earned cash to buy an ultralight. Her response was priceless: a falsely enthusiastic, "that's great, son!" accompanied by a very mechanical smile.

I think she must have immediately panicked and called my dad at work because she approached me shortly thereafter and suggested, "What if instead of buying an ultralight you used your money to start flying lessons in a real airplane? If you did, dad and I would match what you've earned."

They ended up more than matching my funds because flying was expensive even back in 1997 when you could still rent a C-152 for $42/hr wet. I am eternally thankful to my parents for their financial support. Earning my Private Pilot certificate in high school gave me a foundation of experience that helped me excel in subsequent flying opportunities. It was a critical start to what has been a wonderful flying career so far.

If I could go back in time, I would have looked for jobs at the airport. This is a cliche I'd heard about my whole life, but I guess I just didn't think it could work back then. However, I've met many pilots who got their start throwing chocks, filling gas tanks, and towing airplanes. These jobs pay, and sometimes even include tips. On top of that, if you work for a flight school, they'll occasionally grant you a free hour of flight instruction for every 8-10 hours you work.

Whether you work for a flight school or not, airport jobs are also the ultimate form of aviation networking for an aspiring aviator. You'd be surprised at how many offers you get to go flying. You may not be able to log the hours, but the experience is worthwhile. If the person taking you flying is a CFI, or you're in a category and class of aircraft for which you're already rated, then you will be able to log the time. An extra half-hour of flying in your logbook, endorsed by a CFI, is the equivalent of a $75 tip, or more. I don't know of many jobs where tips come anywhere close to that.

As a now long-time pilot and an aircraft owner, I wish I'd found a way to earn an Airframe and Powerplant mechanic (A&P) certificate at some point in my past. If I were looking for an airport job, I'd start by going to every maintenance shop on the field and begging to be a shop assistant. I'd gladly take a job that involved hard work and physical discomfort to gain the experience of working with mechanics every day and gleaning even a little of what they know. If I was a high schooler again, I'd take minimum wage in a job like that over an easier one that pays more money because the experience is that valuable.

If you get a job like this, keep a logbook of all your maintenance experience, and have your A&P supervisor sign off each entry. You'll be able to use that experience to qualify for your own A&P certificate some day. That certificate is a plus for getting any flying job, it's extremely useful if you want to own an airplane, and it gives you a great backup job or side-hustle. There is always a demand for A&Ps, no matter where you go.

While you're hunting for or working in a job to save up flying money, you should also be pursuing another source of funds: scholarships.

We think a lot about scholarships for college, and you should apply for as many as you can find. However, there are also a surprising number of flying scholarships available in the world. You could get one or more of your ratings completely paid for by other people. This is such an important thing for you to pursue that I'm dedicating an entire webpage to listing good flying scholarships. You should go to www.pilotmathtreasurebath.com/scholarships[60] for a more complete and updated list, but here are a few great ones to get you excited:

- The Soaring Society of America offers the Kolstad Scholarship worth $5000 toward college expenses. The eligibility criteria include some specific glider flying experience.[61]
- If you're looking for a scholarship that will help you get the glider experience needed to qualify for the Kolstad, Costello Insurance, an aviation insurance provider popular among glider owners, has a scholarship for $2000 toward earning glider ratings.[62]
- The charitable arm of the Aircraft Owners and Pilots Association offers several scholarships each year.[63]
- The 99s is an organization that promotes aviation for women. They have Amelia Erhart scholarships in several different

---

[60] www.pilotmathtreasurebath.com/scholarships
[61] https://www.ssa.org/Youth?show=blog&id=2390
[62] https://www.ssa.org/Youth?show=blog&id=4459
[63] https://www.aopa.org/training-and-safety/flight-schools/flight-training-initiative/flight-training-scholarships

areas.*[64]

- Women in Aviation International is another women's flying organization that offers several scholarships.[65]
- The FAA Commercial Helicopter Pilot Scholarship is worth up to $50,000 toward that rating![66]
- Legendary flight instructors John and Martha King have joined with the National Association of Flight Instructors to offer $5000 (and access to the entire library of King Schools' online courses) toward obtaining a CFI rating.[67]

Although many of these organizations are geared toward specific demographics, some of their scholarships are open to any aspiring pilot. You should read the full rules for any scholarship before deciding you aren't eligible.

I've also written about two less-common strategies for starting out your aviation career. If you start by earning a Glider Flight Instructor (CFIG) or Sport Pilot Flight Instructor (SPI) rating, you can start earning money to teach others to fly with as few as 25, or 150 total flight hours, respectively. These strategies require to you live near or move to places with active glider or Light Sport Aircraft (LSA) operations, but they have the potential of saving you tens of thousands of dollars.

If one of these strategies sounds good to you, I recommend reading my series of articles about them on The Pilot Network. You can find the first post in that series on The Pilot Network's community website.[68]

Once you've secured funding through your own work, possible

---

[64] https://www.ninety-nines.org/scholarships.htm

[65] https://www.wai.org/education/scholarships

[66] http://www.helicopterscholarships.com/us-faa/

[67] https://www.kingschools.com/nafinet/king-schools-nafi-scholarship-information.asp

[68] https://community.thepilotnetwork.org/posts/i-want-to-be-a-pilot-but-i-need-cash-now-part-1

You can also get to this series through the free TPN-Go app: https://pilotmathtreasurebath.com/tpn-go/.

family contributions, and hopefully some scholarships, you can start thinking about flight training.

It'd be exciting and motivating to just hop in an airplane and start flying, but you need to make sure you lay the foundation first. You need to get some ground school done before you start spending any serious money on flying.

There are all kinds of ways to get this done. There are in-person and online courses available with prices in the low hundreds of dollars. You can also cover the material you need piecemeal with your CFI during training. If he or she charges you for time spent on ground instruction (you want him or her to do this) then it may end up costing you more than if you'd done a formal ground school course.

However, before you do any of these courses, you can and should do some self-study. The FAA publishes free handbooks covering much of the knowledge you need as a pilot.[69] You should start by reading the Airplane Flying Handbook cover to cover.[70]

You may not understand everything at first, but between Google searches and YouTube you can probably clear up most questions. If you show up to your ground school with at least a decent handle on everything in that Handbook, the course will feel much easier to you. If you're doing any sort of pay-as-you-go course, you'll save hundreds of dollars by studying on your own first. (For more details on self-study, please take a look at Part 3 of my series on The Pilot Network, or in the TPN-Go app.[71]

I remember not loving ground school as a young pilot. Of course we'd all rather just go flying. However, you'll quickly realize that your flying performance is heavily influenced by your preparation on the ground. You will learn and perform better in the air if you've prepared for and completed ground school before you start flying. This also means you'll require fewer hours to get proficient and save a lot of money.

---

[69] Go download everything you can from this website. It's hundreds of dollars of flight training materials for free: https://www.faa.gov/regulations_policies/handbooks_manuals/aviation/.

[70] Seriously. This has most of the knowledge that you'll need to obtain a Private Pilot License: https://www.faa.gov/regulations_policies/handbooks_manuals/aviation/airplane_handbook/.

[71] https://community.thepilotnetwork.org/posts/i-want-to-be-a-pilot-but-i-need-cash-now-part-3, or https://pilotmathtreasurebath.com/tpn-go/

Frustratingly, the FAA also has minimum ages for pilots to solo an aircraft, and earn each level of pilot rating. You can (and should) start flying before you reach any of those ages, but before a certain point this only makes sense if your parents own an airplane. However, there is no restriction on the age at which you can start ground school. You can start early, for free, and accrue most of the knowledge you need long before you're old enough to solo a glider at age 14.

Once you've completed your self study and at least started ground school, you can finally get to the fun stuff: flying. There are many different kinds of flight schools and they even operate under two separate sets of training rules: Part 61 and Part 141.

Larger, more structured programs operate under Part 141. The major benefit of these programs is that you don't need as many hours to get your ratings, potentially saving hundreds or even thousands of dollars. However, we need to be realistic and admit that most student pilots require more than the minimum number of hours anyway. The structure and standardization of a Part 141 program can mean your training is more efficient. However, sometimes these programs charge extra fees or higher rental prices, making them about as expensive as other programs even though they require fewer total flight hours.

By default, if a program doesn't operate under Part 141, then it falls under Part 61. (You can and should read that entire portion of the Federal Aviation Regulations.)[72] This could be a single instructor teaching in a single aircraft, or even a fairly large flight school. Part 61 operations are far more common than Part 141, and these programs offer a lot of flexibility. Unfortunately, the lack of structure can mean some headaches associated with scheduling, and instructor or aircraft availability.

Take the time to interview any potential program. Ask them to introduce you to some past or current students, and talk to those students away from the school itself. Don't bother with a program known for maintenance or instructor availability issues, bad attitudes, or widespread accusations of making students fly far more hours than necessary for their ratings.

It will be tempting to go with a program that has shiny, new,

---

[72] https://www.ecfr.gov/cgi-bin/text-idx?SID=393ba3f6489b82c6a63da2800b1bf56e&mc=true&node=pt14.2.61&rgn=div5

technologically-advanced aircraft. I recommend you avoid them though! You'd think that new aircraft would have fewer maintenance issues than old ones, but I haven't found this to be true...especially in fleets used for flight training. (It turns out student pilots tend to be hard on airplanes.) You'll spend most of your career learning to deal with technology and automation in aircraft, but your primary flight training is one of the few times when it's acceptable and beneficial to have less technology so you can focus on stick and rudder flying. Your flight school will also have to charge more to cover the astronomically high costs of purchasing new aircraft these days. (A 40-year old Cessna C-172 in great shape can be obtained for $30,000-40,000. A factory new C-172 costs at least ten times that much. A brand-new Cirrus SR22 with all the options now costs more than $1,000,000!)

I say find the oldest, cheapest training aircraft possible. They need to be safe, but as long as they are, instrumentation doesn't matter at all. Learn to fly by looking outside the airplane and listening to the air and your engine. If you were born in the last 40 years and know how to use a smartphone, you'll have no trouble figuring out fancy glass-panel avionics when you move up to newer aircraft later in your career.

Ideally, you want to train with a company that has at least 2 or 3 of the model aircraft you're flying. This lets you continue flying when (not if) one does down for extended maintenance or gets stuck far away on a cross-country trip.

Before we go further, I want to mention one more source of discounted flight training: the Civil Air Patrol.[73] Officially an auxiliary of the US Air Force, the CAP does search & rescue, assists with firefighting, helps coordinate disaster relief, and many other missions all over the country. Anyone can join, and as a member you're allowed to get flight training in their aircraft. The rates they charge are subsidized by tax dollars, meaning they're ridiculously cheap. The aircraft are generally new and maintained in accordance with very strict regulations.

If you have enough flight hours, you can get checked out as a Mission Pilot for CAP. Then you get to fly for free when carrying out official CAP missions. Not only are those free flight hours valuable, the flying is rewarding and more engaging than just boring holes in the

---

[73] https://www.gocivilairpatrol.com/

sky.

CAP isn't a totally free lunch. You have to endure all kinds of paperwork and training just to join up. They'll expect you to get qualified as a Spotter and/or Observer to ride in the aircraft on missions before they let you train as a Mission Pilot.. You'll have to buy some uniforms and attend meetings. It's actually even more work than it sounds here, and not to be taken lightly. If you're interested in serving your community, then CAP is a great organization to spend time with while you're doing your flight training. However, if you're only looking for cheap flying, you will hate CAP. It's enough work that it won't be worth the discounted flight hours.

I offer some more thoughts on making CAP a mutually beneficial experience in a post on TPN.[74]

Your first priority in pursuing a pilot career should be to get a pilot's license. You need to make sure that you enjoy flying and don't get airsick. You need to make sure that you're willing to put in the study and practice, and that you can handle the pressure of taking a checkride. You need to make sure you're okay with the idea of spending hours or days scraping together enough money to cover an hour of flying.

Most pilots verify all of this as they work toward a Private Pilot Certificate. This will require at least 40 hours of flight time in a Part 61 program. If you can find a school with LSAs, I recommend earning your Sport Pilot Certificate on the way to Private Pilot. You can do that with as few as 20 hours, then take your friends and family flying with you as you gain experience toward your other ratings.

A few years ago, the FAA also instituted a new program that allows you to simultaneously work on your Private Pilot Certificate and Instrument Rating all at the same time. Talk to people who have gone through a program like this, as well as people who did more traditional flight training, before you decide to go this way. It could

---

[74] https://community.thepilotnetwork.org/posts/i-want-to-be-a-pilot-but-i-need-cash-now-part-5

or

https://www.pilotmathtreasurebath.com/tpngo

potentially save you money, but don't let it impinge on the amount of basic stick & rudder flying you get to do.

Whether you combine Private and Instrument or not, you need to work on your Instrument Rating as soon as you can. Instrument flying is the bread and butter of professional aviation and having that rating lets you go flying on days when the weather keeps basic Private or Sport pilots grounded.

With Private and Instrument ratings in hand, your next step is to fly as much as possible until you get 250 hours. This magic number makes you eligible for a Commercial Pilot Certificate. Getting to Commercial is critical because, other than scholarships and a couple other exceptions, you have to cover the cost of all your flying up to that point. Aircraft rental most places starts well above $100/hr, so even if you don't account for the costs of flight instructors, training materials, equipment like headsets, etc., you're looking at a minimum of $25,000 to get to that point. Scholarships will help, but you need to start finding a way for someone else to pay for your flying ASAP!

I already mentioned earning ratings and working as a CFIG and/or SPI as ways to start making money for flying before you hit 250 hours. When you take a good look at the costs, it's easy to see how advantageous these two options could be. Even if you don't want to (or can't) start your flight training as a glider pilot, it might be worth obtaining some of these ratings as you're working toward 250 hours anyway. If you have to pay for those hours no matter what, why not add a few more ratings during the process? Your eventual airline application will always look better with a greater number and variety of pilot ratings on it. You'd also be surprised by the opportunities that arise when you're in the right place, at the right time, holding the right pilot certificate. Either of these paths could allow you to get paid while you accrue the last 100+ hours toward your Commercial Airplane Single Engine Land rating. That's a potential savings of at least $10,000, plus the $2000-$3000 you could earn in instructor fees while you fly those last 100 hours.

Although earning a Commercial Pilot Certificate is an important and noteworthy milestone, it isn't as good a deal as you think. It'd be nice if you could call up all your friends and family and say, "I'm a Commercial Pilot now, so I'll fly you wherever you want to go, at cost. Fly with me instead of the airlines!" Unfortunately, this isn't allowed and the FAA will hammer you to the wall for trying to do it...even though your pilot's license now has the word "commercial" on it. Instead, you're going to spend the next 750-1,250 hours scraping for flying jobs.

Most of these jobs aren't glamorous. Some will end up just being something you get through. When faced with the choice between an undesirable flying job or no flying job you must ask yourself: what is my ultimate goal? If professional aviation is what you want to do, then I assert you need to take advantage of every opportunity you can get for professional flying, as long as the operation is safe. You'll be looking for the following types of jobs:

- Pipeline patrol
- Jump plane
- Banner/glider tow
- Part 135 corporate or charter operations (500 hours total time for VFR-only operations, 1,200 hours total time for IFR operations.)
- Civil Air Patrol
- Flight instruction (for a big school, small school, or freelance)
- Ferry pilot

The point of these jobs is to accumulate enough hours for an Airline Transport Pilot certificate (ATP.) You'll may be eligible for a Restricted ATP at 750, 1000, or 1250, depending on where you did your flight training. Worst case, you can always get a full ATP at 1500 hours total time.

Once there, the next step is to start flying for a regional airline. That job is still a lot of work, but the pay and working conditions at these operations have improved drastically over the last few years. We've already seen how Pilot Math works out for regional airline pilots...it's outstanding! Starting your aviation career on this path will eventually result in millions of dollars filling your Treasure Bath.

The regional may be your first job flying a jet, and you should take advantage of every chance to build that experience for at least your first 1,000-2,000 hours. At most regionals, you should expect to upgrade to Captain either the moment you get 1,000 hours of Part 121 airline time, or within your first two years at the company. Multi-engine turbine Pilot In Command (PIC) hours are very important for getting hired by a major airline, so I wouldn't rest until I had at least

500-1,000 regional airline PIC hours. A pilot with at least 3,000 hours total time, of which 500-1000 are multi-engine turbine PIC, will be increasingly competitive for major airline jobs over the next 5-10 years.

As we've said, this path isn't quick or easy. It's actually a lot of hard work and sacrifice. However, if you have the discipline to put in that work, and focus on doing what it takes to advance along this path, you'll be richly rewarded. If you take advantage of scholarship and employment opportunities to reduce or eliminate costs, you can absolutely complete this path without a large debt burden.

The following table is a simplistic summary of the major steps you need to follow in your pilot career development. You can succeed if you skip the glider and sport pilot parts, but just realize that you'll also be skipping a $12,000+ discount on your flying costs.

Step	Minimum Total Flight Hours	Comments
Private Glider	10	
Commercial Glider	25	Limited opportunities for paid flying
CFIG	25	Plentiful paid flying, 225 hours before you're eligible for a Commercial ASEL rating
Sport Pilot	20	Build hours/experience while flying with friends and family. (You may split flying costs evenly.)
Private Pilot ASEL	40	Same ability to split flying costs with passengers
Instruement Rating	50	Possible to combine much of this training with Private Pilot
Sport Pilot Instructor (SPI)	150	Paid flying, 150 hours before you're eligible for a Commercial ASEL rating
Commercial Pilot ASEL	250	Limited opportunities for paid flying
CFI/CFII	250	Lots of paid flying available
Commercial Multi-Engine	250	
Multi-Engine Instructor (MEI)	250	
Restricted ATP	750/1000/1250	Hours required depend on military service or type of civilian training program. Plentiful work as a regional airline pilot.
ATP	1500	

Flight training is fun and exciting. You can start at almost any age and start soloing in gliders at age 14. However, if you want to end up in a top-tier professional flying job, you need to get a 4-year college degree. Aside from scholarships, there are several ways you can minimize the costs of college...leaving you more money for flight training, or just reducing the amount you have to raise through scholarships, work, grants, and loans.

In high school you should take as many Advanced Placement (AP) classes as possible.[75] If you study hard and do well on the associated AP exam, most colleges will give you at least some college credit. Every credit you earn through an AP exam represents hundreds or thousands of dollars of savings. Some schools offer International Baccalaureate (IB) courses in addition to, or instead of, AP courses.[76] You can receive college credit for good grades in the IB program, though this isn't as widely accepted as AP exam scores. One of the factors in choosing the college you attend should be their acceptance of the AP and/or IB credits you earned at your high school.

In addition to AP and IB, you should consider studying for and taking some CLEP exams. The College Level Examination Program offers tests in 33 different subject areas, and passing scores are widely accepted by colleges for credit.[77] A quick search online will reveal study guides for these exams. They're far cheaper than paying for and then spending hours of your life in an entry-level college class.

One final way to start tackling college is to take advantage of dual enrollment programs where you can take one college-level class and receive both college and high school credit. These courses are usually free or steeply discounted for high school students.

A carefully planned combination of AP, IB, CLEP, and dual enrollment could potentially help you finish high school with a year or more of college already complete.

Another important part of saving on college costs is not being a moron when you pick what school to attend. Yes, big names like Harvard and Yale will open doors that other colleges won't. However, that effect is greatly diminished in aviation. As long as you have the right combination of pilot ratings and experience, where you went to school and what you studied aren't all that important.

If I were starting from scratch, I'd strongly consider doing my first two years at a community college. The costs are much lower and they're more likely to give credit for AP/IP/CLEP. I'd spend my time there accomplishing as many general education requirements as possible. Why pay Harvard prices for core classes when I can

---

[75] https://ap.collegeboard.org/
[76] https://www.ibo.org/
[77] https://clep.collegeboard.org/

accomplish the same thing at a cheap community college? (Just make sure that your credits will actually transfer to your eventual 4-year university.)

Many small towns have some sort of community college and it may be possible to further reduce costs by continuing to live with your parents for a couple years. If you maximized your AP/IB/CLEP/Dual enrollment opportunities beforehand, you may only need to stay at home or a year or less anyway.

My hometown even had a community college with an aviation program nearby.[78] A program like this would be a fantastic place to start college and get some flight training.

After completing two years of community college, I'd transfer to a 4-year school. We've already decided that the aviation community doesn't really care which school that is. I'd pick one based on cost and location. I'd want it to have a flying program, or be near airports where I could get flying jobs and further my flight training.

There are many aviation-focused college programs throughout the country. Some, like Embry Riddle and the University of North Dakota, have big, fancy, well-known programs. They're fantastic schools, but they're also extremely expensive. Those names carry a little extra weight in the aviation community, but I'm not sure they're worth the bigger price tag. There are plenty of schools throughout the country that offer great programs with flight training at lower cost. I'd shop among those first.

If you're trying to minimize debt and overall college costs, you need to consider working during college, just like you did in high school. Sure, part of college is about having fun, drinking, and looking for love, but what is your ultimate goal? You could pursue all those things while working as a shift manager at a fast food joint for the rest of your life. If you want easy living, worldwide travel, and a Bathtub brimming with Treasure as a professional pilot, you need to prioritize your application of Pilot Math over those short-term frivolities. This doesn't mean there's no place for fun or relaxation...far from it! It's possible to hit college hard, pursue flight training, and work at least part-time while still enjoying a good social life. It's certainly easier if

---

[78] One of my first exposures to aviation was a week-long summer class called something like: "So you want to be a pilot" at Aims Community College. If I were starting over as a civilian pilot, I'd definitely look at doing my first two years of college there: https://www.aims.edu/academics/aviation/.

you can find friends involved in the same activities.

If you can't learn to live a balanced life when you're young, you'll end up as a disgruntled pilot with a sky-high income, but very little actual wealth...just like Poor Old Joe. Don't be like Joe.

Now that age 65 airline retirements are on the verge of kicking into high gear, some airlines are realizing that they have to do more effective recruiting if they want any hope of staffing their companies for the next 30 years. These airlines are starting to offer a variety of programs that help young pilots pay for college and get the experience they need. They're even starting to offer essentially guaranteed employment to pilots years before they'll qualify for a major airline job.

JetBlue has had several Pilot Gateway Programs available for a while.[79] Delta Air Lines recently became the first major US airline exploring this concept with their Propel Pilot Career Pathway Program.[80] Many of these programs require participants to attend one of a few select aviation universities. If I were starting from scratch, I'd absolutely consider going to a one of those schools and applying to the associated airline's program.

It's important to note that Delta's partners include expensive schools like ERAU, but also much more affordable options like Middle Georgia State University.[81] I'd choose a school like Middle Georgia over an expensive place like Auburn, UND, or ERAU any day, unless I had scholarships or other ways to cover the costs without going into greater debt.

Once you get to college, there are many ways to reduce peripheral costs. I'd definitely consider some sort of shared housing arrangement. Traditionally referred to as just "having a roommate," some online communities have adopted the term "house hacking," implying that it's a way to beat a wasteful system. If you're interested in using house hacking to save money, I recommend listening to the Bigger Pockets

---

Money Podcast as they do a great job covering the subject.[82]

There are also many ways for a college student to reduce the costs of food, transportation, and more. Bigger Pockets Money and the ChooseFI Podcast are both great places to start getting ideas.[83]

Whether it's flight training or college, be smart about obtaining funding and choosing where to spend it. There's no reason to chase more expensive options just because they look fancier or sound more prestigious. Pilot Math works because of the earning potential of pilots at *major* airlines and your best bet is to get there as soon as possible. Up to that point, your focus should be on flying and avoiding the need to incur large debts on your way.

---

[82] A well-done podcast done as an effort of Bigger Pockets branching out just a little. The hosts are friendly, enthusiastic and approachable. It's a good listen: https://www.biggerpockets.com/moneyshow.

[83] Already a couple hundred episodes in, the hosts are going beyond the traditional podcast model and forming an active community around their ideas. Every Monday is a "standard" episode, then on Friday they release a follow-up that discusses the material from Monday and brings in a lot of listener feedback and input. It's a great resource: https://www.choosefi.com/podcast-episodes/.

CHAPTER THIRTEEN

Flying Solo - Single Pilot Math

I've chosen to primarily address this book to pilots with families because I feel like most of us eventually end up in that situation. Sadly, some pilot communities (and especially the military) tend to give preference to married couples at the expense of single pilots because it seems convenient. I'm not that guy, and this chapter is dedicated to all of you pilots who haven't yet found the right person.

If you aren't single you might think that this chapter is not for you. Don't necessarily skip over it though. Unfortunately, married pilots are notorious for failing to maintain balance in their lives, and marriages don't always work out. Whether you're in the position to help a friend, or you realize that there's a (hopefully very small) chance that you could be in this situation yourself someday, I feel like this chapter is important for married pilots as well.

If you're single, you should be excited that you're reading this book right now. You are in the best possible situation for applying Pilot Math to start setting up your future! Take advantage of this opportunity while you can, because you never know when you're going to find love and lose a lot of options for optimizing the deluge of money pouring into your Treasure Bath.

That said, I'm not advocating anyone avoid romance to make this work. If I were a single pilot I'd definitely put time and energy into looking for someone special. The great thing is that if you have a solid understanding of Pilot Math before you meet that person, you'll be able to make sure that you're both on the same sheet of financial music right from the start. This is a formula for increased harmony in any relationship! Also, if you have systems in place for automatically investing your money, you won't be tempted to blow it all on lifestyle creep to impress the new and exciting person you just met.

If I could go back in time and have a chat with my younger self, here's some of the advice I'd give:

Live frugally

Your life will only get more expensive when you eventually add other people to it. Live frugally while you can. Take advantage of every opportunity right now to optimize expenses and maximize your savings rate and your earnings. We use an arbitrary annual spending number of $57,758 in this book. This number is based on a full family living a traditional upper-middle-class lifestyle. As a young, single pilot you should be able to have an awesome life while only spending a fraction of that amount each year. The more money you can save and invest early in your career, the sooner your Treasure Bath will start overflowing with bounteous wealth!

That said, there is a critical difference between being frugal and being cheap. Frugal is optimizing your life to balance saving for your future with getting maximum value from the money you spend now. Being cheap is a form of financial extremism that yields minimal returns and comes with steep opportunity costs. Being frugal is a process that challenges you to always improve yourself while you enjoy your life. Being cheap is counter-productive deprivation, and it's not fun. You don't need to be cheap to make Pilot Math work for you.

I recommend that you allow yourself to appear successful enough to attract a spouse. Ideally, living frugally will show the world that you're a focused and capable person, who effectively optimizes life. This may be a turn-off for the types of spendthrift people who wouldn't understand Pilot Math and would drain every last penny out of your Treasure Bath in just a few years. That's a victory!

You should avoid associating with those people at all costs, let alone getting emotionally involved!

Ideally, living a frugal and enjoyable life will attract the type of person who has habits and values similar to yours. Your handle on Pilot Math will be part of what makes you irresistible. That type of relationship will supercharge the rate at which you accumulate Treasure in your Bath.

Finding someone who shares or willingly adopts your financial mindset will also lead to more harmony in your relationship. Couples frequently cite money as a source of arguments and contention. If you can avoid fighting over money problems, you can focus your efforts on better things...like why she refuses to wash dishes. (Oops, TMI. As long as you remember to enjoy the making-up process, there's nothing wrong with finding something to argue about every now and then ;-)

Fly like crazy!

The toughest part of being an airline pilot is that you have to leave your family to do your job. If you don't have a family yet, you should take advantage of your opportunity to fly without leaving anyone behind. Be adventurous, bid layovers in places you've never been and see the world on your company's dime, take an early upgrade to captain or aircraft commander to start accruing turbine PIC hours, volunteer for deployments.

If you're a young pilot, this will mean you accumulate hours faster than your peers. You'll get to a major airline faster than them, and you'll be senior to them for the rest of your career. At the airlines, seniority is everything!

If you're already at a major airline, you should still take advantage of opportunities to fly as much as possible. Use this time to chase extra trips for premium pay and pour every extra dollar into your Treasure Bath. The more you do this now, the less you'll need to add later when you've found someone who gives you a reason to fly less and spend more time at home.

A single person who figures out how to optimize premium pay flying can make outrageous money and still enjoy enough time off to avoid going crazy. It still won't be the most balanced life, though, so I recommend only planning to employ this strategy for a fixed amount of time. It's a lot easier to get through a period of especially hard work when you have a defined end date in sight. Give yourself plenty of long breaks between periods of hard work to recharge. During those breaks, use travel hacking to inexpensively spend time in the mountains, at the beach, or wherever it is that relaxes you the most.

Save like crazy

As we mentioned in #1, a single person can potentially live an extremely frugal life. Mr. Money Mustache supports an entire family with a great life on $25K per year. You definitely don't *need* a large family home, two cars, or $92 worth of new drapes every year. You could easily beat MMM's $25K figure. All the numbers we use in this book assume you spend every penny you make, up to $57,758 each year. If you're only spending $25K or less, you can supercharge your savings and fill up your Treasure Bath that much faster.

If you do this right, you will reduce your taxable income to incredibly low levels. There are lots of (perfectly legal) loopholes you can exploit if your taxable income drops that low. They're beyond the scope of this book, but you can check out the Bigger Pockets Money and ChooseFI podcasts,[84] as well as a mind-blowing post on Root of Good,[85] for more about them. (A cornerstone post at Go Curry Cracker also has some principles that could help early on,[86] though you'll eventually make so much money that most of these ideas won't apply to you.)

Don't spend money frivolously

Yes, in a way this is the same as "live frugally" and "save like crazy." However, we have to look at it from a new angle or your mind will trick you into making bad choices anyway.

It's easy to spend money when you don't have to get the purchase approved by a spouse or significant other. It's also easy try spending money to cure loneliness or chase excitement. If you feel like buying something or just "going shopping" for its own sake, recognize the warning sign and do something else.

You should already have at least some hobby or side-hustle to work on. It might even be related to your ultimate Why. When all else fails, go work on that project instead of spending money. Barring that, joining a club, a sports team, or a service organization can be a great way to enjoy your free time and meet other people. Instead of consuming, go and do something productive or fun.

---

[84] https://www.biggerpockets.com/moneyshow and https://www.choosefi.com/podcast-episodes/

[85] This is some next-level tax optimization strategy: https://rootofgood.com/make-six-figure-income-pay-no-tax/.

[86] https://www.gocurrycracker.com/never-pay-taxes-again/

This means you really do need a side-hustle.

You're allowed to use other types of flying for this, but some variety in life is good. Also, some side-hustles will help you meet attractive people. If you have a good idea for a business you can pursue in addition to flying, you'll never have more time than now to make it happen. If you put forth extra effort to set up systems now, it'll be easier to keep them going in the future when family or the rest of life threatens to get in the way.

Many potential side-hustles start as hobbies. One of the great things about being single is that there's no pressure to perform. If your hobby or budding business fails, you're not negatively impacting the well-being of a spouse or children. This can actually give you the courage (or disregard) to work harder and be bolder in your efforts...and that's a recipe for business success.

Stay healthy

Use your free time to stay fit, and teach yourself the habit of eating healthy food. This can potentially be part of your side hustle. Just going to the gym or running are great, but this might be the time to learn a martial art, yoga, rock climbing, or some other skill that is both fun to do and offers the possibility of becoming an instructor someday.

My wife happens to look extremely hot wearing a pair of boxing gloves and whaling on a bag. If you want a future spouse that is interested in staying fit and attractive, you could do worse than meeting him or her at a yoga class, in a rock climbing gym, or at a triathlon.

If you find that you're a good cook, you could publish recipes, broadcast cooking classes on YouTube, teach classes in your community, or even sell your food. If you want to hear a fascinating story of this in action, listen to the episode of the *How I Built This* podcast where Guy Raz interviews Seth Goldman of Honest Tea.[87] Goldman built a multi-million dollar company (that he eventually sold to Coca Cola for many more millions) because he couldn't find a beverage he wanted to drink after working out. If that story doesn't do it for you, try the episode about how Gary Erickson developed Clif Bar

---

[87] https://www.npr.org/2018/06/08/618252345/honest-tea-seth-goldman

in his mom's kitchen.[88] (He's also a multi-millionaire.)

Educate yourself

This is also the time to pursue educational opportunities that will either be more useful to you later in life, or make you more competitive on major airline applications. A master's degree is a plus. So are safety courses, business school, programming skills, language skills, etc. You will never have more time to spend on these pursuits. Don't waste it all on television, video games, or alcohol!

Travel, but be frugal

There's a lot of talk along the lines of: "Buy experiences, not things" these days. YOLO! Right? Those are great sentiments, but don't waste exorbitant amounts of money on experiences if you don't have to. If you're an airline pilot, use your non-revenue travel privileges whenever you can. Use travel hacking to cut your costs. As a single person, it's much more acceptable to sleep on a friend's couch instead of paying for a hotel.

If you're traveling with friends, you can share expenses. Take the lead in planning activities and meals that don't break the bank while you're on the road. Make an adventure out of it.

Chances are your singularity won't last forever, even if you want it to. We pilots are hard to resist and someone will likely fall for you. Fly a lot while you can. Set up systems for saving and living frugally. Then, when you meet that other person, roll him or her into the life you've set up and you'll be able to make it a Treasure Bath for two.

—

We all start off single, but, far too frequently, professional pilots find themselves single again after a divorce.

I'll start off by saying that I've been there and done that. I know it sucks and I'm sorry you had to endure it as well. If you're going through it right now, saying this won't help much at the moment, but

---

[88] https://www.npr.org/2018/02/06/572560919/clif-bar-gary-erickson

your life will be immeasurably better once your divorce is official!

There are as many potential causes for divorce as there are marriages. Sometimes, a pilot or spouse betrays the other. Sometimes we're just supremely incompatible. Sometimes it turns out one of us is just a bad person. You may or may not be at fault in your divorce, but once it's happened there's no point in punishing yourself for past mistakes. I'm even less of a marriage counselor than I am a certified financial counselor (that is: not one at all) so I won't presume to address all of your issues here.

I highly recommend searching out good books and the help of professional counselors if you feel like things aren't working for you. Sometimes couples just need to learn to communicate and things can work out fine. Other times they can't, and talking to someone can prompt the kinds of useful introspection that leads you to make tough decisions, and then prevent repeat performances.

I will say that it's not infrequent for us pilots to get so enamored with aviation that we forget the need for balance in our lives. Don't let that happen to you! Chasing hours, money, or ratings can be thrilling and addictive. If there are other people in your life, give them their due...even if it means you all have a little less money available to spend.

Speaking of money, divorce is extremely expensive in the short- and long-term. The best thing you can do for your financial and emotional well-being is to choose your spouse correctly in the first place and make that relationship your top priority!

If it's too late for that, you should be very excited about the career opportunity you've just handed yourself. (It's okay to simultaneously feel bad about your lost relationship and excited about flying.)

First off, now is not the time to jump into another relationship! Let's be honest with ourselves: divorce means that your marriage was a failure. Even if the failure was mostly the fault of the other person, you still played some part. At the very least, you owe it to yourself and to any future relationships to take some times and figure out what your part you played in that failure. I'm not saying you have to become a celibate monk or nun for the rest of your life, but at least give yourself a few months before starting another serious relationship. A year is probably better.

Giving yourself this period of introspection has another benefit: it gives you a chance to reset your life and save like crazy. By definition, you don't have anyone to impress. Adjust your life, quickly, and go back to the strategies listed at the start of this chapter.

If you're recently divorced, I recommend you spend a while doing a lot of flying for work. This has several benefits unique to your situation. You can spend time in self-evaluation just as easily from cushy layover hotels as you can from your cheap new apartment full of cardboard boxes containing painful memories. For me, the spartan furnishings of a hotel room are always less distracting than home.

This is the time to be the narrowbody FO who makes $380,000 per year, or the most junior narrowbody Captain in New York City. Even just one year of that will trigger a titanic flood of Treasure into your Bathtub. If this happens early in your major airline pilot career, the long-term financial gains will be staggering.

This will have an added benefit of helping you understand what it's like to go maximum effort at work. I don't think it's a sustainable long-term lifestyle, but you won't know your tolerance for it until you've tried it. During that year, you'll learn how to optimize every part of your contract for maximum gain. Even if you never work that hard again in the future, you'll be able to use many of the techniques you learned to improve your Quality of Life and/or make more money for less work.

Even if you spend a year or so working extra hard, you need to make sure you don't burn yourself out. Take time to visit friends and family. Take a vacation or two. If you haven't started travel hacking yet, now is absolutely the time!

Once you've figured yourself out a little, you've optimized your life for maximum Pilot Math, and you've experimented with working way too hard, you'll be in the perfect place to dial things back and enjoy a brand new life. This is the time to start seriously dating again, if you so desire. When you find someone special, you'll have a much better understanding of what you need to do to make that relationship more successful than your last one. Be careful here. Having been married you'll be hungry for the type of serious, committed relationship that your last marriage probably was (for at least a while.) Don't expect every new relationship to be like this and don't be afraid to walk away if you encounter another Mr. or Miss wrong.

When you do find someone worth considering for another serious relationship, you'll be able to explain Pilot Math to that person and show him or her what your Treasure Bath looks like so far. You need to make sure that he or she is on board with what you're doing because a spendthrift spouse will destroy your life. (I've seen it happen to a friend of mine. It's tragic.)

Being "newly single" feels horrible at first. I don't mean to be glib about this, but you will get past it. When you do, recognize it for the opportunity it is! Take advantage of the chance to reset things and you'll be back on track before you know it.

Unfortunately, many divorces impact more people that just you and your spouse. If you have children, be sure to take time amidst all this introspection and working to be with them. Work like crazy when your spouse has your kids, but be 100% there for your kids any time you get to be with them. Getting over a failed romantic relationship is one thing. You will never get over a failed relationship with a child if it happens because of a lack of effort or attention on your part.

If you're obligated to pay child or spousal support, then do it! Don't play games or use it as leverage. Do exactly what the judge ordered. You do not want to deal with legal trouble because you haven't upheld your part of a divorce decree. It will cost you time and money, and could impact your job. If your ex is the one playing games, you absolutely must have the moral justification of obeying all of the judge's orders when your lawyer goes back to complain.

This is one of the reasons I believe it's so important to set up financial support for your kids as soon as they're born. If you can show a divorce judge that each of your kids already has a fat 529 account balance just waiting to fund his or her college education, your child support payments should get reduced accordingly.

The same may go for retirement accounts and spousal support. It will suck to lose large chunks of your savings, but if they're large enough you may not have to pay as much month-to-month going forward. Also, if your spouse was on board with Pilot Math and doing his or her own saving, you may each have sizable savings in your own accounts. It won't feel as bad losing access to those shared assets if they were earned by your spouse and deposited into a retirement account that was always in his or her name.

Human beings are not meant to live alone. Finding yourself single because of a failed relationship is never fun. However, as a single pilot you have a unique opportunity to optimize Pilot Math to your advantage. Take advantage of this opportunity while you can because it won't last forever. I hope you succeed wildly in your solo optimizing efforts, and that you run out of time for doing it before long.

CHAPTER FOURTEEN

Dead Zoners

This book exists because the state of our industry fills me with optimism. US airlines are expanding, retirements are looming, pilot supply is insufficient to meet demand, and our world is addicted to air travel. All of that is good news for someone starting out a career as an airline pilot.

Sadly, history shows that I need to spend at least a few moments trying to temper my unrelenting enthusiasm. All it takes is one bad day to go from what we have now to a really terrible decade in this industry. Whether we are talking about health scares, a financial crisis, or a major terrorist attack, there are numerous threats to the good life that we enjoy.

Should something cause the music to stop, we could all find ourselves in a very different environment. If (or perhaps more likely when) this happens, it will affect the way we employ Pilot Math. I'm going to start illustrating this by using the current generation of "deadzoners" as an example. Here's today's history lesson:

At the end of the 20th century, the US economy was booming. The dot com bubble was still inflating, deregulation meant that airlines were free to figure out how to actually make money, and airline pilots were still treated with deference. Times were fantastic!

Pay rates for a senior widebody captain were sky-high. In today's dollars, they were in the ballpark of $600,000 per year, or more. In addition, every major airline had a pension fund that promised to pay 60% of a pilot's Final Average Earnings (FAE) for the rest of his or her life. During their working years, pilots spent money like it was going out of style, knowing that they'd still be pulling in more than six figures every year in retirement. Nobody saved for the future because there was no need...60% FAE is a *lot* of money!

Tragically, a lot of bad things happened in relatively rapid succession.

The first problem was Uncle Sam's fault. Congress wrote tax law to allow pension plans like those the airlines used to offer. The IRS allows companies to contribute pre-tax money into these funds. That tax treatment is supposed to incentivize companies to do the right thing for their people. Make no mistake though, neither IRS nor Congress wants to give up a single dollar of tax income if they don't have to. They can't afford it. (Someone needs to explain Pilot Math to the US Government.)

In theory, a company like an airline should contribute *more* money into a pension fund than is required to meet their payout obligations. This would protect against a market crash. It would be the morally correct thing to do.

Companies don't want to tie up a bunch of money in a pension fund, but I think many of them would have chosen to fund their plans a little better if they could have. The problem is that he IRS won't let this happen. They only allow a company to put enough capital into the fund to meet payout requirements, after accounting for accrued interest. It's a very count-your-chickens-before-they-hatch situation. There are specialists called actuaries who do the chicken counting. They gaze into mathematical models equivalent to crystal balls, decide what kinds of investment gains a pension plan can expect, and tell a company how much cash it's allowed to put into the pension fund each year.

The IRS watches this process very closely and only allows a pension to be "over-funded" to a certain level. If the company were to over-fund to an even higher level, perhaps expecting bad times ahead, the IRS would accuse the company of tax evasion and start arresting people.

As we just mentioned, the stock market was on a tear through mid-2000. It was called the "Dotcom boom" until it became the "Dotcom bubble" then the "Dotcom bust." Over several months, the stock market experienced one of the largest drops in history. Companies went bankrupt, investors lost billions.

Suddenly, all the pension plans that had been anywhere from

healthy to legally over-funded were in trouble. The value of the assets in which they were invested wasn't even enough to pay out their obligations. The retirees drawing on the pension fund continued to decrease the principle available, exacerbating the situation.

As companies looked toward the future, it was mathematically impossible to fulfill all their pension obligations without huge cash infusions into those funds. The problem was that in the crashed economy, spending on air travel had dropped and the airlines weren't making enough money to do that. It didn't help that they were still trying to figure out how to make money in the first place, with deregulation not that far in the past.

Then things got worse.

Some evil men corrupted the minds of some religious zealots and used them to crash airplanes into the Twin Towers and the Pentagon...and the world panicked.

Commercial airlines resumed operations fairly quickly after 9/11, but it took a long time for the American public to feel comfortable flying again. The problems that the Dotcom Bust was causing for the airlines only got worse.

Many deadzoners will tell you that airline executives jumped with joy when this happened. There was simply no way they could continue to meet their pension fund obligations in this environment. The cynics say that the airlines used this situation as an excuse for getting rid of the pension plans altogether. I have no way to know if this was the case, but it doesn't matter. It doesn't take a math genius to realize that the economics of this situation left companies with no choice.

A series of bankruptcies preceded a series of mergers that left us with three major airlines (Delta, American, and United) and Southwest as the fourth major domestic player. As part of those bankruptcies, the US Government allowed these companies to simply give up on trying to fund their pension plans.

Some companies got to "freeze" the plans. The funds would remain invested and each pilot would get a payout when he or she retired; however, the company didn't have to contribute any more money to the plan.

Other companies had to fall back on the Pension Benefit Guarantee

Corporation.[89] The PBGC is a government-run insurance agency just for pensions. Airlines (and other companies) had been paying premiums to the PBGC, and it had in effect insured their pension plan. The problem here is that, as with most insurance policies, the benefits the insurance company paid out weren't anywhere near what had been promised. Most pilots who will receive PBGC money in place of their expected pension will receive pennies on the dollar for what they were promised. Many will receive even less.

This was a rough time for the entire industry. The mergers and bankruptcies continued for the better part of a decade. It didn't help that SARS, bird flu, swine flu, and the 2008 financial crisis continued to...uh...challenge...the airlines throughout this time.

Another part of the bankruptcy process involves cost-cutting measures mandated by bankruptcy court. At my company, management told the pilots that they had to take a large pay cut if the company was to survive. The pledge was that they were only going to cut pay once. It'd be a huge amount, but it do the trick. The pilot group accepted reality and voted to approve the cuts.

Shortly thereafter, management came back and said that the pilots would have to take another pay cut if they wanted the pension plan to remain solvent. In the end, the pilots accepted nearly a 50% pay cut...and lost the pension anyway.

Naturally, with times this tough, everything scaled back and many pilots were furloughed. The ones that survived furloughs were stuck with almost zero progression for years. Every pilot at Delta Air Lines knows the name of the guy who was at the bottom of the seniority list during these years because he was stuck there *for a decade*!

Before the pension finally died, the company offered early retirement to many pilots. Take a lump-sum or a reduced payment now and you still get your pension, or you can stick around for a few more years and roll the dice. Many pilots took the early out, for better or for worse.

However, most pilots weren't eligible for that golden parachute, and had no choice but to stick things out. These are the deadzoners - the pilots who were employed at a major airline the day it went bankrupt. They lost their pension, but unlike us, they have less time to use new

---

[89] https://www.pbgc.gov/

401K plans to build up retirement savings. They were immediately behind the retirement savings power curve because they'd lived the last decade (or two or three) thinking that they didn't need to save. They'd always had a pension to look forward to.

Today's deadzoners will tell you that their companies could have preserved their pension funds. Some of them accuse their companies of intentionally pushing things toward bankruptcy. We'll never know if those accusations are true or not, but we do know that the current generation of deadzoners will never be "made whole."

I feel bad for them. I wish there was more we could do for them. I would even support policies that paid them a little extra at my expense because I realize that I would not have the great job I do today if not for their sacrifice. We'll see if our companies and our pilot groups have the creativity and moral backbone to make that happen.

When I look at our industry today, I can't help but perceive a shadow of doom looming over my sea of optimism. Pay and benefits are high. The economy is booming. People are happy. All it will take is one bad day and we could find ourselves hurting, much like the deadzoners.

Thankfully, few airlines still have a pension, so none of us has been deceived into thinking that someone else will take care of retirement for us. Anyone starting at a major airline these days has plenty of time to take advantage of 401K plans and other savings to put away enough to enjoy a comfortable retirement. However, if things were to go bad and we saw another round of 50% pay cuts, the Pilot Math equations would get out of balance very quickly.

I hope that this doesn't happen. I hope things will stay good for a very long time. However, we need to be realistic about the fact that things could go wrong. If they did, we'd each have to take some significant action.

One of the reasons the term "deadzoners" even exists is that they can't help telling everyone they meet about how badly they got screwed. In their defense, they did get screwed. Unfortunately, as many of them approach retirement, they're starting to worry that they'll run out of money before they die.

I feel terrible for that generation of deadzoners. I hope they're taking advantage of these good times to make up as much of their shortfall as they can, within reason. Unfortunately, some of them spent too long clinging to hope of a restored pension and failed to take the action necessary to protect their families financially.

Poor Old Joe falls into this group. When his company went bankrupt and he took his massive pay cut, he had just closed on a gorgeous "captain's house." This house had it all...4,500 square feet, 5 bedrooms, a home theater, a pool, new furniture to fill it all up, with tennis courts and a golf course just down the street (and a $500/month Homeowners Association fee to cover their upkeep.) He'd treated himself to a brand-new Corvette to park in the driveway. He'd raised some smart kids and they all got into top private schools. His daughters had been taught that they deserved to dream big for their weddings and had spent accordingly.

Having taken a 50% pay cut, Joe couldn't afford any of this, but he refused to give it up. He told himself: "My family is accustomed to a certain standard of living. I refuse to deny them that. It's not their fault we're in this situation. It's the damned airline's fault!"

Sadly, Old Joe never realized that it doesn't matter who was at fault. The money was gone and it's still not coming back.

Joe attempted to fund all this with two bad choices. First, he took on debt. Second, he chose not to maximize his contributions to his new 401K plan because he needed the cash elsewhere.

You've seen the spreadsheets. You know that Pilot Math doesn't work if you are spending like crazy and/or not saving. Poor Joe was immediately doomed.

Eventually, he realized the dire straits he was in. He pared back his expenses slightly, and started increasing his savings. However, he still didn't want to give up his house or his toys. He felt at least a little bit entitled and had a tough time facing reality. (Funny, I thought those were exclusively the traits of young whippersnappers who don't know how hard we old graybeards used to have it....) Although the government, or the market, or the company, or...*someone*...screwed him, Poor Old Joe also played a role in his current financial emergency.

I'm not telling you about Joe's generation to pick on him. He was a victim on many fronts: severe macroeconomic turbulence, a lifetime of consumerist brainwashing, and a company that had to declare bankruptcy because it had no mathematical way to honor the promises it had made. I hope my generation of airline pilots can figure out a way to help Joe as he enters retirement. However, we need to understand the severity of his situation so we don't make the same mistakes.

If (or when) our industry again hits hard times, we cannot afford to ignore reality like Poor Old Joe. In the event of a bankruptcy or other catastrophe that cuts our pay or benefits, we need to adjust our Pilot Math to protect our families' future.

What follows here is essentially an emergency procedures checklist. None of this is fun, or desirable. I imagine I'd be very angry and feel wronged at finding myself in this situation.

Unfortunately, like some emergencies in aviation, my feelings about the situation don't matter. If my aircraft catches on fire, my choice is to try to put the fire out and land ASAP...or burn up. If I lose all my engines, my options are to find a suitable runway...or crash.

If I suddenly become a deadzoner, my options are to follow this checklist...or crash financially. So, here goes. In case of economic tragedy, do this:

Cut housing costs

Houses are expensive. There's mortgage, interest, taxes, utilities, maintenance, furnishings, and more. If I'm living in a house that I can barely afford on my current salary, it would be simply illogical to continue living in that house after taking a massive pay cut. Even a house that may have been "sensible" in the past might end up being too much to handle in a severe downturn.

As a new deadzoner, I would consider moving to a new part of town, or even a completely different part of the country. If I was previously commuting to my airline job, I'd consider moving to my airline base to make myself available for the extra pay opportunities that will eventually arise when things recover. If I lived in a state I loved with high taxes, I'd consider moving to one I don't love as much to pay less tax. This move doesn't have to be forever. If times improve, I could move back to a place I like more. However, the fire marshal has to agree that the emergency is over before I get to taxi back to parking, right?

I've mentioned BiggerPockets.com repeatedly throughout this book. Their community is truly a wealth of ideas for minimizing housing costs. Before I moved, I would start spending a lot of time there reading about ways to help make ends meet.

One of the reasons I love including real estate as part of my Treasure

Bath is that it opens up some great opportunities if things go bad. If I'd been studying real estate for years on the day of a market crash, I'd already have an education that would equip me to move quickly and find a better housing situation. If I already own some smart rental properties, I'll have a recession-proof stream of income to help support my family while my wages are low. One of those properties could even be a fallback plan. This is exactly how I view one home that my family owns.

My wife bought a house when she got assigned to Ellsworth AFB, SD, in 2006. We were only there a few years and didn't have enough equity to justify selling it when we moved away. It's a nice 4/2 with a big yard, located within walking distance of one of the best elementary schools in Rapid City. It's an ideal rental, and we've had tenants in it ever since.

We don't owe that much money on the house. Though we're waiting to pay that mortgage off for the tax benefits, we have a pot of money earmarked for just that purpose if it became necessary. If everything went to hell, we could have that house paid off in a matter of days and move our family there. We love the area and the cost of living there is very low, as long as you're not a tourist. I'd have to commute for work, but our family could survive there very happily, even if I took a giant pay cut.

This is the power of having a Treasure Bath. It gives you options to stand in the worst possible storms and brush the water off your jacket like it's just a trickle.

Cut car costs

We don't realize it because many of the costs are easy to overlook, but owning a car is extremely expensive. If you don't believe me, there's a free calculator on Edmund's that you can use to prove me right.[90]

If economic disaster strikes, there is no excuse to be making payments on and driving expensive cars. If I suddenly got hit with a 50% pay cut, I'd sell at least one of my cars. If we were making payments on two new cars, I might consider selling both and buying a used Toyota Corolla or Nissan Leaf. My wife and I can share a car.

---

[90] https://www.edmunds.com/tco.html

When our kids get old enough, they can become the family taxi service.

If you've already figured out Pilot Math, you'll be way ahead of the game here too. Worst case, you're only making payments on one car at a time. You realize that tying your ego to your car will only drown you in a flood of economic disaster. You have affordable, efficient cars that minimize (optimize) the costs of car ownership as much as possible. These cars have high resale value and become increasingly desirable in bad economies. You'll have no trouble getting your money's worth if you decide to sell one. If you have more than one car, and they're all efficient and paid off, you may be able to keep them anyway.

Get rid of toys

I own an airplane - a 1950 C-170A. It's a lot of fun, but it's a frivolous expense. You could describe a boat, jet skis, RVs, pickup trucks, and many other toys the same way. In the face of an economic disaster, my toy would go immediately. Worst case, it'd get parked in a hangar and I'd stop insuring it for flying operations until I could afford to fly it again.

There is simply no excuse for drowning in the depths of financial disaster with your hands holding white-knuckled to your toys.

Have "The Talk" with your family

History and literature are replete with stories of families reaching financial ruin because the a spouse or parents were ashamed to explain their hard times to their families. They tried to ignore the truth and let their families live (and spend) as if nothing had changed. Willfully avoiding this truth will never help you.

In this situation, you absolutely must sit down with your entire family and explain your new financial reality. This could have some severe lasting impacts. Elective shopping trips will be cancelled. Kids may have to give up spots on expensive traveling sports teams. Our society seems stuck on the idea that a child is entitled to attend any college that will admit him or her. This won't be the case for your kids, and they must understand that. (If you're having trouble coming to terms with this, you need to read Malcolm Gladwell's fantastic book,

David and Goliath.[91] He argues very convincingly that going to a big name school isn't all it's cracked up to be.)

Your kids will need to pursue scholarships. They may need to start at a local community college. They may need to work to fund some part of their education. There is no unlimited free ride. You'll have to adopt a similar mindset for school trips, home remodeling, and weddings. (You just read the chapter on Baby Pilot Math, so you've hopefully started brainwashing your kids to favor these strategies anyway.)

As a guy and a cheap-ass pilot, I'm scandalized by all the wedding-themed TV shows around today. One show features girls who walk into stores planning to spend thousands of dollars on wedding dresses...and they almost all end up going over budget. Others highlight a stream of increasingly over-the-top weddings that cost more that most American families spend on college. The hosts of these shows gush over how wonderful everything is and always assure the bride that she has "earned" her special day.

If a child's parents are paying for the wedding, or if the wedding is being funded with debt, then almost by definition, the child hasn't earned anything. If your family is in financial chaos, you cannot afford to spend an unlimited amount of money on a single party.

That said, the existence of these TV shows, and the rest of the wedding "industry," show that our society still values the institution of marriage. Weddings are important ways for us to celebrate a milestone in our kids' lives, and gather families together. In discussing this section, my wife informed me that simply refusing to pay anything here probably isn't an option. The cheap and unsentimental pilot in me resists this notion, but I'll defer to her superior judgement in this case, like I do in most cases.

If you're going to help pay for a child's wedding, and I won't fault you if you do, the important thing is to have a plan. When you decide it's time to have kids, you and your spouse will need to start having a series of conversations. When can you kid get a smartphone and will he or she have to pay for it? Will you provide a car for him or her to drive? Will you pay for college, and if so, then how much? Do you

---

[91] Here's an Amazon Affiliate link. Warning, you won't be able to put this book down! https://amzn.to/30UmXs5

plan to provide money toward your kid's eventual wedding.

As long as you're thinking about these things early, you can use Pilot Math to designate a mini-Treasure Bath set aside for each of these purposes. If you want to pay toward an eventual wedding, then start putting a few dollars each month into a specifically designated investment account early in that kid's life, just like you should have done with a 529 plan for his or her education. This wedding investment account will be subject to taxes, but at least it'll be earning interest for a couple decades first.

We're talking about this situation based on the assumption that we've fallen on hard times and money is suddenly tight. One of the most beautiful, enduring principles of Pilot Math is that if you save as much as you can while times are good, your family will be okay when times aren't. If you suddenly have to come up with a bunch of money on short notice, it's an emergency. If the money has been sitting in an investment account for a decade or more, a furlough or other catastrophe doesn't change anything. The money is still in that account. If the economy tanks, the balance in this account might decrease, but it would take a very bad recession to wipe out a decade or more of investment gains.

When the time comes, don't simply ask your kid, "What do you want for your wedding?" This open-ended question runs the danger of suggesting that there are no cost limits. Instead, I'm hoping to go with something along the lines of, "We love you, we're proud of you, and we're happy that you've found someone to marry. We want to help you celebrate. Here's the amount of money we've saved up to contribute. How can we help you make this enough?"

Hopefully, you've been teaching your kid about Pilot Math for his or her entire life. He or she should at least understand how to look at this little Bath full of Treasure and budget it out. With my kids, I'm hoping that if his or her desires exceed the amount we've offered, he or she will work to fund things in other (debt-free) ways. If they're going to ask me for money, they'd better be willing to ask the in-laws. I hope I'll also be able to inspire enough of a work ethic in my kids that they'd take pride in going out and earning some of the money they need themselves. (I have, thus far, failed miserably at my goal. Thankfully, I still have some time.)

I also plan to suggest that my kids get creative about how they do things. The blogosphere has a seemingly infinite number of writers who talk about how to do a wedding on a budget. I won't insist that a child uses all of the ideas out there, but there's nothing wrong with considering some of them. My wife and her friends made centerpieces for the tables at our wedding. We hired the spouse of a friend from my squadron to take pictures. She did a fantastic job for a very reasonable price. These are just a couple ways we saved a little money while still enjoying a fantastic experience with our friends and family.

I feel that between planning and saving ahead, encouraging your kids to find at least some of their own funding, and encouraging them to be creative, it's possible to help your son or daughter have a wonderful wedding experience, without having to simply say "No!" to everything or bankrupt yourself.

For better or for worse, things like weekend entertainment and family vacations will need to get a lot cheaper in this situation too. It turns out that human beings knew how to have fun long before the advent of theme parks and international airline travel. You'll need to work with your family to find ways to have fun without spending a lot of money. I'd expect to spend a lot of time enjoying the mountains or beaches near my house.

Side Hustle

I made side hustles part of Pilot Math (next chapter) more because they enrich our lives, than because we airline pilots need the cash. In the face of economic disaster, that changes. A pay cut or furlough at a major airline is the perfect excuse to start or expand on a lucrative side hustle.

If you've been enjoying something as just a hobby or doing low-volume business, you should look for ways to start monetizing your efforts more effectively. If you've already adopted this Pilot Math principle, you might have something profitable already in place. In a best-case scenario, you might be able to increase your profitability enough to make up for your lost airline pay.

Although I'm pretty hard on deadzoners like Poor Old Joe, not every pilot in his position made such bad decisions. I've flown with more than one senior captain who started or already had a side-hustle when our company went bankrupt. Many of them now have an overflowing Treasure Bath thanks to these businesses, and in spite of the same economic challenges that still give Joe fits. There was no functional difference between these deadzoners other than the fact that the ones who are currently solvent went out and did something to improve their situation instead of avoiding the truth and complaining.

For some deadzoners, the military was this side hustle. Whether they went back onto active duty to fight the war in 2001, or they were just able to pick up full-time orders in the Guard or Reserves, the military saved their families. I've heard that Southwest even worked with the Air Force to help make sure that some of their pilots got activated, precluding the need to furlough them. Having military service as a fallback in case of economic crisis is one of the many reasons I believe the ultimate career path for a military pilot includes joining the airlines ASAP while keeping a foot in the Guard or Reserves.

Continue Saving!

A market crash is the worst possible time to panic and stop saving. (It's also the worst possible time to sell!) When the market is down, it means that stocks are on sale. Over the very long-term, the stock market always goes up. No matter how hard it falls, it will beat all previous record highs in the future. One of the reasons to cut so many costs in hard times is to protect your ability to continue investing while assets are cheap.

If you take a 50% pay cut, you must realize that it will take a very long time for your pay to get back to where it was. (Adjusting for inflation, today's wonderful pay rates are still only starting to approach the levels they were at before 9/11 and the waves of bankruptcies.) You will spend many years not making as much money and you won't be able to pump as much into your retirement accounts as you'd like. This means that the power of compounding interest is even more important. You need to do everything you can to get money into your accounts ASAP to give it the maximum amount of time to grow before you need to start drawing on it.

You also need that money to be in the market when the recovery starts to happen. You'll spend the rest of your life kicking yourself if you miss out on that opportunity. Ask anyone who panicked in 2009, sold everything, then waited until 2012 to start investing again.

[End of Checklist]

194

This certainly isn't an exhaustive list. There are many other useful things your family may be able to adjust if (or when) our industry has another bad day. I feel that it's important to have frank and open discussions about finances with your spouse. He or she needs to understand Pilot Math, and you two need to know exactly what your financial plans are. I believe that you should also discuss your emergency plan for a worst-case scenario. This list should be taken as a starting place from which you build a plan specific to your family's situation.

While another black swan event would really put a damper on the fun of our career, this discussion only continues to prove the power of Pilot Math. If you've worked hard to fill up your Treasure Bath as quickly as possible, you can potentially make yourself invulnerable to a bad day.

If your Treasure Bath is so full that a 4% withdrawal rate can cover all of your family's needs, then who cares if you take a pay cut? We've already discussed the idea that you could declare FIRE and quit mandatory full-time work once the volume of your treasure bath equals 25x your annual spending.

Take a moment to think about how powerful you'd feel in that situation.

(Yes, if the market just tanked, 4% of your current account balance probably won't cover your spending like it would have the day before. If you're already drawing from your Treasure Bath you'll need to adjust your spending for a while. If you have a side hustle, or even reduced pay at a full-time airline pilot job, you should still be able to make ends meet. Times will get better, and your portfolio will end up worth more than it has on the day the market crashed. You'll be able to raise your spending again at that point.

It's also important to note that it would take terrible timing on a really, really bad day to affect your Treasure Bath catastrophically. People a lot better with money than you or me have examined the entire history of the stock market. There are only a few 30-year periods where a Treasure Bath containing 25x annual spending would not survive even the worst collapses in US history...even when those periods included the Great Depression. In most of those cases, the balance of those savings doubled by the end of the 30-year period. Michael Kitces has studied this extensively and you can read his research if you want a second opinion.)[92]

Imagine that Joe is your neighbor. On the day that disaster strikes he'll be shell-shocked, walking around on the verge of tears. He and his family will be overwhelmed with fear and uncertainty. Everyone will be angry, but there will be nowhere to turn for help. From that day forward, Joe will be at work *all the time*. He'll have to be because of all the expenses he has to cover. He'll miss out on important family events, his health will suffer, and his job will become an obligation instead of a passion. Poor Old Joe.

In contrast, you have a Treasure Bath full enough to support all of your family's needs, you won't have to worry about anything. You may have to forego some luxuries, but you won't be facing deprivation or the embarrassment of having any of your property repossessed. Whether you get to keep your major airline job, you end up furloughed at a regional airline, or you end up elsewhere, you won't have to be frustrated about your pay cut. You won't have to work extra hours...all because you won't need the money. Sure, you won't turn down the drastically reduced paychecks, but they'll only add to the comfortable depths of your Treasure Bath. You'll even have the option to work less than full-time, allowing Joe to pick up all your extra flying, and continue enjoying time with your family.

We'll discuss later how to present the ideas behind Pilot Math to your non-pilot spouse. If you're finding it difficult to get him or her onboard, illustrating this type of financial security in the face of an economic crisis should help. Your spouse might not understand the potential benefits of turning your full-time airline job into a side hustle, but he or she will absolutely support a plan that means your kids don't go hungry if you lose your job.

You may have no intention of abandoning mandatory full-time work now while times are good. However, if things suddenly change, having that Treasure Bath ready to go gives you all the options. It's like having an extra hour of fuel in the tanks when you get to your destination to find that a thunderstorm has popped up, or having an extra 5000' of altitude between you and the mountains when an engine failure forces you to drift down. I cannot overstate the sense of power

---

[92] https://www.kitces.com/

and security that comes from maximizing your application of Pilot Math as early as possible in your career. Having a Bath full of Treasure makes you invulnerable to many threats that keep most pilots up at night.

I hope we get to ride these high times for decades, but if something happens, Pilot Math can make sure you weather the storm in comfort.

CHAPTER FIFTEEN
Side-Hustles

There's a good reason that it took so long to get to the chapter about side-hustles in this book. I think they're an important part of achieving a balanced life, but it's a good idea to not get too serious about them before you have the rest of your Pilot Math working for you.

I've been a flight instructor for years, and got to fill the role of chief pilot a couple times. I believe strongly that if a person is going to go to the trouble of becoming a pilot, that flying has to be his or her first professional priority. You absolutely do not want to be the most interesting person in the world, with all kinds of pots on the fire, if it means you suck at your primary flying job.

When I joined the Air Force, I blithely assumed that everyone there would treat flying as the priority and pursue excellence at it as a lifelong passion. It's an understatement to say that I was disappointed. On an individual level, most of the pilots I knew worked hard to be good at flying. However, on an organizational level, the Air Force prioritized everything but flying. I will never forget the day when my base commander gathered all the officers in the wing and explained how, "It doesn't matter whether you can fly or not. Your ability to get promoted in the military depends entirely on your ability to get a master's degree and complete your Professional Military Education."

The infection of this mentality had already spread throughout the rest of the Air Force. I later found myself as an instructor pilot in a PC-12 one night in Afghanistan as my copilot tried to land our aircraft without any awareness of or attempt to correct for strong crosswinds. He had more than 900 hours and was slated for upgrade to aircraft commander, yet he had let a fundamental pilot skill slip away...like the topsoil blowing across the runway in that gusty Afghani dust bowl. None of that mattered to the Air Force though. This guy looked great on paper! He had a master's degree and he'd completed Squadron Officer's School. He as on the path to command!

I saw similar patterns in other pilots throughout my Air Force career. It didn't cause immediate problems in the Air Force because an officer's career really does depend on things other than flying. However, for a future airline pilot, all those non-flying distractions (you could even think of them as side-hustles) were getting in the way of what really mattered.

Some of the Air Force pilots I know who prioritized these side-hustles over flying are still on active duty. They revel in positions of great responsibility. Unfortunately, they completed staff and school assignments to go back and command flying squadrons not realizing that their lack of basic flying chops erodes their authority and credibility as leaders. (I take this dim view of their priorities realizing that they look down on me for prioritizing flying over pursuing the command track. Since we're all pilots on some level, each of us knows, objectively, that he is better than the other. I guess that's fair, and I always enjoy debating the principles behind our decisions together over frosty beverages.)

The point here is that while you're a young pilot, your priority must be flying. Get all the hours and experience you can. Yes, you need hobbies to keep you from going crazy, but you should not let other things like a time-intensive side-hustle impact your development as a pilot.

You also need to make sure that you focus on reaching a point where your pilot job pays real money before you start chasing side-gigs that may or may not pay well.

If anyone chooses to criticize the ideas behind my Pilot Math, they'll pick side-hustles as an easy target. A pilot might make a few hundred dollars for photographing a wedding on a Saturday. As a major airline pilot on second year pay, I made more than $1000 for every day that I spent at work. If I just picked up one extra trip per month at regular pay, I'd make more in one day than I could with a whole month of photography. And at my company, that extra day of work can frequently be obtained at premium (double) pay!

There are very few side-hustles more lucrative than just doing extra work at your major airline job. If some other side-hustle is going to keep you away from your family for the day anyway, you're better off just picking up extra flying.

That said, there isn't always extra flying to be had. At most airlines, extra flying gets awarded in order of seniority. If you're junior, you might not get what you want. If your category is well-staffed, there may not be much, if any, extra flying to go around.

It's also possible to find side-hustles that fit into periods of time smaller than a whole day. You can pursue these opportunities on days that you'd be home with your family anyway. Maybe you like building things in the garage. Maybe your kids enjoy helping, and you build planter boxes together to sell on Etsy. Not only do you make money while enjoying time with your kids, you get to teach junior about the value of work and managing a business. You're firing on all cylinders there.

Maybe your kids are all school-aged and your spouse works. You have a few hours to yourself every weekday. What side-hustle could you fit into those hours?

I mentioned that I've been teaching in the A5 for Icon Aircraft. On days that I'm home anyway I can leave early to beat traffic, while my wife drops the kids off at school on the way to work. I have plenty of time to get a flight or two with my students and get home in time to pick the kids up from school. I enjoy flying. I make some money. I lose zero time with my family. It's awesome.

I do not include side-hustles in Pilot Math as a replacement for your day job. I intend them as things you'd be doing in your free-time, when you wouldn't be at work anyway. (And with this statement, I hope I've successfully knocked down any straw men who would oppose my affinity for side-hustling.)

I word this concept as an economic undertaking, a "hustle." However, I use this idea interchangeably with the idea of a hobby. A side-hustle doesn't have to be something that makes money. In fact, many of my hobbies are drains on my time and money. If they bring me joy in life, then I'm happy to trade my limited resources for doing them.

I firmly believe that we all need things like this outside of work. The most disgruntled pilots I know seem to have no hobbies other than haunting Facebook groups and forums where they spend all day talking about their jobs. I feel bad for these pilots.

You need something more than this, even if it's something that will never earn you a dime. The funny thing is, most people I know who are imaginative and disciplined enough to become pilots end up finding ways to make money from their hobbies without even trying.

One example of someone like this is the father of some of my friends. (We'll call him Clark.) He's a talented and hardworking man for whom I have great respect. He had a full-time job of some kind, but I never even understood was it was. I mostly knew him as a photographer.

Clark learned photography as a hobby, like many of us do, but had never pursued it professionally. One day he was asked to speak (about his day job) at a career fair at his daughter's school. When he was done, there was some commotion because the next speaker, a photographer, hadn't showed up. He said, "I know a little about photography." At a loss for what to do, the event organizer sent him back out on stage. The crowd loved Clark's presentation and he realized that he knew more about photography than he'd thought. He decided to see if he could use it to make any money.

He went home, picked out some of his best photos, and entered them in some contests. He won prizes. He offered to take senior pictures for some friends who had a child approaching graduation. The pictures were good and word spread. He got asked to photograph at a wedding. His work was great, and word spread. By the time he took my senior pictures, he'd built an entire studio onto the side of his house. Every square inch of the studio's walls was covered in gorgeous, award-winning photographs. Over his career, he probably did senior pictures for hundreds of kids in our town. He did dozens, if not hundreds, of weddings and family photo shoots. He had to turn away lucrative offers because his work ended up in such high demand.

He had not originally set out to become an award-winning professional photographer, but he did anyway. He loved his side hustle. He would have wanted to spend his nights and weekends taking pictures anyway. His family benefited greatly from his skills.

I don't expect you to monetize all of your hobbies, but you would be surprised at how easily it can happen.

Another reason I think involved hobbies and side-hustles should wait until you're established in a real pilot job is that they tend to involve expense or risk. Maybe you aspire to be a champion wakeboarder. That's a great hobby for a major airline pilot, but far too expensive for a young lieutenant or regional airline FO with nothing more than a few pennies in your Treasure Bath.

Many side-hustles do end up as business ventures, and that comes with a lot of pressure. The vast majority of small businesses fail within a few years. If a business venture is pivotal to your family's solvency, it immediately transforms from hobby to chore. The venture itself is less fun, and the increased stress in your life just makes everything worse.

On the other hand, if you can approach a side-hustle from a position of financial strength, it can be a blast. If your financial future is assured whether your business succeeds or not, you can afford to try big innovations and take risks with the potential for large payoffs.

When I applied for my job at Icon, I didn't even know how much it paid. It didn't matter. My airline job more than covered my family's needs and my wife and I already had a Treasure Bath available in case of trouble. I applied to teach in the Icon because I loved the aircraft, I loved teaching, and I wanted to spend my free time flying it. My interview was extremely low-stress because failing to get the job would have had zero impact on my family's well-being. Instead of being nervous and tripping all over my words, I was able to exude my love for the company, the product, and flight instructing in general. Apparently my enthusiasm wasn't too obnoxious because they hired me. I've enjoyed flying the A5 ever since.

It turns out the money is far better than I would have ever imagined, but since I'm not desperate for it, I get to work largely on my own terms. I explained up-front that I already have a full-time job and that it necessarily had to get scheduling priority in all cases. I didn't present this as an ultimatum, and I have been willing to adjust my airline schedule when possible to help out, but this was a take-it-or-leave-it proposition from me.

I would have never dreamed of approaching a potential employer with this attitude without the safety of a full Treasure Bath. Having applied Pilot Math gives me ultimate power in making my side-hustles exactly what I want them to be.

Although small business ventures carry a lot of risk at first, they can be an additional source of strength once they get established.

All it takes is one bad day for an airline pilot career to become a nightmare. A medical issue could prevent any one of us from flying for months or even years. On an industry-wide scale, we're subject to economics, weather, terrorism, and other threats. If, for any reason, a pilot's main job goes away, it's sure nice to have a side-hustle to fall back on.

An established side-hustle won't immediately provide enough money to replace your airline pilot salary, but it's a lot better than sitting around your house in your boxer shorts complaining about being unemployed. The profitability of many side-hustles is limited by the time and energy we have available to invest in them. Losing your day job, even temporarily, gives you plenty of time to work on scaling-up a part-time venture. If you're later able to return to flying you then have the option of scaling back your efforts, or hiring help to maintain or even continue growing your business.

I've tried to give some specific, actionable advice in this book. I could write volumes about side-hustles, but I've already covered the topic in some detail on The Pilot Network.[93] I'm also building a list of side-hustle ideas and opportunities at pilotmathtreasurebath.com/side-hustles.[94]

If these resources aren't enough for you, there's an overwhelming number of blogs and podcasts available for free about this topic on the internet. A site called Side Hustle Nation is a good place to start.[95]

Real estate also makes a great part-time job for airline pilots. I know a few pilots who also work as real estate agents. I know some who own rentals and others who flip homes. Two of them have given up professional aviation entirely because they enjoy real estate so much and the money is too good. I don't know that I could ever go that far, but having a Bathtub brimming with Treasure absolutely gives you the option. At that point, it's just a game to see how long it takes you to make enough money selling houses to buy your own amphibious twin Aircam. (Look it up on YouTube. Your spouse will hate me!)[96]

You don't have to make money with a side-hustle, but you need something to enjoy in your life other than work. Don't let it distract from your primary flying job before you're established at a major airline, but you need something to help you achieve balance. If you

---

[93] https://community.thepilotnetwork.org/posts/soside-hustles
[94] http://pilotmathtreasurebath.com/side-hustles
[95] https://www.sidehustlenation.com/
[96] https://www.youtube.com/results?search_query=aircam

choose to monetize a hobby, it can provide some welcome adventure in your life and potentially increase your financial security in case of an economic downturn.

Of course, if you can make money from a side-hustle without earning less at your primary job, it will only increase the rate at which your Treasure Bath fills up. I'm not counting on income from any of my side-hustles when I try to prognosticate my financial future, but I don't mind noticing that I'm ahead of the power curve when the extra income shows up.

CHAPTER SIXTEEN

Debrief

Thank you for sticking with me this far. We've covered all the required maneuvers and it's time to debrief this little sortie into setting you up for financial freedom.

I've presented my body of ideas under a framework that I call Pilot Math. I've been pretty liberal with my metaphor of a Treasure Bath, hoping that using a light-hearted mental image would help us not to take ourselves too seriously. This is not some get rich quick scheme. It's not some guy with slicked-back hair and an $3000 suit selling you a ticket to an expensive course where he spends half the day reversing the flow of hot air through your compressor section. The ideas I'm presenting take time, effort, and discipline to succeed.

I hope I've supported my claims and estimates sufficiently for you. I spelled out your potential career earnings as a professional pilot. They're based on real data, and my experience as both a military officer and a major airline pilot. I tried to be conservative to avoid painting too rosy a picture for you. I honestly believe my airline compensation estimates to be so much lower than average that it'd be fair to call them inaccurate. That should give you comfort. If you're willing to work hard in the short-term, your Treasure Bath will fill up even faster than I've shown here. Even if things in our profession slow down quite a bit, these numbers should still be in the ballpark. If that's the case, you have the potential to earn $8-10M, or more, over the course of your career as a pilot.

Don't let that money go to waste!

If you start applying Pilot Math as early as possible in your career, your Treasure Bath will rapidly reach a level where you achieve complete financial freedom. The passive income from your investments will be more than enough to cover your family's needs, and all work will become optional for the rest of your life.

I want you to have that option!

The pursuit of a Treasure Bath isn't about having a bunch of money. I hope the picture on the cover of this book illustrates how ridiculous I think it is to make money a goal, in and of itself. Having a Treasure Bath is all about giving you the choice to do whatever you want in life. If you're like me, you'll want to continue working even after you get to that point. I think the FIRE movement gives us some very valuable perspective on life, but I am the last person on Earth who will advocate you hit your number and then immediately jump into what mainstream America views as "retirement."

However, the moment you cross the threshold on not needing to work, everything about your job changes. Do you remember how Peter Gibbons changed in the movie *Office Space* the day he realized that he no longer needed his job? When your Treasure Bath fills up enough to support your family's needs, you get to enjoy the exact same feeling.

Yes, there will still be long days, frustrating company policies, and difficult coworkers. However, once you no longer need your job, none of that matters as much. Having the option to adjust the amount of work you do, or just walk away from it whenever you want, makes all the tough times more bearable.

I worry that we pilots make the mistake of spending more time at work than we have to...and our families suffer greatly as a result. I believe that they'd rather have more time with us than own a housefull of stuff.

When you have a Treasure Bath, you can still enjoy fulfilling work while spending far more time with your family. You get the best of both worlds. If anything, I expect to someday find myself in the situation where my wife starts pestering me to go pick up an airline trip because I'm home too much. That would be a nice problem to have, wouldn't it?

Speaking of spouses, I haven't even mentioned the possibility of having an employed spouse anywhere in my calculations. It should seem significant to you that one pilot is enough to fill a Treasure Bath deep enough for the whole family.

I absolutely don't mean to imply that your spouse can't or shouldn't work if he or she wants to. Having two working parents makes it more difficult to take adequate care of a family, but it is possible. My wife and I overlapped active duty military service for 11 years, part of which included raising two terrorists...uh...kids. The Air Force made it enough of a hassle that we both decided to leave active duty, and we're glad we did. It's been much easier to find time together and take care of our kids as civilians. (We still both work. My wife works Monday and Tuesday, and I schedule my airline trips Wednesday through Sunday, averaging about 10 total days of work per month.)

You've seen the power that Pilot Math has when it's fueled by a single income. If you add the income of a second person to that mix, the results can be amazing. Your spending needs shouldn't increase significantly, meaning you'll have even more money to dump into savings. Remember that your spouse will also become eligible for another complete set of tax-advantaged retirement accounts. Even a (tragically) low-paying job like school teacher can help significantly accelerate your progress toward financial freedom.

If you're blessed by being married to a spouse with a job, congratulations! Sock away those savings while you can, but make sure to balance your life. Don't over-do encouraging a spouse to work if he or she is resistant to the idea. Don't over-influence a spouse to not leave a bad job that he or she hates. It's easy to get used to the luxury of a double income, but you're far better off married with one income than divorced!

Remember, we based all of the Pilot Math in this book on single-income numbers. If your spouse enjoys work and your family lives a balanced life, he or she will probably end up finding a way to make money at some point. There's no need to push.

I'm blessed by being married to someone with more talent and diligence than me. She also makes more money than I probably ever will. I freely admit that our annual spending exceeds those of the average upper-middle-class family that I used in this book. To be honest, our spending is a lot closer to what I allow for a major airline captain.

I've rationalized this for myself two ways: 1) Although I've always tried to live frugally and been onboard with the idea of a large savings rate, I only recently discovered the math that I've shamelessly stolen and rebranded here as Pilot Math.[97] 2) As a family, my wife and I made double officer pay (plus pilot and dentist bonuses) while we were in the military, and we're both making more now as civilians. Our combined income is certainly on par with that of a major airline captain, so I suppose we're justified in spending as much as I allowed for that captain. I'm still learning to apply these principles in my own life, but I'm not perfect yet. Please forgive me for that. I promise that I'm constantly working to spend less and save more.

I could have waited until my life was so optimized that I had full moral authority to preach to you about spending, saving, and investing. At best though, that would have cost you years of progress on your own Treasure Bath. I've decided to go with General Patton's adage: "A good plan violently executed now is better than a perfect plan executed next week." If my personal shortcomings detract from anything in this book, please focus on the ideas and take from them what you can. The math doesn't lie.

For the examples we looked at in this book, I chose $57,758 as an average amount of spending. It allows all kinds of luxuries, to include:

- A mortgage on a house.
- Owning two or more reliable cars, making payments on one new car at all times.
- Keeping the major appliances in your home up-to-date.
- Budgets for restaurants, entertainment, pets, almost $100 to spend on drapes every year, and much more.

None of that should feel like a life of deprivation. It's more than the average spending of all Americans who earn as much as $69,999 per year. It's a ridiculous amount of spending compared to most of the human beings on our planet.

If you start to feel deprived as you try to optimize your spending, you've gone too far. There is no point in being miserable for a decade...just to produce a passive income that is only capable of

---

[97] Here's the source document: http://www.mrmoneymustache.com/2012/01/13/the-shockingly-simple-math-behind-early-retirement/. This is quite possibly the most important blog post in the history of the Financial Independence movement. Once you read it, you will never view money or personal finance the same way again. Enjoy!

keeping you at the same level of misery for the rest of your life. Chances are that you can find a way to get what you feel like you're missing out on for less. However, sometimes you really do get what you pay for. Don't feel bad if you have to adjust your spending back up just a little for the sake of your own sanity.

Being frugal is not the same as being cheap. Frugality isn't about misery. Spend money on the things that matter to you, and optimize where you can. You'll find that you get better at frugality as time goes on. You may not even notice it, but you won't be able to stop yourself.

I firmly believe that every person in the world is capable of living an amazing life with the annual spending figures that we chose here. This doesn't mean you're entitled live anywhere you want no matter what. It doesn't mean you're entitled to have whatever you want.

There's a fascinating and talented FIRE blogger named Paula Pant who writes a blog called Afford Anything.[98] You can probably figure out her theme from the blog's name, and I believe it's true. If you want to fill up a Treasure Bath while living in downtown New York City, you absolutely can. However, you can't afford that while you and your spouse drive a pair of brand new Teslas, eat in fancy restaurants all the time, constantly buy expensive clothing, and go to Broadway shows every night, etc. You have to identify the things that matter to you and focus on them.

You're entitled to decide your own attitudes and actions. You're entitled to the consequences of those actions, good or bad. You are not entitled to a single material thing in this world. If you take exception to that, you have a lot of things to figure out before this book can do you any good.

We showed that with a realistic career progression and unrealistically conservative numbers, a major airline pilot can reach financial independence at 10 years. You can even double your spending when you upgrade to major airline captain and become financially free at the 17-year point.

This assumes that you have a net worth of $0 the day you start your last full-time job. I hope that's not the case! If you can apply Pilot Math while starting your career at a regional airline or in the military, you

---

[98] https://affordanything.com/

get a head-start that can reduce the time it takes for your Treasure Bath to fill up.

In order to make this happen you need to:

1. Live frugally (not cheaply.)

Track your expenses and/or budget to keep yourself honest.

2. Eradicate bad debt.

Reasonable home, reasonable collegiate or vocational education, payments on one reasonable car at a time. No other consumer debt allowed. You will never, ever carry a credit card balance past the end of the month.

3. Invest the maximum possible amount into tax-advantaged accounts each year.

This includes:

$3,500 - $7,000	HSA
$0 - $6,000	Roth IRA
$0 - $19,000	Roth TSP or Roth 401K (if your total income is low enough make Roth accounts advantageous
$37,000 - $56,000	Traditional TSP or 401K

Depending on which of these items you're eligible for, your total tax-advantaged savings could be as high as $69,000 each year. You may also want to invest in 529 plans for tax-advantaged funding of your kids' higher education, though I didn't include those numbers in this list.

4. Invest the rest.

We've spoken for $57,758 (later $115,516) in spending and up to $69,000 in tax-advantaged investments for a total of $126,758 each year (or $184,516 once you upgrade to major airline captain.) Every other penny you earn each year goes into a taxable brokerage account at a large investment firm like Vanguard. (While you make less than $126,758, you cover your expenses and do your best to invest what's left over. There's no shame in this. A little patience and hard work will eventually boost your income.)

5. Invest Simply.

The vast majority of your investments should be in low-fee index funds. 50-100% should be in a total stock market index fund like Vanguard's VTSAX, and 0-50% of your investments can be in a low-fee bond fund like Vanguard's VBTLX if volatility scares you. Your TSP investments should be in the C Fund, or a Lifecycle fund.

6. Alternative Investments, If Desired

You're welcome to research alternative investment strategies, including various forms of real estate investing. However, there is almost nothing as low-effort for generating passive investment returns as a good index fund.

7. Side-hustles and Balance

Spend more of your life with your family and pursuing hobbies that you love. You may be able to turn a hobby into a lucrative side-hustle. This just means your Treasure Bath fills up even faster.

And that's it. If you do this, you almost can't help filling your Bath with so much Treasure that work becomes optional for the rest of your life. It won't happen overnight, and there will be headaches along the way. However, I hope you were shocked to see how quickly Pilot Math can make this happen for you.

You should note that I have zero interest vested in your choice to apply Pilot Math in your life. You bought my book, or borrowed it from someone who did. I thank you for that. My pledge to you is that at least 25% of my earnings from this book will be going to help non-profit organizations I support. The rest will hopefully go to help fund my flying habit.

Beyond that, I'm not here to up-sell you.

I have a website, pilotmathtreasurebath.com, where you can find more details and resources to help you. I hope to earn some additional revenue there through advertising or affiliate links, but have no plans to charge you money for what I put there.

My wife and I have a nice, cosy Treasure Bath of our own. As far as I'm concerned I'm already "retired" with (at least) four part-time jobs that I do because I enjoy them. Part of the reason I like those jobs so much is that my family doesn't depend on any of them to survive. Whether you choose to use Pilot Math, or not, you will have zero effect on my ability to support my family and enjoy life.

I enjoy hearing stories of how my writing helps the lives of others, but I'm not after fame either. Remember: we're all pilots...I don't care all that much what you think about me as a person. (Don't feel hurt by that. We both know that as a pilot you know you're better than me anyway, right?)

I don't expect the version of Pilot Math I presented here to work out perfectly for you, to the dollar. You'll need to adapt these numbers based on your actual income each year and your family's needs. I encourage you to build or download copies of the appropriate spreadsheets and get to work! You should not feel that you're a sub-standard human being if your situation fills up your Treasure Bath slower than the scenarios we used in this book. (Though, my numbers were conservative enough that you may be able to beat them!) Optimize where you can, work hard when it makes sense, but be sure to live a life of balance!

You also have the option of ignoring what I say. You can live the traditional life of a US airline pilot: spend like crazy, work like a dog until 65, retire from a job that ceased to be a passion for you long ago, and spend 20-ish years trying not to starve. This is the best that Poor Old Joe can hope for. You're welcome to it, but I say we can all do better!

There will be people to criticize the ideas I've presented here. They'll say that my spending figures are unrealistic, that my (and JL Collins') take on investing is naive, that our jobs will be taken over by robots in a matter of years. I hope those nay-sayers are more wrong than I am.

The interesting thing about Pilot Math is that it doesn't matter. Once you have money earning passive income, it continues to work for you forever. If the FAA was only 15 years away from approving fully-autonomous passenger airline operations (um, not likely) there would still be enough time for a disciplined pilot to start at a regional airline and end up with a Treasure Bath full enough to never work again the day he or she finally got replaced by a robot.

There's something else interesting about Pilot Math. It gives us the hope of achieving financial freedom relatively early in life and never suffering through mandatory work again. If all else fails what will we do? We'll go back to mandatory full-time work...just like everyone else has been doing the entire time.

Jason Depew

Our worst case scenario is everyone else's everyday life.

What do we have to lose?

CHAPTER SEVENTEEN

The Way Forward

Okay already Emet, I'm sold. Pilot Math is great. I want a Treasure Bath. So now what?

Unfortunately, the first thing you need to do is be patient. I've already mentioned that this is not a get rich quick scheme. You're looking at 10 years, give or take, after you get to a major airline before your Treasure Bath is full enough to support your annual spending through passive income. You were already planning to be at your airline that long anyway, so we're not talking about any drastic job-related measures.

Follow the steps I outlined throughout this book, and summarized in the last chapter. If you don't know where to start, use those steps to make yourself a checklist. Start by tracking your spending. Once you do, you can't help identifying ways to optimize your life and reduce waste. Check on your existing retirement plan contributions and adjust them as necessary. If it seems daunting, then break each step into sub-tasks and do one of those each day.

I ran cross country in high school because I was never fast enough to be a sprinter. Pilot Math is a marathon, not a sprint.

If you're married, or have a prospect in mind, you'll realize that Pilot Math doesn't work unless everyone in the family is onboard. You're going to have to explain the ideas in this book to your spouse or significant other. Whatever you do, don't treat that discussion like a decree or a mandate. I promise, it won't work.

You even need to be careful enthusiastically presenting these ideas as a sudden revelation. Sadly, these ideas are not mainstream. If you rattle them off in a single bout of zealous fervor, they'll sound crazy. If your sweetheart is a big consumer or spender, it'll be even worse.

In my experience, the best way to get someone onboard with these ideas is to Start with Why. You need to help your partner understand what your lives could look like when supported by a Treasure Bath that makes full-time work optional, and how that life differs from the one you have today.

One of my favorite financial independence bloggers, the Mad Fientist, has an article about this, mostly written by his wife.[99] She started seriously considering his ideas when they were on their honeymoon and he asked her, "What would be your perfect life?"

Answering this question seems like a fundamental part of any human being's life, and certainly of any marriage, yet how many of us have actually tried to answer it in concrete terms? How many of us just grow up, go to school, get a job, have kids, and go through life maintaining that status quo without ever considering what an ideal life would or could look like?

If you want to get your spouse onboard with the idea of Pilot Math, discussing this question is the first step. Once you've done that, everything else gets easier.

When you know your definition of a perfect life, your driving Why, it should be pretty easy to figure out how much money you'll need available to spend each year. Once you know that, you can use the charts from this book as the starting point to calculate exactly how long you'll have to work before the passive income from your Treasure Bath covers all your needs.

If you and your significant other go through that exercise together, I promise you'll be pleasantly shocked when you realize how quickly you can reach that point. Once you see that math, you can't un-see it. With your driving Why in mind, it will be easy to optimize your spending and pour Treasure into your Bath. You won't feel deprived both because you'll be working toward a bigger goal, and because I've still allowed you to spend as much as millions of other Americans who are trapped in our crazy consumerist culture. (Though, I can't promise that you won't do better than them…finding ways to spend less, save more, and reach financial freedom even sooner.)

---

[99] https://www.madfientist.com/spouse-early-retirement/

I've written this book specifically for pilots because sometimes it takes a little fear, sarcasm, ridicule, and self-deprecating humor to get through our thick skulls. However, once your significant other is onboard with the general plan, it may be worth having him or her read through this book. Let him or her know that my feelings won't be hurt by all of his or her eye-rolling at my pilot-focused language.

Finding your Why(s) and explaining the fundamental concepts of Pilot Math are just part of the discussions you need to have with your family. There is no point in pursuing this path if it feels like deprivation, or it leads you to live an unbalanced life.

You need to talk to your spouse and children about what a good, balanced life looks like for your family. How much time is okay for you to spend at work? How long should your trips or blocks of reserve days be? Are there standing days of the week when you need to be home, or can you be flexible from week to week?

You and your spouse will be making most of the big-picture financial decisions for your family, but what are your kids' monetary needs? Do they aspire to play on a traveling sports team? Do they want to pursue a pilot's license, earn welding certification, take programming courses after school, study ballet, or do other potentially expensive activities? What do they want to study in college, and what schools should they consider? How is that education going to be funded?

Very little about these conversations should be one-sided. You are opening discussions, not presenting. You also need to realize that some of these discussions will happen in bits and pieces, over time. Don't rush through any of it.

You also need to make a conscious effort to maintain balance in your personal life. I oppose extremism in almost all forms. It's good that Pilot Math is something you can't un-see; however, it's easy to get carried away with it. Don't get so enthusiastic about saving that you become cheap. Frugal is good enough. Don't get so excited about earning more money to invest that you spend all of your time on your job and side-hustles, at your family's expense. Don't spend so much time on everything else in life that your health and physical fitness suffer.

You'll be far better off reaching financial independence five years later in good health with a happy family than reaching it right away, but as a single pilot in bad health.

Once you have your family onboard and you have a plan to keep your life balanced, you go back to the checklist we talked about at the start of this chapter. If nothing else, take one idea related to reducing spending, increasing income, or investing, and execute it. Then move on to the next one. Reduce your cable bill. Open a Vanguard account. Research legal requirements for your side-hustle. Reduce your cell phone bill. Find out about backdoor Roth options for your 401k.

You could batch these tasks, doing several of them on a layover or a Saturday at home, or just do one each day. Even if you only did one item on your checklist every week, Pilot Math would still work for you in the long run. Remember, this is a marathon rather than a sprint.

All of this has the added benefit of helping you stay patient. If you're busy obsessing about all these little life changes, you won't be obsessing about the fact that you're suddenly dumping so much money into savings. When you finally get a large portion of your plan implemented, you'll be able to go back and look at your new savings rate and you'll be very pleased. It is incredibly motivating to see your account balance fill up more rapidly than ever before. It'll motivate you to find ways to live more frugally and inch your savings rate even higher.

Once you have your plan in place and you're patiently filling up your Treasure Bath, you'll find you have lots of time for further study. If you're interested, you could spend years digging deeper into every aspect of Pilot Math and further optimize your life. I've posted what I jokingly call The Pilot Math Bible on this book's companion website.[100] This collection is a list of the books, blogs, podcasts, and other resources that I referenced in formulating my ideas. Most of them are as entertaining as they are informative and you could spend many pleasant layovers digging through them.

As a pilot, you'll immediately notice that some of the people who write or speak on theses topics are morons. Some don't know enough to be pontificating on the subject at all, some are too extreme for anyone else to follow, and some are more whiny than helpful. Don't

---

[100] http://www.pilotmathtreasurebath.com/bible

give up on the resource just because you've realized that you're a vastly superior human being, compared to the author. (Especially this one!) As a pilot, you also possess the skills to pick out hidden gems of wisdom in what these people present. Take what's good and leave anything you don't like.

I don't recommend actually obsessing about any of this, but you should review your progress from time to time. Applying Pilot Math is a lot like instrument flying, which can be summed-up in 7 words: "Establish power and pitch. Trim. Crosscheck. Adjust." Check your spending on Mint, Personal Capital, or YNAB to see if any adjustments need to be made. Review your investments and revel in the increasing depth of your Treasure Bath. Talk with your spouse and kids to make sure you haven't accidentally pushed yourselves past frugality into deprivation, and that your time spent on work or side-hustles hasn't fallen out of balance. Spend time thinking and talking about the ultimate Why that is driving you to do all this.

At some point along this path, you'll reach a point where your Treasure Bath is deep enough to cover even more than just your basic needs. Chances are, you'll still be earning a generous major airline pilot salary, meaning you aren't even drawing anything from that Treasure Bath yet.

There will also be a point somewhere along the line where your quest for balance will lead you to wonder if it's really worth your time doing menial tasks like mowing the lawn and cleaning your own toilets. Until your Treasure Bath is deep enough for passive income to cover your annual spending, the answer is a resounding "YES! It's worth your time to do these tasks yourself!" However, once you've reached a point of financial freedom I feel like it's okay to spend a little extra money to give yourself more time for meaningful, big-picture things and fewer chores.

I assert that you're always better off paying your kids to do these things. Pay them a fair wage, let them learn the value of hard work, and use the situation to teach them the principles of Pilot Math at an early age. However, if you don't have access to this kind of labor, you're allowed to go buy it on the market.

We accounted for this happening throughout this book by assuming that your annual spending doubles when you upgrade to captain at a major airline. I hope you won't arbitrarily start spending like crazy the moment that happens. I hope you won't let yourself get so lazy that you never do any hard work around your house. Try to let this "lifestyle inflation" happen as slowly as possible. However, I believe that it's acceptable to increase your frivolous spending if you've hit financial freedom and chosen to continue working because you enjoy it.

At this point, I believe I've said enough to get you started. Go reduce your spending and save everything else! Maximize what you put into tax-advantaged accounts, and then invest the rest in a brokerage account. Take time for family and hobbies, but don't be afraid to turn a hobby into a side-hustle. If you diligently pursue these strategies, you can't help but fill up a Treasure Bath capable of supporting your needs forever.

I plan to continue writing on this topic. If you want more, please stop by pilotmathtreasurebath.com. My goal is take deeper looks at everything I've discussed in this book, and identify useful strategies for making all this happen.

I hope your Treasure Bath fills up quickly. Fly safe and I'll see you in the world!

Acknowledgements

I'm good at explaining things, but this book would not exist without the help of many others.

First off, I need to thank Bryan el "Padre" Graddy for first introducing me to the concept of a Treasure Bath. If you buy me a drink sometime, I'll do my impression of how he sounded when he says the phrase. (Better yet, buy him a drink and hear it first hand!) You may or may not be shocked to find out that the amount of money he regarded as an overflowing Treasure Bath at the time, earned for 100 days of deployment away from his family, equals a slow month's worth of pay as a major airline captain.

Thanks to my wife for encouraging me to write this, and being the first person to read it. She suggested changes that will hopefully make Pilot Math a lot more realistic for people other than computer engineer pilot nerds. Her suggestions will probably also prevent me from getting fired.

Thanks to Marc Himelhoch, the author of Cockpit2Cockpit,[101] for inspiring and encouraging me to publish this myself. I wish my book was as good as his!

Thanks to the many big thinkers who planted the seeds that would eventually become Pilot Math in my brain. In no particular order: Mr. Money Mustache, The Mad Fientist, JL Collins, Pretired Nick, Mr. Root of Good, Paula Pant from Afford Anything, Jeremy from Go Cury Cracker, Brad and Jonathan from Choose FI, Mindy & Scott from Bigger Pockets Money, everyone else at Bigger Pockets, Michael Kitces, and others that I probably forgot to mention.

Thanks to Michael Hicks for blogging and responding to my emails about how to self-publish a book. I used tools and techniques he wrote about to create and launch Pilot Math Treasure Bath. He also happens to write some fun science fiction. Like any good drug dealer, he offers the firsts book in each series for free.[102]

Thanks to the readers of AviationBull, The Pilot Network, BogiDope, and many random Facebook comments for your feedback over the years. Writing is a skill that requires development. I cringe

---

[101] If you're in the process of applying for airline jobs, you need this book: https://amzn.to/339f3ME.

[102] http://www.authormichaelhicks.com/

when I look at my first posts on AviationBull. If the quality of my writing has improved (and for your sakes I hope it has) then it's thanks to you putting up with my work for so many years.

Thanks also to Ted Erickson, Adam Uhan, Matt Swee, and John McFarland for letting me work with them on those projects.

Most importantly, thank you for reading this book!

About the Author

Jason "Emet" Depew is a pilot for a major US airline. He does some part-time flight instructing in the Icon A5, his 1950 C-170A, and whatever else he can get his hands on. He also publishes regularly as a Staff Writer for The Pilot Network, a group of more than 25,000 pilots dedicated to helping each other enjoy great careers, and on BogiDope.com.

While on active duty, Emet flew the TG-4A, TG-10B/C/D, B-1B, U-28A, T-6A, and E-11A. He flew more than 300 combat missions over Afghanistan, Djibouti, and elsewhere. The proudest moments of his military career were times when he made a difference in protecting good men and women with boots on the ground, and making bad guys go away forever. He now does a non-flying job in the USAF Reserve.

Married with two kids, three dogs, a hamster, a parakeet, and certainly many more animals to come, Emet and the other Depews enjoy travel, swimming, eating delicious food, building things, and escape rooms.

Made in the USA
Monee, IL
14 November 2024

70125642R00128